Cisco Networking Academy Program
Fundamentals of Java Programming
Lab Companion

Cisco Systems, Inc.
Cisco Networking Academy Program

Cisco Press

201 West 103rd Street
Indianapolis, IN 46290 USA

Cisco Networking Academy Program
Fundamentals of Java Programming
Lab Companion

Cisco Systems, Inc.
Cisco Networking Academy Program

Course Sponsored by Sun Microsystems

Published by:
Cisco Press
210 West 103rd Street
Indianapolis, IN 46290 USA

Printed in the United States of America   1 2 3 4 5 6 7 8 9 0

First Printing   March 2003

ISBN: 1-58713-090-4

Warning and Disclaimer

This book is designed to provide information on Java programming. Every effort has been made to make this book as complete and as accurate as possible, but no warranty or fitness is implied.

The information is provided on an "as is" basis. The author, Cisco Press, and Cisco Systems, Inc. shall have neither liability nor responsibility to any person or entity with respect to any loss or damages arising from the information contained in this book or from the use of the programs that may accompany it.

The opinions expressed in this book belong to the author and are not necessarily those of Cisco Systems, Inc.

 This book is part of the Cisco Networking Academy™ Program series from Cisco Press. The products in this series support and complement the Cisco Networking Academy Program curriculum. If you are using this book outside the Networking Academy program, then you are not preparing with a Cisco trained and authorized Networking Academy provider.

For information on the Cisco Networking Academy Program or to locate a Networking Academy, please visit www.cisco.com/edu.

Trademark Acknowledgments

All terms mentioned in this book that are known to be trademarks or service marks have been appropriately capitalized. Cisco Press or Cisco Systems, Inc., cannot attest to the accuracy of this information. Use of a term in this book should not be regarded as affecting the validity of any trademark or service mark.

Feedback Information

At Cisco Press, our goal is to create in-depth technical books of the highest quality and value. Each book is crafted with care and precision, undergoing rigorous development that involves the unique expertise of members of the professional technical community.

Readers' feedback is a natural continuation of this process. If you have any comments regarding how we could improve the quality of this book, or otherwise alter it to better suit your needs, you can contact us at networkingacademy@ciscopress.com. Please be sure to include the book title and ISBN in your message.

We greatly appreciate your assistance.

Publisher	John Wait
Editor-in-Chief	John Kane
Executive Editor	Carl Lindholm
Cisco Systems Representative	Anthony Wolfenden
Cisco Press Program Manager	Sonia Torres Chavez
Manager, Marketing Communications, Cisco Systems	Scott Miller
Cisco Marketing Program Manager	Edie Quiroz
Production Manager	Patrick Kanouse
Acquisitions Editor	Sarah Kimberly
Project Coordinator	Tracy Hughes
Project Editor	San Dee Phillips
Copy Editor	Karen A. Gill

CISCO SYSTEMS

Corporate Headquarters
Cisco Systems, Inc.
170 West Tasman Drive
San Jose, CA 95134-1706
USA
http://www.cisco.com
Tel: 408 526-4000
    800 553-NETS (6387)
Fax: 408 526-4100

European Headquarters
Cisco Systems Europe
11 Rue Camille Desmoulins
92782 Issy-les-Moulineaux
Cedex 9
France
http://www-europe.cisco.com
Tel: 33 1 58 04 60 00
Fax: 33 1 58 04 61 00

Americas Headquarters
Cisco Systems, Inc.
170 West Tasman Drive
San Jose, CA 95134-1706
USA
http://www.cisco.com
Tel: 408 526-7660
Fax: 408 527-0883

Asia Pacific Headquarters
Cisco Systems Australia,
Pty., Ltd
Level 17, 99 Walker Street
North Sydney
NSW 2059 Australia
http://www.cisco.com
Tel: +61 2 8448 7100
Fax: +61 2 9957 4350

Cisco Systems has more than 200 offices in the following countries. Addresses, phone numbers, and fax numbers are listed on the Cisco Web site at www.cisco.com/go/offices

Argentina • Australia • Austria • Belgium • Brazil • Bulgaria • Canada • Chile • China • Colombia • Costa Rica • Croatia • Czech Republic • Denmark • Dubai, UAE • Finland • France • Germany • Greece • Hong Kong • Hungary • India • Indonesia • Ireland Israel • Italy • Japan • Korea • Luxembourg • Malaysia • Mexico • The Netherlands • New Zealand • Norway • Peru • Philippines Poland • Portugal • Puerto Rico • Romania • Russia • Saudi Arabia • Scotland • Singapore • Slovakia • Slovenia • South Africa • Spain Sweden • Switzerland • Taiwan • Thailand • Turkey • Ukraine • United Kingdom • United States • Venezuela • Vietnam • Zimbabwe

Table of Contents

Introduction

This manual was developed for use with the *Cisco Fundamentals of Java Programming* online curriculum and the *Cisco Networking Academy Program Fundamentals of Java Programming Companion Guide* textbook. These labs are based on those in the current Cisco Networking Academy Program with some additional information.

Cisco Networking Academy Program Fundamentals of Java Programming Lab Companion is designed to act as a supplement to your classroom and laboratory experience with the Cisco Networking Academy Program, whose curriculum is designed to empower you to enter employment or further education and training in the computer programming field.

The book is designed to further train you beyond the online training materials that you have already used in this program, along with the topics pertaining to the Sun Java 2 Platform certification exam. The book closely follows the style and format that Cisco has incorporated into the curriculum.

All the labs are hands-on, and the additional paper-based labs are practice exercises for complex topics that are included to supplement the online curriculum.

Who Should Read This Book

This book is written for anyone who wants to learn about Java programming. The main target audience for this book is students in high schools, community colleges, and four-year institutions. Specifically, in an educational environment, this book could be used both in the classroom as a textbook companion and in computer labs as a lab manual.

This Book's Organization

This book is divided into 15 chapters covering various lab tasks related to the following:

- Chapter 1, "What Is Java?" – This chapter presents lab exercises covering the location of resources, managing editors, and interfacing with the console window. It includes lab activities on creating and running your first Java class, accepting input from the user at runtime, debugging and correcting errors in predefined classes, exploring the BlueJ IDE, and introduction to the JBANK threaded case study application.

- Chapter 2, "Object-Oriented Programming" – This chapter presents lab exercises covering the definition of a Java class and creation of an object of that class. Students identify the attributes of a Student class and use a main method to create and operate on Student objects. It also includes lab activities on designing and describing classes using the Unified Modeling Language (UML) and designing the initial banking classes for Phase I of the JBANK case study.

- Chapter 3, "Java Language Elements" – This chapter presents lab exercises covering the documentation of classes and the Core API, including the use of javadoc parameters for creating documentation. It also includes lab activities on defining variables, applying access modifiers, using constructors, and creating the classes for Phase I of the JBANK case study.

- Chapter 4, "Java Language Operators and Control Structures" – This chapter presents lab exercises covering the use and precedence of operators, and the implementation of control structures. It includes lab activities on arithmetic operators, use of operators, String concatenation, if statement, switch statements, loops (do while, while, for), the java.lang.System class, and the Console class.

- Chapter 5, "Basics of Defining and Using Classes" – This chapter presents lab exercises covering the steps, processes, and syntax necessary to define a class and then create an object of that class. It includes lab activities on the four steps to creating objects, encapsulation concepts, attributes, constructors, methods, overloaded methods and constructors, scope of variables, and the completion of Phase I of the JBANK case study.

- Chapter 6, "System, String, StringBuffer, Math, and Wrapper Classes" – This chapter presents lab exercises covering the use of the API documentation to implement the methods and attributes of Java core classes. It includes lab activities on reading input using System.in, String and StringBuffer methods, casting and conversion, wrapper classes, Math class, Math package, working with dates and the Date class, and the Console class.

- Chapter 7, "Arrays" – This chapter presents lab exercises covering the creation, initialization, and use of arrays. It includes lab activities on creating and traversing through arrays, passing an array to a method, searching and sorting an array, traversing a multidimensional array, and implementing arrays in the JBANK case study.

- Chapter 8, "Classes and Inheritance" – This chapter presents lab exercises covering the design and implementation of classes using inheritance. It includes lab activities on extending classes from abstract and concrete classes, implementing interfaces, polymorphism, and implementing abstraction and polymorphism in the JBANK case study.

- Chapter 9, "Understanding Packages" – This chapter presents lab exercises covering the organization of classes into packages, including how to access classes in a package. In addition, this chapter provides an introduction to AWT (Abstract Window Toolkit). It includes lab activities on exploring the API packages, building a banking package for the JBANK case study, and identifying graphic components to build an ATM GUI and Teller GUI for the JBANK case study.

- Chapter 10, "Creating GUIs Using AWT" – This chapter presents lab exercises covering the implementation of GUIs in the JBANK case study using AWT. It includes lab activities on creating components, selecting containers, using layout managers to add components, implementing event handling, and utilizing the Model View Controller Pattern for the JBANK case study.

- Chapter 11, "Applets and Graphics" – This chapter presents lab exercises covering the design and launching of applets that display and run in a web browser. It includes lab activities on creating an applet, GUI components in applets, changing the location of the components in an applet, and creating an ATM applet for the JBANK case study.

- Chapter 12, "Exceptions" – This chapter presents lab exercises covering the use of the Throwable class, for handling errors. This includes the use of the keywords try, catch, finally, throw, and throws to manage exceptions. It includes lab activities on testing for runtime exceptions, using the finally block, creating user-defined exceptions, and implementing exceptions in the JBANK case study.

- Chapter 13 , "Files, Streams, Input and Output" – This chapter presents lab exercises covering the input and output of data (into and from a program) provided through the use of classes in the java.io package. It includes lab activities on displaying file statistics, using the RandomAccessFile class to seek positions within a file, and writing and reading Customer objects to and from a file for the JBANK case study.

- Chapter 14   "Collections" – This chapter presents lab exercises covering the classes in the java.util package that provide the programmer with prebuilt classes to manage a collection of objects. It includes lab activities on the ArrayList class, the ListIterator class, creating a collection to store Integer objects, implementing file I/O using collection classes in the JBANK case study, and implementing a SortedSet (to hold a collection of Customer objects) and an Iterator in the JBANK case study.

- Chapter 15   "Threads" – This chapter presents lab exercises covering the use of the Thread and ThreadGroup classes and the Runnable interface to perform operations concurrently. It includes lab activities on thread priorities, controlling threads using methods of the Thread class, and creating a digital clock.

This Book's Features

Many of this book's features help facilitate a full understanding of the Java programming language covered in this book:

Objectives and Scenarios—Each lab in this manual provides an objective or a goal of the lab. The equipment required is listed and a scenario is provided that allows you to relate the exercise to real-world environments.

Reflection Questions—To demonstrate an understanding of the concepts covered, a reflection question is provided at the end of the lab. In addition, there are questions included that are designed to elicit particular points of understanding. These questions help verify your comprehension of the technology being implemented.

The conventions used to present command syntax in this book are as follows:

- [ ] or < > indicate that enclosed information is optional.

- ( ), ; {} indicate symbols required in the location specified.

- Italicized words indicate data provided by the programmer.

- Bold words or symbols indicate keywords that must be typed exactly as shown.

- Ellipses represent information that can be repeated.

Chapter 1 Labs – What Is Java?

Lab 1.5.1: Locating Resources, Managing Editors, and Console Windows

Estimated Time: 30 Minutes

Learning Objective

- In this lab activity, students locate the resources used to develop Java programs. Students also locate and learn how to use the Notepad editor and the MS-DOS console window.

Description/Scenario

- Use Windows Explorer to find the window for locating javac.exe and java.exe.

- Use Windows Explorer to navigate to jdk1.3.1 directories.

- Open Notepad.

  ⇒ Open Notepad using the taskbar.

  ⇒ Open Notepad at the desktop.

- Open a console (MS-DOS) window.

  ⇒ Open the MS-DOS window from the Run command.

  ⇒ Open the MS-DOS window from the taskbar.

Tasks

Step 1: Locating Resources

a. Click on the **Start** button, located at the lower-left corner of the screen.

b. Position the mouse arrow over **Programs**, which is located on the menu.

c. Click on **Windows Explorer**.

Note: On some computers (Windows 2000 and Windows XP), Windows Explorer might be located under the Accessories tab. A simple way to locate Windows Explorer is to use the shortcut keys. Press the **Windows** key located in the bottom row of keys on the keyboard while pressing the **E** key. Windows Explorer opens.

Step 2: Locating jdk1.3.1 Directories

    a.   Locate the **JDK1.3.1_02** folder and click on it.

    b.   Locate the **bin** folder and click on it.

    c.   Locate **javac.exe**.

    d.   Locate **java.exe**.

Step 3: Opening the Notepad Editor

    a.   Opening Notepad using the taskbar.

        1.   Click on the **Start** button.

        2.   Position the mouse arrow over **Programs**, which is located on the menu.

        3.   Position the mouse arrow over **Accessories**, which is located on the menu.

        4.   Click on **Notepad**.

    OR

    b.   Opening Notepad on the desktop

        1.   Click the **right mouse button** on the desktop while it is not positioned over an icon.

        2.   Position the mouse over **New**, which is located on the menu.

        3.   Click on **Text Document**, which is located on the menu.

        4.   Double-click the newly created text document icon.

Step 4: Opening a Console (MS-DOS) Window

    a.   Opening a console window from Run

        1.   Click on the **Start** button, which is located in the lower-left corner of the screen.

        2.   Click on **Run**, which is located on the menu.

        3.   Type **cmd** (Windows 2000) or **command** (Windows 98) in the text box to the right of the word run. Then press **Enter** or click on the **OK** button.

OR

    b.   Opening a console window from the taskbar (Windows 98)

        1.   Click on the **Start** button, which is located in the lower-left corner of the screen.

        2.   Position the cursor over **Programs**, which is located on the menu.

        3.   Click on the **MS-DOS** prompt.

OR

    c.   Opening a console window from the taskbar (Windows 2000)

        1.   Click on the **Start** button, which is located in the lower-left corner of the screen.

        2.   Position the cursor over **Programs**, which is located on the menu.

        3.   Position the cursor over **Accessories**, which is located on the menu.

        4.   Click on the **Command Prompt** prompt.

Lab 1.5.4: Creating and Running the HelloStudent1 Class

Estimated Time: 15 minutes

Learning Objectives

- In this lab activity, students create their first Java program, called HelloStudent1.java, by using Notepad.

- At the DOS command prompt, students use the javac command to compile the HelloStudent1.java file, creating a HelloStudent1.class file. Students then use the java command to run the HelloStudent1.class program.

Description/Scenario

- The three steps to create and run a Java program are as follows:

    1. Create the source code using an editor. The source code is stored in a .java file.

    2. Compile the source code to create the byte code using the program javac. The byte code is stored in a .class file. The name of the compiler program for Java is javac. This program will create a byte code file with the same name as the source code file but with the suffix of .class. Remember when compiling the program that Java is case sensitive. Verify that the .class file has been created.

    3. Start the JVM and run the program (the .class file) using the program java. To execute the program SayHello, type the command java SayHello.

- Understanding the basic syntax, keywords, and identifiers of the Java programming language. Java keywords used in this lab are public, class, static, and void.

Tasks

Step 1: Coding HelloStudent1.java

a. Open **Windows Explorer** and find the C drive.

b. Create a folder/directory named **Labs** on the C drive.

c. Launch **Notepad** and type the code using the sample HelloStudent1 class. Refer to the sample code that follows. The javadoc comments that are shown in the sample code will be covered in future chapters.

d. The keyword public, located in front of the class definition, means that access to the objects of this class is unrestricted. The opening brace ({) marks the beginning of the class definition, and the closing brace (}) marks the end of the class definition.

e. The main method is the entry point for the application. It contains the instructions for the Java Virtual Machine (JVM).

f. The identifier "name" is used to store the student name. In the program, replace 'John Doe' with any student name.

g. The System.out.println() method concatenates and prints the literal string "Hello Student" message and the student name:

```
/**
* Java Program: HelloStudent1.java
* @author Student
* @version
*/
public class HelloStudent1{
        public static void main(String args[ ] )
        {
                String name = "John Doe";
                System.out.println("Hello Student " + name);
        }
}
```

Step 2: Saving the HelloStudent1 Class in the HelloStudent1.java File

a. Click on **File**, which is located in the upper-left corner of Notepad.

b. Click on the **Save** button.

c. Click on the **down arrow** to the right of the Save In text box.

d. Click on local disk **C**.

e. Locate the **Labs** folder and double-click on it.

f. Type **HelloStudent1.java** in the text box to the right of File Name.

g. Click the **down arrow** to the right of the text box next to Save as Type.

h. Click on the **All Files [*.*]** option; otherwise, the file will be stored as a .txt file.

i. Click on the **Save** button.

Step 3: Compiling the HelloStudent1.java

a. Open an **MS-DOS** window.

b. At the C:\ prompt, type **cd \Labs**, and press the **Enter** key.

c. At the C:\Labs prompt, type **dir** to list the files and directories and ensure that the HelloStudent1.java file exists.

d. At the C:\Labs prompt, type **javac HelloStudent1.java** and press the **Enter** key. The javac command creates a byte code file called HelloStudent1.class in the C:\Labs directory.

e. Make sure there are no compilation errors. If there are, use Notepad to edit the HelloStudent1.java file, make necessary corrections, and recompile.

f. At the C:\Labs prompt, type **dir** to list the files and directories and ensure that the HelloStudent1.class file exists.

Step 4: Executing the HelloStudent1 Class

a. At the C:\Labs prompt, type **java HelloStudent1** and press the **Enter** key. The java command is the Java Virtual Machine, and it will execute the byte code of the class file.

b. The program output should be Hello student *<student name>*.

c. At the C:\Labs prompt, type **exit** to return to Windows.

Step 5: Review Questions

a. What symbol was used to concatenate (or join in order) "Hello Student" to the identifier name?

_____

b. What symbol is used to end a Java statement?

_____

Lab 1.6.1: Modifying the HelloStudent1 Program to Accept Input from the User at Runtime

Estimated Time: 10 minutes

Learning Objective

- In this lab activity, the student will create HelloStudent2.java to accept the student's first name and last name at runtime.

Description/Scenario

- Main features of the Java programming language.

- Basic syntax for the Java programming language.

- Keywords in the Java programming language.

- The console window used to compile and run Java programs is, in fact, a program that is running on the computer. The command line accepts text as an input message and can pass that message to other programs. In particular, the command line can pass the message to the next Java program. In this lab, the Java program will be executed by supplying a name. This name will be received as input to the program from the console and stored in two variables (data locations): args[0] and args[1]. The main method provides access to input from the console through the use of the String array args.

- The main method outputs Hello *<student first name>* *<student last name>* to the screen. The key to sending a message to the main method is the String[] args inside the parentheses.

There are several key points to know for this lab exercise:

- All methods receive data as input in the form of an argument list. The *argument list* is the text inside the parentheses after the name of the method. For the main method, the argument list is String[] args.

- The argument list for a method is a list of word pairs, separated by commas. The first word identifies what type the argument must be, and the second word is the identifier, or name, of the argument. In the main method, the identifier for the input data is args and its type is String array.

- An *array* is a list of elements, all of the same type. A *String array* is a list of objects that are all strings. A String object contains text, such as "Sam Smith" or "123-34-1234". The brackets ([]) denote an array in Java. They can appear next to the identifier of the array, or they can appear next to the name of the type of elements in the array. In this example, String[] args or String args[] both mean an array of String objects. Now it is clear why there are two ways to write the main method.

- Because an array is a list of objects, there must be a way to tell the program to look at the first, fifth, or hundredth element in the list. You can access any element in the array by using an index. An *index* is a number that corresponds to the element's position in the array. The numbering for arrays starts at 0, not 1, which can cause confusion for new programmers. The first element in the String array called args is args[0], not args[1]. The reference args[1] refers to the second element in the array. The thirty-seventh element in the array is referenced with args[36], not args[37]. The reasoning for array indices starting at zero will be studied in more detail in Chapter 3.

Tasks

Step 1: Modifying HelloStudent1.java to a HelloStudent2.java File

a. Open the **HelloStudent1.java** file created in Lab 1.5.4 using Notepad.

b. Click on **File**, which is located in the upper-left corner of Notepad.

c. Click on the **Save As** button.

d. Click on the down arrow to the right of the Save In text box.

e. Click on local disk C:.

f. Locate the **Labs** folder.

g. Type **HelloStudent2.java** in the text box to the right of File Name.

h. Click the **down arrow** to the right of the text box next to Save as Type.

i. Click on the **All Files [*.*]** option.

j. Click on the **Save** button.

k. Modify the class name HelloStudent1 to **HelloStudent2**. Refer to the sample code that follows.

l. In the main method, replace the line name = "John Doe"; with **firstName = args[0];** and add a second string **String lastName = args[1];**. Values are passed to the main method through the identifier args. The values are entered on the command line when the program is executed. The identifier args is an array of Strings whereby args[0] refers to the first element in the array and args[1] refers to the second element in the array. Arrays will be covered in later chapters.

m. Include the **System.out.println()** method to print Hello Student followed by the first name and the last name.

n.   Save the file before compiling. Click on **File** and then **Save**.

```
/**
* Java Program: HelloStudent2.java
* @author Student
* @version
*/
public class HelloStudent2{
    public static void main(String args[ ] )
    {
        String firstName = args[0];
        String lastName = args[1];
        System.out.println("Hello Student " + firstName + " " + lastName);
    }
}
```

Step 2: Compiling the HelloStudent2.java

a.   Open an **MS-DOS** window.

b.   At the C:\ prompt, type **cd \Labs** and press the **Enter** key.

c.   At the C:\Labs prompt, type **javac HelloStudent2.java** and press the **Enter** key.

Step 3: Executing the HelloStudent2 Class

a.   Make sure there are no compilation errors.

b.   At the C:\Labs prompt, type **java HelloStudent2 *<first name> <last name>*** and press the **Enter** key. At the command line, the first word is interpreted as the name of the program; the rest of the words are interpreted as input parameters to the program.

c.   Output of the program should be Hello Student *<first name> <last name>*.

Step 4: Review Questions

a. When first name and last name were typed at the command line, where were they placed as inputs to the program?

_____

(*Hint*: Refer to section 1.6.1 in the chapter.)

b. If a first and last name were not supplied on the command line, would this program have executed?

_____

Lab 1.7.2: Debugging and Correcting Errors in Predefined Classes

Estimated Time: 15 minutes

Learning Objective

- In this lab, students are given several predefined classes with errors (Auto.java, BlueJay.java, HelloStudent.java, Beam.java) located in the c:\javacourse\resource\chap1 folder. Students will debug and correct the errors.

Description/Scenario

- Correcting syntax errors in a Java program

Sample code with errors (referenced in Review Question):

```
/**
 * Java Program: YourData.java
 * @author Student
 * @version
 */
public class YourData
{
        public static void Main(String[] args)
        {
                String firstname = args[0]
                String lastname = args[1];
                int postalcode = 45356;
                String FavoriteColor = "Blue";
                System.out.println("Hello " + firstName + " " +
lastName);
                System.out.println("Your postal code is : " +
postalcode);
                System.out.println("Your favorite color is " +
Favoritecolor) :
        }
}
```

Tasks

Step 1: Correcting Compilation Errors

a. Open **Notepad** and use **File/Open** to access the c:\javacourse\resource\chap1 folder and change Files of Types to **All Files**. Select one of the programs that have errors to be corrected. Click **Open** and **Save As** using the same filename to save the file in the c:\Labs folder.

b. Open an **MS-DOS window**.

c. Compile the program to see a list of errors given by the JVM. Some common errors might appear:

Java keywords or class names spelled incorrectly.

Inconsistently referencing identifiers. Remember that the Java language is case sensitive.

Forgetting to close braces ({}), brackets ([]), or parentheses (( )).

Missing the dot operator (.).

Missing semicolons (;).

d. Make a note of the errors, make corrections, and recompile the program. Repeat the process until no errors are listed.

e. Repeat the process for all programs until no errors are reported for all programs.

f. After all the programs are error free, have the instructor view the execution of the programs to confirm that the tasks were completed correctly.

Step 2: Review Question

What are the errors in the red lines of code in the previous YourData class?

(Each line has an error.)

_____

_____

_____

_____

_____

13

Lab 1.8.2: Creating HelloStudent3 with BlueJ

Estimated Time: 15 minutes

Learning Objective

- In this lab activity, the student will use BlueJ to create a HelloStudent3 program using the sample program shown next. (javadoc comments will be discussed in detail in future chapters.)

Description/Scenario

- Creating and running the HelloStudent3 program using BlueJ.
- The program should display the "Hello Student" screen.

```
/**
* Java Program: HelloStudent3.java
* @author Student
* @version
*/
public class HelloStudent3{
    public static void main(String args[ ] )
    {
        System.out.println("Hello Student");
    }
}
```

File Management

- Students will use the supplied file structure to save the labs.
  Note: Use Windows Explorer to validate that the file structure exists on the system.

  If not, create the file structure on the hard drive.

Tasks

Step 1: Programming by Using BlueJ

a. Open **BlueJ** by double-clicking on the desktop icon. Then click on **Project** from the BlueJ main menu and select **New**. In the New Project window and in the Look In list box, select **C:**. Double-click the **javacourse** folder listed in the text window. A different New Project window will open with javacourse in the Look In list box. Double-click the **chap1 folder** listed in the text window, and a different New Project window will open with chap1 in the Look In list box. Type **lab1.8.2** in the File Name text box to create a lab1.8.2 subfolder in the chap1 folder.

b. Click on the **New Class** button and type **HelloStudent3** in the Create New Class pop-up window. Click **OK**. Right-click on the **HelloStudent3** (the yellow box) and select **Open Editor**. BlueJ provides a constructor and sample method that are not needed at this point. Remove this code.

c. Type in the **HelloStudent3** sample code shown in the Description section earlier. Compile the program by clicking on the **Compile** button at the top of the BlueJ window containing your code. Next, close the BlueJ window containing your code and run the program. Remember: To run the program in BlueJ, users must right-click on the **HelloStudent3** class (the yellow box) that is displayed in the BlueJ window, and then in the pop-up window, users must select the **void main (args)** option. When the Method Call dialog window appears, click the **OK** button and the program will run. Look for the output in the terminal window.

Lab 1.8.3: Exploring the BlueJ Tutorial

Estimated Time: 30 minutes

Learning Objective

- In this lab activity, the student will explore BlueJ by working through the tutorial that is provided with the IDE.

Description/Scenario

- The BlueJ integrated development environment (IDE) is used to build Java programs. It is important to understand that the BlueJ program merely makes the process of editing, compiling, and running programs easier and faster than using the command line. BlueJ automates several of the tasks for the programmer. To compile a Java program, BlueJ still uses the javac program. An example of this was done when compiling the HelloStudent program from the command line. BlueJ also uses the same JVM (java) that has been used at the console window when it was told to run a program.

- BlueJ has an online tutorial that is simple to follow and well written. However, you might encounter some terms that are specific to Java. Some of these terms have not been covered because the tutorial assumes the reader is an accomplished Java programmer. Do not worry about these terms for now. They will become familiar as the course proceeds.

Figure 1-8-3-1: BlueJ Online

Tasks

Step 1: Opening BlueJ

    a.   Locate the **BlueJ** shortcut on the desktop.

Figure 1-8-3-2: Opening BlueJ

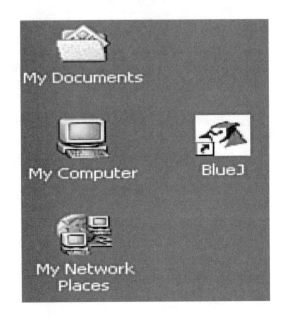

    b.   Double-click the **BlueJ** icon to start BlueJ.

    c.   In the opening window, move to the far right of the menu bar and select **Help**.

Figure 1-8-3-3: Starting BlueJ

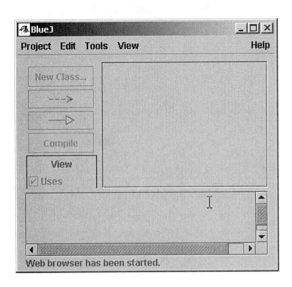

Step 2: Starting the BlueJ Tutorial

a. In the pop-up list, select **BlueJ Tutorial** and start the tutorial. *Note:* If the Internet connection is not available, the tutorial .pdf is available in the resource folder (c:\javacourse\resource).

Figure 1-8-3-4: BlueJ Tutorial

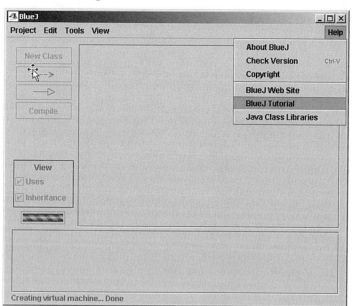

b. After selecting tutorial, the web connection is made and the tutorial will be made available through the use of an Adobe .pdf file. *Note:* Adobe Acrobat Reader is required to view this file (see http://www.adobe.com/acrobat for additional information).

Figure 1-8-3-5: BlueJ .Pdf

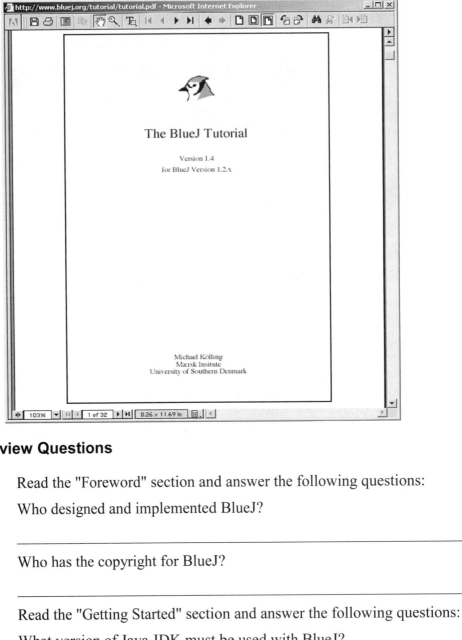

Step 3: Review Questions

a. Read the "Foreword" section and answer the following questions:
    Who designed and implemented BlueJ?

    _____

    Who has the copyright for BlueJ?

    _____

b. Read the "Getting Started" section and answer the following questions:
    What version of Java JDK must be used with BlueJ?

    _____

    What is the meaning of JDK?

    _____

What is the meaning of SDK?

_____

What is the meaning of JRE ?

_____

How is BlueJ started at the command line?

_____

c.   Read the Basic- edit/compile/execute section and answer the following questions:

Where is the examples directory located?

_____

What method is used to start an application?

_____

How is the editor opened for a class?

_____

How is a class compiled?

_____

_____

_____

How is an application executed?

_____

_____

_____

Lab 1.8.4.1: Create and Run the Teller Class

Estimated Time: 15 minutes

Learning Objective

- In this lab activity, the student will use BlueJ to create and run the Teller class with the variables custName and tellerName. Refer to the sample code shown next.

Description/Scenario

- Increase the understanding of BlueJ and develop foundational skills in creating classes.
- Develop the Teller class.
- The main method of the Teller class prints the output to the screen:

```
/**
* Java Program: Teller.java
* @author Student
* @version
*/
public class Teller{
    public static void main(String args[ ] )
    {
        String custName = "John Doe";
        String tellerName = "Betty Smith";
        System.out.println("Customer Name is " +
            custName + " and the teller Name is " + tellerName);
    }
}
```

File Management

Using BlueJ, create a Teller Class in the folder c:\javacourse\chap1\lab1.8.4_1 using the following instructions:

Open BlueJ. Click on Project from the BlueJ main menu and select New. Select C:\ In the New Project window and in the Look In list box. Double-click the javacourse folder listed in the text window. A different New Project window opens with javacourse in the Look In list box. Double-click the chap1 folder listed in the text window and a different New Project window opens with chap1 in the Look In list box. In the File Name text box, type lab1.8.4.1 to create a lab1.8.4.1 subfolder in the chap1 folder.

Tasks

Step 1: Building the Teller Class Using BlueJ

a.   Click on the **New Class** button and type **Teller** in the Create New Class pop-up window. Click **OK**. Right-click on the Teller class (the yellow box) and select **Open Editor**.

b.   In the main method, add the two variables custName and tellerName of the String data type. Assign **custName = "John Doe";** and **tellerName = "Betty Smith";**.

c.   In the main method, add a System.out.println() method to print the custName and tellerName.

d.   Compile and run the program.

Note: Functionality will continue to be added to the Teller class as the course progresses.

Lab 1.8.4.2: Case Study: Modify the Teller Class to Accept Runtime Data

Estimated Time: 20 minutes

Learning Objective

- In this lab activity, the student will modify the Teller program to accept runtime input so that he can set the custName and tellerName.

Description/Scenario

- Accepting input data for the Teller class at runtime.

File Management

Using BlueJ, create a Teller class in the folder c:\javacourse\chap1\lab1.8.4.2 using the following instructions:

Open BlueJ, click on Project from the BlueJ main menu, and select New. Select C:\. in the New Project window and in the Look In list box. Double-click the javacourse folder listed in the text window. A different New Project window opens with javacourse in the Look In list box. Double-click the chap1 folder listed in the text window, and a different New Project window opens with chap1 in the Look In list box. In the File Name text box, type lab1.8.4.2 to create a lab1.8.4.2 subfolder in the chap1 folder.

Tasks

Step 1: Modifying the Teller Class by Using BlueJ

a. Click on **Project** from the BlueJ main menu and select **Import**. In the Select Directory to Import window, select **lab1.8.4.1** and click on the **Import** button. In the Import Status window, click the **Continue** button. Right-click on the **Teller** class (the yellow box) and select **Open Editor**.

b. Modify the Teller class main method to accept data at runtime by using this code:

```
String custName = args[0];
String tellerName = args[1];
```

c. Display the fields as in the previous Teller lab.

d. Compile and run the program.

e. To run the program with runtime input data, right-click on the class and select the main method as usual. This time, in the Method Call dialog window, place the input data between the braces as strings {"John Doe", "Betty Smith"}. Click **OK**.

Step 2: Review Question

Into which variables are the run-time data John Doe and Betty Smith placed?

_____

_____

Chapter 2 Labs – Object-Oriented Programming

Lab 2.2.6: Teacher Class Calls Student Class

Estimated Time: 20 minutes

Learning Objectives

- In this lab activity, the students will identify the attributes of the Student class.

- Students will develop a Teacher class with the main method to create and operate on Student objects.

Description/Scenario

- Defining classes of an object.

- All objects have attributes and exhibit behaviors. Attributes are also known as *data*, whereas behaviors are referred to as *methods*.

- To create an object, a special method known as a constructor is used. A *constructor* is a block of code that defines procedures for how to create an object. The constructor has the same name as the class. The request to create an object is made by using the keyword new.

- Objects interact with each other by sending messages and performing operations or procedures. These actions occur in methods. For one object to interact with another object, it must know the identifier (the name given by the programmer) or object reference (the location in memory). The request for that method is a *message*. The message is sent to an object using the method signature. The method signature identifies the name of the method and provides the method with the data defined in the method signature. A method signature provides the method name, the data it needs to complete the procedure, and the results it will return.

- Current object-oriented designing methods use Unified Modeling Language (UML) to define object-oriented constructs and models. UML is a result of efforts to standardize the terminology and diagramming of object models. Many software products provide graphical tools to create UML diagrams.

- *UML* is a collection of symbols and patterns of symbols. It is used to describe objects, the relationship between objects, the use of objects, and the state of objects.

- UML has many different types of diagrams that can be used to describe object models.

- The symbols that are associated with a UML diagram are as follows:

  Rectangles to describe the class

  Lines to describe relationships

  Special symbols to describe accessibility and strength of relationships

"+ "	public: Any other object can access the data or the method.
"-"	private: Only methods that are defined within the class can access.
"#"	protected: Only objects that are in the same name package (directory) can access.
" "	No symbol indicates default access.
italic	Represents an abstract class or method.
underline	Represents a static method or attribute.

- Students should use the following UML diagram for the Student class definition. The symbols – and + declare the data or method as private or public. The constructor is underlined and has the same name as the class. This UML defines two constructors for the Student class. The arguments for the methods are defined inside the parentheses, and the return type is listed after the method signature:

```
Student
- studentName   : String
- studentGrade  : String
+Student()
+Student(name: String, grade : String)
+setStudentName(name : String) : void
+setGrade(newgrade : String) : void
+getStudentName() : String
+getStudentGrade() : String
```

- The following is a UML diagram for the Teacher class definition. This class defines a static member data of the type String. The keyword static must be included in the declaration of the data:

```
Teacher
-teacherName : static : String = "Miss Daisy"


+getTeacherName() : String
+Teacher()
+main(args: String[]) : void
```

Students should use the sample code for the Student and Teacher class:

```
/**
*JavaProgram: Student.java
* @ author ciscostudent
* @version
*/
public class Student{
  private String studentGrade;
  private String studentName;

  public Student()
  {
  }
  public Student(String name,
String grade)
  {
    studentName = name;
    studentGrade = grade;
  }
  public void
setStudentName(String name)
  {
    studentName = name;
  }
  public String getStudentName()
  {
    return studentName;
  }
  public void setGrade(String
```

```
/**
* JavaProgram: Teacher.java
* @author ciscostudent
* @version
*/
public class Teacher
{
  private static String teacherName =
"Miss Daisy";

  public Teacher()
  {
  }
  public String getTeacherName()
  {
        return teacherName;
  }
  public static void main(String args[])
  {
    Student s1, s2;
    s1 = new Student();
    s1.setStudentName("Mary");
    s1.setGrade("A");
    System.out.println("The student " +
      s1.getStudentName() +
      " has a grade of "+
s1.getStudentGrade());
```

```
newgrade)                                   s2 = new Student("John", "B");
    {                                       System.out.println("The student  " +
    studentGrade = newgrade;                    s2.getStudentName()  +
    }                                          " has a grade of "+
    public String                          s2.getStudentGrade());
getStudentGrade()                             }
    {                                  }
    return studentGrade;
    }


}
```

File Management

Using BlueJ, create a Student Class and a Teacher Class in the folder c:\javacourse\chap2\lab2.2.6 using the following instructions.

Open BlueJ, click on Project from the BlueJ main menu, and select New. Select C:/ in the New Project window and in the Look In list box. Double-click the javacourse folder listed in the text window, and a different New Project window will open with javacourse in the Look In list box. Double-click the chap2 folder listed in the text window and a different New Project window opens with chap2 in the Look In list box. Next, in the File Name text box, type lab2.2.6 to create a lab2.2.6 subfolder in the chap2 folder.

Tasks

Step 1: Creating the Student Class

a. Click on the **New Class** button and type **Student** in the Create New Class pop-up window. Click **OK**. Right-click on the **Student class** (the yellow box) and select **Open Editor** or double-click on the class (the yellow box).

b. The Student class defines the common features of Student objects. studentName and studentGrade are the attributes of the class. Operations to set and get studentName and studentGrade are the class methods.

c. Use the UML and sample code provided to create the Student class first.

Step 2: Creating the Teacher Class

a.   Similar to Step 1, create the Teacher class using the UML and sample code provided.

b.   The Teacher class has the main method. In the main method of the Teacher class, create two Student objects by using statements like the following:

```
Student s1, s2;
s1 = new Student();
//or
s2 = new Student("Joe Doe", "B");
```

c.   The identifier s1 references a student object created without a name, after instantiating using the default constructor. The Teacher class uses setName() to set the name for s1 and uses the setGrade() method to set the grade for s1.

d.   The identifier s2 references a student object created with a studentName and a studentGrade by using the second constructor.

e.   The Teacher class prints the studentName and studentGrade of Student objects through the accessor methods getStudentName() and getStudentGrade().

Step 3: Running the Teacher Class

a.   Compile the Student class.

b.   Compile the Teacher class.

c.   The Teacher class defines the main method, which is the entry point for this application. Run the Teacher class.

d.   What is the code in the Teacher class that is used to print the student's name and grade?

_____

In the main method of the Teacher class, why can't the code access Student name by using s1.studentName instead of using the method s1.getStudentName()?

_____

_____

Lab 2.6.1.1: Designing and Describing Classes by Using UML

Estimated Time: 15 minutes

Learning Objectives

In this lab activity, the student will identify the features of the JBANK classes by using the UML diagram provided next. The UML diagram presents Phase I of the JBANK application.

Students will describe the accessibility to the attributes and methods of the Customer and Account classes.

Description/Scenario

- Current object-oriented designing methods use Unified Modeling Language (UML) to define object-oriented constructs and models. UML is a result of efforts to standardize the terminology and diagramming of object models. Many software products provide graphical tools to create UML diagrams.

- UML is a collection of symbols and patterns of symbols. It is used to describe objects, the relationship between objects, the use of objects, and the state of objects.

- UML has many different types of diagrams that can be used to describe object models.

- The symbols associated with a UML diagram are as follows:

    Rectangles to describe the class

    Lines to describe relationships

    Special symbols to describe accessibility and strength of relationships

"+"	public: Any other object can access the data or the method.
"-"	private: Only methods that are defined within the class can access.
"#"	protected: Only objects that are in the same name package (directory) can access.
" "	No symbol indicates default access.
italic	Represents an abstract class or method.
underline	Represents a static method or attribute.

Preparation

- BlueJ, paper and pencil, or any GUI text editor.

Task

Step 1: UML Review Questions

Answer the questions by using the UML diagram shown in Figure 2-6-1-1-1:

a.   Which class is the entry point for the application and why?

_____

_____

_____

b.   Which class includes a custom method that is other than an accessor or mutator method, and what is the method signature?

_____

_____

_____

c.   Identify the accessor method signatures for the Account class.

_____

_____

_____

d.   Identify the mutator method signatures for the Customer class.

_____

_____

_____

_____

_____

_____

e.   Which class stores each of the following data and what is its accessibility?

Attribute	Class	Accessibility
balance		
email		
lastName		
firstName		
custID		

31

*** Figure 2-6-1-1-1: JBANK Application—Phase I*

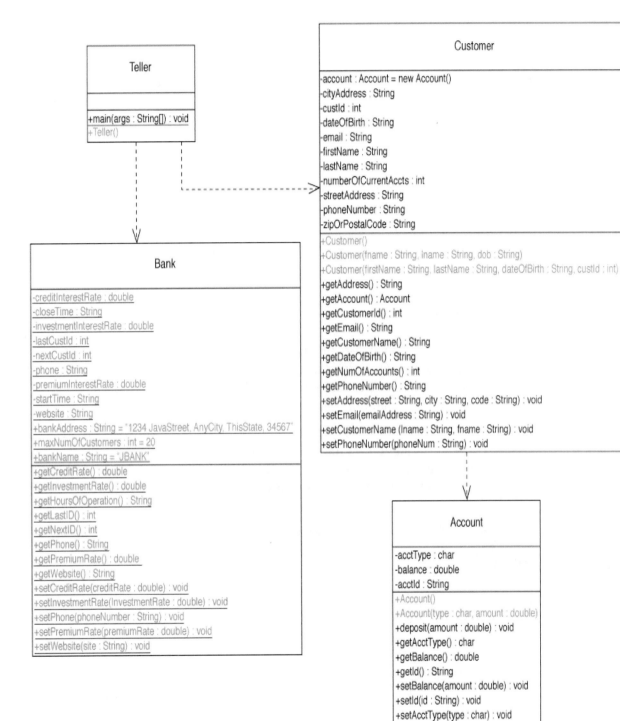

Lab 2.6.1.2: Developing the Banking Classes for Phase 1

Estimated Time: 30 minutes

Learning Objectives

- In this lab activity, the student will begin to work on Phase1 of the JBANK Banking Application.

Description/Scenario

- This activity requires that students use the UML diagram to design and develop JBANK classes according to set business rules. Students will also be using these classes in the subsequent chapters.

- A UML test tool is also provided, which can be used to verify that the created classes match the UML diagram that is defined.

Business Rules

1. The Customer class maintains information on a specific customer. The customer information maintained includes last name, first name, customer ID, address, phone, e-mail, and date of birth. The customer account information is maintained in an Account object. This data is not accessible to other objects. There are mutator and accessor methods to set and get the customer information.

2. The Account class maintains the account balance. This class is used to define account objects that hold data on customer bank accounts. An account has an ID, type, and balance. These are not accessible to other objects directly. The Account class provides methods to deposit or withdraw funds.

3. The Teller class has a main method and is the entry point application.

Preparation

- BlueJ

File Management

Using BlueJ, create Customer, Account, and Teller classes in the folder c:\javacourse\chap2\lab2.6.1.2 using the following instructions.

Open BlueJ, click on Project from the BlueJ main menu, and select New. Select C:\ in the New Project window and in the Look In list box. Double-click the javacourse folder listed in the text window and a different New Project window opens, with javacourse in the Look In list box. Double-click the chap2 folder listed in the text window and a different New Project window will open with chap2 in the Look In list box. In the File Name text box, type lab2.6.1.2 to create a lab2.6.1.2 subfolder in the chap2 folder.

Task

Step 1: Create an Account Class

a.   Click on the **New Class** button and type **Account** in the Create New Class pop-up window. Click **OK**.

b.   Right-click on the **Account class** (the yellow box) and select **Open Editor**.

Step 2: Implement Methods for the Account Class

a.   Use the UML diagram provided in Figure 2-6-1-2-1 to create the Account class.

b.   Implement all the set and get methods for the Account class. The mutator methods or the set methods set the private attributes to the argument passed in the set method. Accessor or get methods return the required attribute.

c.   The custom methods are deposit and withdraw. In the withdraw method, set the balance to (balance minus amount), and in the deposit method, set the balance to (balance plus amount).

Step 3: Create a Customer Class

a.   Similar to Step 1, create the Customer class using the UML provided.

b.   Implement all the set and get methods for the Customer class. The getAddress() method concatenates the streetAddress, cityAddress, and the zipOrPostalCode and returns the customer's address. The getAccount() method returns the Account, which is defined as an attribute in the Customer class.

Step 4: Create a Teller Class

a. Again, similar to Step 1, create the Teller class using the UML provided.

b. The Teller class has the main method, which will be used to create and maintain customer information in future labs.

Step 5: Documentation

a. Using the Document "How to Use UML TestTool," follow the instructions to verify that the JBANK classes created in this lab match the JBANK UML diagram shown next.

Figure 2-6-1-2-1: JBANK Application—Phase I

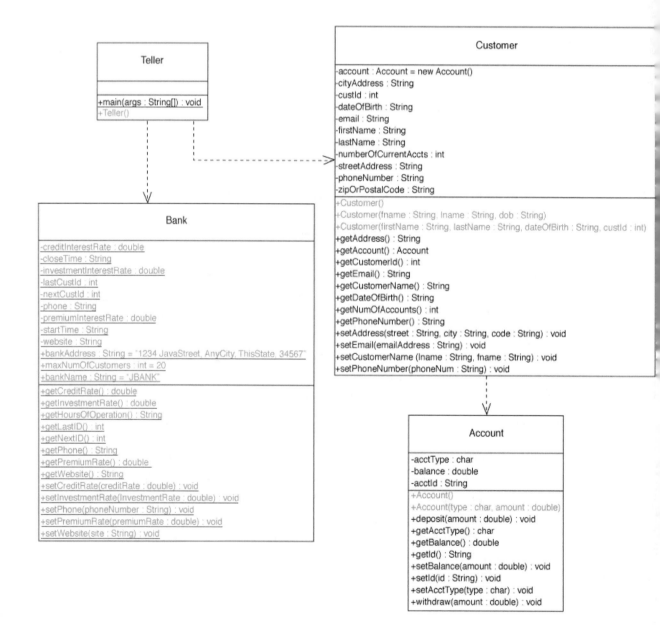

Chapter 3 Labs – Java Language Elements

Lab 3.1.3: Exploring Javadoc Parameters

Estimated Time: 20 minutes

Learning Objective

- In this lab activity, the student will generate javadocs for an existing Java file called Day.java and review the HTML documents generated for the Day class.

Description/Scenario

- Javadoc comments are used specifically for creating the HTML documents for the class. These comments are also known as *block comments* because they can span more than one line. These comments are used to explain the purpose of the class, what its methods do, what the arguments represent, and so on. The javadoc comments are enclosed within the symbols /** and */. As with other comments, the compiler ignores these comments. Whereas general comments can be placed anywhere in a source file, comments used to generate HTML documents using the javadoc utility have specific guidelines and symbols.

- Review the javadoc parameters in Java source files.

- Generate Java documents using the javadoc utility and review the HTML documents that are generated. After comments and javadoc tags have been inserted into class definitions, you can then use the javadoc tool to generate the documentation. To do this, open an MS-DOS or console window and type javadoc at the prompt followed by the name of the Java file.

File Management

Open BlueJ, click on Project from the BlueJ main menu, and select New. In the New Project window and in the Look In list box, select C:\. When you double-click the javacourse folder listed in the text window, a different New Project window opens with javacourse in the Look In list box. If you double-click the chap3 folder listed in the text window, a different New Project window opens with chap3 in the Look In list box. In the File Name text box, type lab3.1.3 to create a lab3.1.3 subfolder in the chap3 folder.

Tasks

Step 1: Reviewing javadoc Parameters in the Day.java File

a. Go to the Resource folder and find the chap3 subfolder. Copy the Day.java file to the lab3.1.3 folder.

b. Open the **Day.java** source file using BlueJ (using the Open Non BlueJ option). Open the **editor** and review the javadoc comments. Identify the various javadoc tags used, such as these:

@author is used for _____

@version is used for _____

@param is used for _____

@return is used for _____

What is the difference between javadocs and multiline comments?

_____

_____

_____

Step 2: Creating the javadocs

Open the **MS-DOS window** and type **javadoc** at the command prompt. A listing of all the options used for the javadoc command is shown. At the C:\ prompt, change the directory by typing **cd\javacourse\chap3\lab3.1.3.** To generate the javadoc for Day.java, type **javadoc Day.java** after the prompt. Several HTML files and associated style sheets will be generated in the same directory unless a different directory option was selected.

The javadoc utility does not automatically insert the version and author information. To include this information use the –version and –author options at the command line as shown:

javadoc –version –author Day.java

Step 3: Reviewing the HTML Documents Generated

Using the Windows Explorer, find the index.html document in the folder c:\javacourse\chap3\lab3.1.3. Click on the **index.html** document and review the contents of the document.

Review the class description. _____

What is the version and who is the author? _____

What is in the Constructor summary? _____

What is in the Method summary? _____

Lab 3.1.5: Reviewing the API Documentation

Estimated Time: 15 minutes

Learning Objective

In this lab activity, the students will review the Java API documentation and familiarize themselves with its structure and content. The API enables the student to review the documentation provided for the core classes—classes that can be used to create applications that solve simple as well as complex problems.

Description/Scenario

- Explore the Core API documentation.

- Students can get to the documentation for the core Java classes by locating the API docs on the desktop or opening the browser to http://java.sun.com/j2se/1.3/docs/api/index.html.

- The information for a Class in the API documents includes the following:

  ⇒ The actual class definition statement.

  ⇒ Links to other related words or phrases.

  ⇒ Version and author information.

  ⇒ A description that includes information on the proper use of the class and restrictions.

  ⇒ A section for locating sample code.

  ⇒ A field summary describing the types of data that the object stores.

  ⇒ The constructors that are the specific methods for constructing objects (Classes that do not describe constructors use a "null" constructor. These are also known as *default constructors*.)

  ⇒ A method summary displays the method signature and the return value for the method.

  ⇒ The class hierarchy, starting from java.lang.Object down to the class being documented.

- This lab will also show students where to find key Java constructors, fields, and methods. In addition, it will give insight into which classes and methods to use to achieve the necessary results.

Tasks

Step 1: Locating the Java API Documentation

a. Find the local copy of the Java API (a shortcut should be located on the desktop) and open it with the browser. You can also point the browser to **http://java.sun.com/j2se/1.3/docs/api/index.html**.Install the HTML files that form this extensive documentation in C:/javadocs/docs/api/index.html.

b. After the API is open, review the different sections. Go to the **Packages** frame in the upper-left corner and look at the packages that are available. Note the different packages.

Step 2: Browsing the java.lang Package

a. Click on the **java.lang** package. Go to the **Classes** frame just below the Package frame and click on **String**. Notice that String has a tree structure that describes inheritance. Scroll down and notice the Field summary. The documentation refers to Class or Object data that is member data as Fields. This section will inform you of the data that the object or class will store. Next you will find the Constructor summary and then the Method summary. This is an important section, and you will need to become intimately familiar with the operations or methods of the objects you use. Note that in general, field data is hidden or encapsulated. You use the methods to access the field data.

b. What is the concatenation operator? (See the String description following the tree structure.)

    _____

    _____

c. Are String objects mutable or immutable?

    _____

d. How many constructors does the string class have? (Look in the Constructor summary.)

    _____

e. How many constructors are deprecated? (Look for the reason the constructor has been deprecated.)

    _____

f. There are two substring() methods listed. (Look in the Method summary.) What is the difference between these two?

_____

g. What will the length() method do?

_____

h. Find the methods equals() and equalsIgnoreCase(). These will be useful in future labs.

i. What is the difference between equals() and equalsIgnoreCase()?

_____

_____

Step 3: Browsing the System Package

a. Go to the **Classes** frame and click on **System**. Just like the String class, this class has similar information for Fields, Constructors, Methods, and Inheritance. What are the fields for the System class? Now click on the **Field Out** link. What is the typical way to write a line of output data?

_____

b. Next click on the See Also link **PrintStream.println(java.lang.String)** and read some of the detailed methods for print and println.

c. How many print and println methods are there? _____

d. Why would so many variations of println or print methods be needed?

_____

_____

Lab 3.1.6.1: Inserting Documentation for the Classes in the JBANK Application

Estimated Time: 20 minutes

Learning Objectives

- In this lab activity, the student will add or update comments in the Customer, Account, and Teller classes.

- Students will add or complete the associated "@" tags for author, version, and method parameters.

Description/Scenario

- Demonstrate the usage of line comments, block comments, and javadoc comments along with several javadoc parameters.

- Programmers must get into the practice of embedding documentation in all of their code. Although single-line and block comments are useful to review personal source files, they are not visible to other programmers who only have access to the class files. For a program to be useful, it must be well documented, which includes javadoc comments. Only information that is public should be commented for javadoc purposes.

- Because the banking application used in this course has multiple classes, it is important that students document each class.

- The importance of documentation is emphasized here by including specific instructions for documenting the classes in each phase of the banking application. Every time students change the code of a class, they should rerun the javadoc utility to generate updated HTML documents.

- In the following lab, students will begin by inserting specific documentation tags in the Customer and Account class.

File Management

Open BlueJ, click on Project from the BlueJ main menu, and select New. Select C:\ in the New Project window and in the Look In list box. When you double-click the javacourse folder listed in the text window, a different New Project window opens with javacourse in the Look In list box. Then double-click the chap3 folder listed in the text window, and a different New Project window will open with chap3 in the Look In list box. In the File Name text box, type lab3.1.6.1 to create a lab3.1.6.1 subfolder in the chap3 folder.

Tasks

Step 1: Adding Comments to the JBANK Application

    a.   Use the UML diagram provided in Figure 3-1-6-1 as a reference.

    b.   Click on **Project** from the BlueJ main menu and select **Import**. In the Select Directory to Import window, select **lab2.6.1.2** and click on the **Import** button. In the Import Status window, click the **Continue** button. Students will find the classes they created in lab2.6.1.2.

    c.   Open **Editor** and insert descriptions about the class for Customer, Account, and Teller classes. Open the editor for each class to add descriptions and comments.

    d.   For each class, in the "@author (your name)" line, add your name. Will the name automatically be displayed?

           _____

    e.   For each class in the "@version (a version number or a date)" line, put in the current date.

    f.   Add or update the javadoc comments for all of the methods in the Customer, Teller, and Account classes. Javadoc comments are used specifically for creating the HTML documents for the class. They are enclosed within the symbols /** and */.

    g.   What is the difference between javadoc comments and multiline comments?

           _____
           _____
           _____

    h.   Include the method name and a detailed description of the method's purpose or function, using the following template as a sample:

```
/**An example of a method - replace this comment with your own
 *
 * @param  y   a sample parameter for a method
 * @return     the sum of x and y
 */
public int sampleMethod(int y)
{
    // put your code here
    return x + y;
}
```

i. The javadoc tags are used to create various sections, links, or text styles. The @author and @version tags have been used in previous labs. The @author name-text tag adds an "Author" entry with the specified name-text to the generated documents when the Author option is used. Add or update @param tags to all method parameters and @return tags with descriptions for all get methods. Group the @tags together.

j. Within several of the methods, include a line comment. These comments are not executed when a program runs. Use the comments to describe the operation that is taking place.

k. In the Account class, add a block comment to describe the Account class and methods described in the Account class. When the comment is on multiple lines, the comment is referred to as a *block comment*. The symbol /* precedes the first line or is the first character on the first line and ends with the */ on the last line or after the last line. How many lines can the block comment use? _____

l. Add a line comment showing the end of each class, after the last }. How many lines can a single line comment use? _____

43

Figure 3-1-6-1: JBANK Application—Phase I

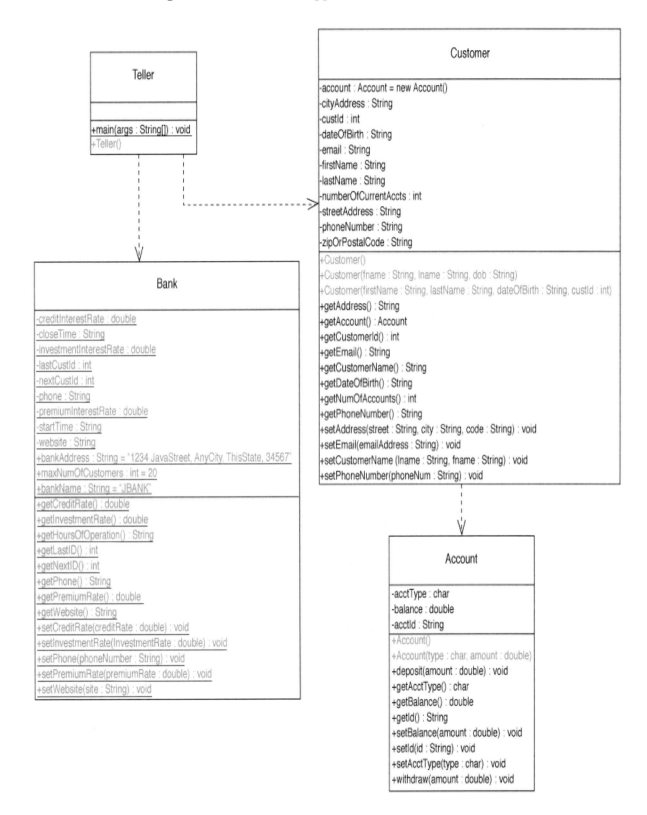

Lab 3.1.6.2: Generating API Docs for JBANK Classes Using the Javadoc Tool

Estimated Time: 15 minutes

Learning Objective

- In this lab activity, the student will generate API docs using the javadoc tool for the JBANK classes.

Description/Scenario

- Generating HTML documentation for JBANK classes using the javadoc utility.

- Java provides a way to share the information about classes through the javadoc tool. Students will use the javadoc tool to create the HTML documentation for their Account and Customer classes.

Tasks

Step 1: Generating API Docs for JBANK Classes Using the Javadoc Tool

a. Make sure javadoc comments were added along with the @param and @return
tags to lab3.1.6.1. Whereas general comments can be placed anywhere in a source file, comments that are used to generate HTML documents must be placed before declarations.

b. Using Windows Explorer, open the **lab3.1.6.1** directory that contains the Customer, Account, and Teller classes. Now open a **DOS window** to the same directory, lab3.1.6.1.

c. With the DOS window opened to the lab3.1.6.1 directory containing the Customer and Account classes, enter the command **javadoc** followed by the two class filenames, including their .java extension. *Note:* To see a listing of all the options for javadoc, enter **javadoc** at the prompt. The HTML files will be generated in the same directory unless a different directory option was selected.

d. Note the events that occur.

e. Using Windows Explorer, examine what is in the lab3.1.6.1 directory.

f. Double-click on **index.html** to open it with the browser.

g. Review the contents.

h. The javadoc utility does not automatically insert version and author information. To include this information, repeat task c using **javadoc –author –version Account.java Customer.java** in the DOS command line.

i. Repeat tasks d through f and note the changes in the documents.

Lab 3.5.1: Defining Variables

Estimated Time: 20 minutes

Learning Objective

- In this lab activity, the student will practice defining variables and using them in a Java program.

Description/Scenario

When a variable is declared, the allocation of storage for a variable is being requested. If the variable is defined as part of the object data, default values are assigned to the variable when the object is created. (Remember: Numeric integrals have a default of 0. All numeric floating-point data have a default of 0.0, Boolean default to false, and char default to Unicode \u0000.). If the variable is a local or method variable, the programmer must assign the variable's values as part of the method definition.

- The syntax for declaring variables is as follows:

```
<modifiers> datatype identifier;

example :    private int length;
```

- In this lab activity, the students will create a class called Rectangle. In this class, variables called length and width of the data type int are declared, and the area of the rectangle is computed.

File Management

Open BlueJ, click on Project from the BlueJ main menu, and select New. In the New Project window and in the Look In list box, select C:\. When you double-click the javacourse folder listed in the text window, a different New Project window opens with javacourse in the Look In list box. If you double-click the chap3 folder listed in the text window, a different New Project window opens with chap3 in the Look In list box. In the File Name text box, type lab3.5.1 to create a lab3.5.1 subfolder in the chap3 folder.

Tasks

Step 1: Creating the Class Rectangle.java

Create a class called Rectangle.java, define a variable called length of type int, and define another variable called width of type int. The syntax for declaring variables is <modifiers> datatype identifier. Assign the length equal to **10** and the width equal to **2**. In the main method, create an instance of the Rectangle object. Define a variable called area of type int, and compute and print the area of the rectangle.

Here's the sample code:

```
Rectangle rectangle = new Rectangle();
int area = rectangle.length * rectangle.width;
```

A variable declaration is a request for the allocation of storage for the variable. If the variable is defined as part of the object data, default values are assigned to the variable when the object is created. If the variable is a local or method variable, the programmer must assign the variable's values as part of the method definition. In this example, the length and width are part of rectangle object, and the area is local to the main method.

Step 2: Compile and Run the Program

Compile and run Rectangle.java to view the output.

Lab 3.5.5: Applying Access Modifiers

Estimated Time: 20 minutes

Learning Objective

- In this lab activity, the student will create a class and apply access modifiers to both attributes and methods. A program will be designed to test the impact of using these access modifiers.

Description/Scenario

- A class, method, or variable definition can include modifiers. There are two categories of modifiers: access-specifiers and qualifiers.

- *Access-specifiers* define the level of access to the method, variable, or class. The keywords are private, public, and protected. If the access-specifier is left blank, the access is defined to be default.

- *Qualifiers* define the state of the object, variable, or method. The keywords are static, final, native, and transient.

- In the StudentProfile class, studentName and courseNumber have public access. studentID and studentGrade have private access.

File Management

Open BlueJ, click on Project from the BlueJ main menu, and select New. In the New Project window and in the Look In list box, select C:\. If you double-click the javacourse folder listed in the text window, a different New Project window opens with javacourse in the Look In list box. When you double-click the chap3 folder listed in the text window, a different New Project window opens with chap3 in the Look In list box. In the File Name text box, type lab3.5.5 to create a lab3.5.5 subfolder in the chap3 folder.

Tasks

Step 1: Creating the StudentProfile Class

a. Create a class called StudentProfile.java. Define the attribute studentName of String type, and make it public by using the keyword public. The public access specifier allows all other classes and objects to reference the attribute. Define the studentID of int type, and make it private by using the keyword private. The private access specifier allows only the methods within the class to access the attributes. Similarly, define studentGrade of char type with private access.

b. Define the courseNumber of int type with public access and a static qualifier. A static qualifier qualifies the data at class level. No object is needed to use this variable. Assign a value to the courseNumber.

c. Define a public method setStudentGrade(char grade) to set the studentGrade. Similarly, define a public method setStudentID(int id) to set the studentID. Define get methods to get the student ID and grade.

Step 2: Testing the StudentProfile Class

a. Define a class called StudentTest.java. In the main method, create an instance of the StudentProfile class called student1.

Sample code:

```
StudentProfile student1 = new StudentProfile();
```

b. Set the studentName to "John Doe" and use set methods to set the studentID (Sample code: student1.setStudentID(3456);) and studentGrade. Use System.out.println() to print the studentName, studentID, and studentGrade. In the System.out.println(), use get methods to get the studentID and studentGrade.

Sample code:

```
student1.getStudentID();
```

c. You can access the studentName by using student1.studentName because studentName is a public member. The student courseNumber is a public static member; you can access it directly by using the class name, such as StudentProfile.courseNumber.

Lab 3.6.1: Using Constructors

Estimated Time: 20 minutes

Learning Objective

- In this lab activity, the student will define constructors and use constructors to create objects.

Description/Scenario

- All class definitions include a special method that is used to construct objects. The creation of an object requires such a method to be defined, either by the programmer or by using the compiler-created default constructor.

- The syntax for a constructor is as follows:

```
<modifier> Classname(<modifier data-type identifier>, <modifier data-type identifier>, …)
```

- A constructor is a special type of method that does not have return values. The name of the method must be the name of the class. There can be more than one constructor method defined in a class. If the programmer has not explicitly defined a constructor method, the compiler will insert one in the class definition during the compilation of the source code. Constructors can be defined with no arguments—sometimes referred to as the null constructor—or with arguments. Again, there can be more than one constructor method defined in a class with different arguments.

- Define a constructor for the StudentProfile class created in lab 3.5.5. Create StudentProfile objects to demonstrate the use of constructors.

File Management

Open BlueJ, click on Project from the BlueJ main menu, and select New. In the New Project window and in the Look In list box, select C:\. When you double-click the javacourse folder listed in the text window, a different New Project window opens with javacourse in the Look In list box. Double-clicking the chap3 folder listed in the text window opens a different New Project window with chap3 in the Look In list box. In the File Name text box, type lab3.6.1 to create a lab3.6.1 subfolder in the chap3 folder. Import the Student class from lab 3.5.5.

Tasks

Step 1: Defining a Constructor for the StudentProfile Class

A constructor is a special type of method that does not have a return value. The name of the method must be the name of the class. The syntax for a constructor is <modifier> Classname (modifier data-type identifier, modifier data-type identifier, ...). In the StudentProfile class, define a constructor public StudentProfile(String name, int id, char grade), and initialize the studentName, studentID, and studentGrade.

Sample code:

```
public StudentProfile(String name, int id, char grade)
{
    studentName = name;
    studentID = id;
    studentGrade = grade;
}
```

Step 2: Calling a Constructor

a. In the StudentTest class main method, create an instance of the StudentProfile class called student2 using a student name, student ID, and student grade.

Sample code:

```
StudentProfile student2 = new StudentProfile("Betty Smith",
8484, 'A');
```

b. Use the System.out.println() method to print the student information of student2.

Step 3: Run the Class

Compile and run StudentTest.java to view the output.

Lab 3.7.1: Creating the Classes for Phase I of the JBANK Application

Estimated Time: 60 minutes

Learning Objectives

In this lab activity, the student will add the Bank class to the current Phase 1 JBANK classes to match the UML diagram. Part of the Bank class will be provided. The students will complete it to match the UML diagram shown in Figure 3-7-1-1.

Description/Scenario

- Phase I of the banking application creates all the basic classes needed. These are the Customer, Bank, Account, and Teller classes.

- The Teller class is the main entry point for the banking application. This will be the class that creates Customer and Account objects.

- The Customer class is a "data-filled" class. Although the code is lengthy, it will give students practice in managing classes that hold large amounts of data. This is not uncommon in real-world applications. The Customer class will go through additional modifications in later chapters. Here, its primary use is to store customer information.

- The Account class is a simple class that holds account balance information. This class includes methods for depositing and withdrawing from the account. This is a class that will also be modified further in later chapters.

- The Bank class provides for the use of static qualifiers. This is particularly appropriate because all the customers share the information that is pertinent to a bank. Therefore, if a user needs to display information about the bank or an account for a specific customer, he obtains the bank information from the Bank class and the customer and account information from the Customer and Account objects. This important concept states that no objects of the Bank class need to be created to use the data in the class. This class will be loaded into memory as soon as a reference is made to this class.

- In this lab, students also will use a tool to verify the accuracy of their class against the UML provided. This UMLTEST tool is written in Java. This tool will generate a UML diagram of the class, which students can compare with the one that is provided with the course.

- Complete the implementation of all the classes of JBANK Phase I.

- Implement several constructors for Account and Customer classes.

- Demonstrate the creation and use of Account and Customer objects.

-

- Demonstrate the use of static fields. Implement Accessor methods to access these static fields and then print the resulting contents.

- Apply static fields to the Bank class for use by any of the classes.

- Add constructors to the existing Customer and Account classes.

- Create objects of both the Customer and Account classes.

File Management

Open BlueJ, click on Project from the BlueJ main menu, and select New. Select C:\ in the New Project window and in the Look In list box. When you double-click the javacourse folder listed in the text window, a different New Project window opens with javacourse in the Look In list box. If you double-click the chap3 folder listed in the text window, a different New Project window opens with chap3 in the Look In list box. In the File Name text box, type lab3.7.1 to create a lab3.7.1 subfolder in the chap3 folder.

Tasks

Step 1: Add the Bank Class

Add the Bank class to the current JBANK Phase I.

a. Click on **Project** from the BlueJ main menu and select **Import**. In the Select Directory to Import window, select **lab3.1.6.1** and click on the **Import** button. In the Import Status window, click the **Continue** button.

b. Students will be given part of the Bank class. Go to the Resource folder, into the subfolder chap3, and then into the subfolder lab3.1.7.1 where students will find the unfinished Bank class. Import the **Bank** class and compare the class to the UML diagram that follows.

c. Double-click on the **Bank** class and begin to enter all of the fields and methods needed, based on the UML specification. The Bank fields are private static attributes/fields with three exceptions; the bankName, bankAddress, and maxNumOfCustomers are public attributes. When data is to be shared among all objects of a class, the data is declared static and is the same for all instances of the class.

d. Make all of the Bank methods public static. To enter methods, go to **Edit** and then select the **Insert Method**. Repeat this for other methods as needed. Methods of the object perform the operations on the data.

e. Implement the Teller class with a main method that will create several different instances of the Account class and the Customer class. An instance of a class is created, as shown here:

```
Customer newCustomer  = new Customer( );
Account account1 = new Account();
```

f. In the Teller main, create an instance of Customer called customer1, use the set methods defined in the Customer class, and set the Customer fields using the data provided here:

Customer data:

Customer firstName: John

Customer lastName: Doe

Customer street address: Java Street

Customer city address: Java city

"Java City"

Customer zip or postal code: 9999

Customer phone number: 778-888-9999

Customer e-mail: jdoe@java.com

Customer date of birth: 7/8/70

g. Use the System.out.println() statement and the corresponding get methods of the Customer class to display the customer name, address, date of birth, phone, and e-mail address. Similarly create an instance of the Account class called account1. Use the set methods defined in the Account class to set the account information using the data provided next:

Account ID: 1001S

Account Type: 'S'

Account balance: 5000

h. Use the get methods in System.out.println() to display all of the account information.

Step 2: Documentation

Writing javadoc comments to the Bank class:

a. Write a description of the Bank class.

b. In the "@author (your name)" line, put in your name.

c. In the "@version (a version number or a date)" line, put in the version number or current date.

d. Write a detailed description of each method.

Using the Document "How to Use UMLTestTool," follow the instructions to verify that your JBANK classes match the JBANK UML diagram shown in Figure 3-7-1-1.

Figure 3-7-1-1: JBANK Application—Phase I

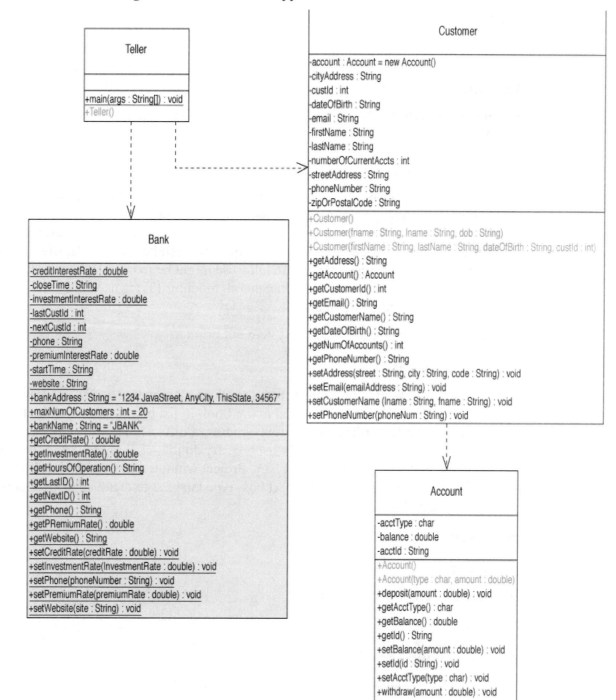

Chapter 4 Labs – Java Language Operators and Control Structures

Lab 4.2.2: Arithmetic Operators

Estimated Time: 15 minutes

Learning Objective

- In this lab activity, the student will build a new class called Time and use the Java language arithmetic operators.

Description/Scenario

- The Java language provides the use of operator symbols that are similar to regular algebraic symbols. Division (/) of integers (variable or constant) results in an integer value; any fraction or remainder is lost. The modulus operator (%) is used to obtain the remainder in integer division. A modulus can also be used to identify whether a number is odd or even. Another modulus use might be to calculate hours and minutes, given a total number of minutes. In general, modulus (%) is used only with integral numbers, not decimal numbers.

- Utilize operators, variables, and System.out.print().

File Management

Open BlueJ, click on Project from the BlueJ main menu, and select New. Select C:\ in the New Project window and in the Look In list box. If you double-click the javacourse folder listed in the text window, a different New Project window opens with javacourse in the Look In list box. By double-clicking the chap4 folder listed in the text window, a different New Project window opens with chap4 in the Look In list box. In the File Name text box, type lab4.2.2 to create a lab4.2.2 subfolder in the chap4 folder.

Preparation

- Open BlueJ.
- Create a new class called Time.

Tasks

Step 1: Creating the Time Class

Create the Time class, including a main method.

Step 2: Creating Three Variables

Within the main method, create three variables of type int. Make one of the int variables minutesWorked. This variable should contain the amount of time to be worked. The other two int variables will hold the resulting hours and minutes.

Step 3: Including Operations

Include the operations that are needed to calculate the hours and minutes.

What would be the expected results if the variables were double instead of int?

_____

Step 4: Adding Print Statements

Add print statements to display the results.

Step 5: Adding Comments

Be sure to add a completed set of comments.

Step 6: Running the Class

Compile and run the class.

Lab 4.2.5: Using Operators

Estimated Time: 15 minutes

Learning Objective

- In this lab activity, students will build a new class named ClassFees. This class will have a main method and several variables. The variables will be private static double class variables. The function of the class will be to add the first two variables and assign the sum to a third variable. The results will be displayed on the screen.

Description/Scenario

- Use operators, class (or static) variables, and System.out.println().

- You must consider some general guidelines when creating arithmetic expressions:

    ⇒ Use parentheses to avoid ambiguity.

    ⇒ Consider the size of resulting values and possible loss of precision.

    ⇒ Multiply before dividing.

    ⇒ When you're using negative numbers with modulus calculation, drop the negative signs from either operand and calculate the result. The sign of the left operand is the sign of the result.

    ⇒ You can use the + operator to add numbers and concatenate String objects.

File Management

Open BlueJ, click on Project from the BlueJ main menu, and select New. In the New Project window and in the Look In list box, select C:\. If you double-click the javacourse folder listed in the text window, a different New Project window opens with javacourse in the Look In list box. By double-clicking the chap4 folder listed in the text window, a different New Project window opens with chap4 in the Look In list box. Next, in the File Name text box, type lab4.2.5 to create a lab4.2.5 subfolder in the chap4 folder.

Preparation

- Open BlueJ.
- Create a new class named ClassFees.

Tasks

Step 1: Declaring Variables

In the ClassFees class, declare three private static variables of type double to hold tuitionFee, bookFee, and the sum of the two. Assign values to the tuitionFee and bookFee variables.

Step 2: Calculating the Sum

In the main method, calculate the sum of tuitionFee and bookFee. Use the System.out.println() method to print the sum.

Step 3: Adding Comments

Be sure to add a complete set of comments.

Step 4: Running the Class

Compile the class and run it.

Lab 4.4.2: String Concatenation

Estimated Time: 15 minutes

Learning Objective

- In this lab activity, the student will build a new class called Concatenate and use String concatenation operations.

Description/Scenario

- The simple definition of a String is a collection of one or more Unicode characters that are stored in an object. String objects are immutable. The + operator in Java is considered an overloaded operator. The + operator can also be used to combine Strings, which is referred to as *concatenation*. The + operator is the sole overloaded operator in Java.

- The + operator in Java is considered an "overloaded" operator. The concept of overloading is explored in Chapter 5. A simple definition of overloading in Java is that the operator or method can perform more than the same action with different types of data. In this lab, the + operator, which was used in adding numeric data, can also be used to combine Strings.

- Guidelines for using String objects:

  ⇒ Create Strings for fixed string data.

  ⇒ Use String s = "text"; or String s = new String("text");.

  ⇒ Strings can be concatenated or combined using the + operator.

  ⇒ String s = "Now ", s2 = " Then";.

  ⇒ String phrase = s + "and" + s2;.

  ⇒ The System.out.println() method accepts a String as its argument: System.out.println(s + "and" + s2);.

- Because String objects are immutable and cannot be changed, concatenation operations on Strings are memory intensive.

- Create a Concatenate class. This class will have a main method and several variables. The variables will be private static char class variables. The class function will be to display all three variables in a single line with periods between each character. This will use the System.out.println() method.

File Management

Open BlueJ, click on Project from the BlueJ main menu, and select New. Select C:/ in the New Project window and in the Look In list box. If you double-click the javacourse folder listed in the text window, a different New Project window opens with javacourse in the Look In list box. By double-clicking the chap4 folder listed in the text window, a different New Project window opens with chap4 in the Look In list box. In the File Name text box, type lab4.4.2 to create a lab4.4.2 subfolder in the chap4 folder.

Preparation

- Open BlueJ.

- Create a new class named Concatenate.

Tasks

Step 1: Creating the Concatenate Class

Create the Concatenate class, including a main method.

Step 2: Creating Static Variables

Create three private static variables of type char and initialize them.

Step 3: Printing Values

Within the main method, use System.out.println() and print all three values separated by periods. Could this have been placed into a single variable and then printed? Note that when concatenation occurs when one of the operands is a String and the other operand is a char (instead of a String), the char is cast to a String first and then concatenated. This is true for all the primitive data types. In the case of an object, a String representation of an object is achieved during concatenation using the toString() method. This method, inherited from the class Object, will be discussed in future chapters. Remember that one of the operands must be a String for the overloaded + operator to perform concatenation.

Step 4: Adding Comments

Be sure to add a complete set of comments.

Step 5: Running the Class

Compile and run the class.

Lab 4.5.4: If Statement

Estimated Time: 30 minutes

Learning Objective

- In this lab activity, the student will use the Java language control structures such as if statements in the method definitions.

Description/Scenario

- A *control structure* is a standard progression of logical steps used to control the sequence of execution. In object-oriented programming, control structures are used only in methods of a class. The three basic control structures are sequence, selection or decision, and repetition. The two selection control structures in Java are if-then-else and switch. The purpose of the control structures is to define the logic flow of the procedure. All of these structures can nest inside each other. A sequence structure can nest inside a selection; a selection and sequence can nest inside a repetition; and so on.

- Conditional statements allow for the selective execution of portions of the program according to the value of some expressions. The Java programming language supports the if statement for two-way alternatives. In an if statement, actions are performed based on a certain condition. The condition is a Boolean expression or a Boolean value. Therefore, the condition must evaluate to true or false.

- The basic syntax for an if/else statement is as follows:

```
if (Boolean expression)
{statement or block;}
else { statements)
```

- Demonstrate decision-making techniques by using condition testing to establish ranking order for grades.

- Update the Teacher class. Use its current main method and add a static testGrade() method that will test a grade set (homeWork and finalTest) using two input arguments. The first argument will be a double, and the second argument will be an int. The function of the testGrade() method will be to take the two arguments and determine if the grades are acceptable or if the student needs to see a counselor. The criteria are as follows:

  ⇒ If the homeWork grade is 3.6 or above and the finalTest is at least 50, display "Grades acceptable!"

  ⇒ If the homeWork grade is 3.0 or above and the finalTest is at least 60, display "Grades acceptable!"

  ⇒ If the homeWork grade is 2.6 or above and the finalTest is at least 70, display "Grades acceptable!"

⇒ If the homeWork grade is 2.0 or above and the finalTest is at least 80, display "Grades acceptable!"

⇒ If the values do not achieve the values shown, a different message needs to be displayed.

File Management

Open BlueJ, click on Project from the BlueJ main menu, and select New. Select C:/ in the New Project window and in the Look In list box. If you double-click the javacourse folder listed in the text window, a different New Project window opens with javacourse in the Look In list box. By double-clicking the chap4 folder listed in the text window, a different New Project window opens with chap4 in the Look In list box. In the File Name text box, type lab4.5.4 to create a lab4.5.4 subfolder in the chap4 folder.

Preparation

- Open BlueJ.

Tasks

Step 1: Opening the Editor

Click on **Project** from the BlueJ main menu and select **Import**. In the Select Directory to Import window, select **lab2.2.6** and click on the **Import** button. In the Import Status window, click the **Continue** button. Right-click on the **Teacher** class and select **Open Editor**.

Step 2: Adding the testGrade Method

Add a private static testGrade() method to the Teacher class (not in the main method).

Step 3: Inputting Arguments

Implement the testGrade() method with two input arguments. The first argument needs to be a double (homeWork), and the second argument needs to be an int (finalTest).

Step 4: Printing

Implement the decision-making process in the testGrade() method. Print "Your grades are acceptable!" if they are; otherwise, print "Please see your counselor!"

What is the difference between & and &&?

_____

_____

Step 5: Verifying the Work

A testGrade() method call is needed in the main method to verify the work.

Step 6: Adding testGrade Method Calls

If the method worked correctly, add four or more testGrade() method calls in the main method to verify the accuracy of the new method.

Step 7: Question

Why wasn't a Teacher object needed to call the testGrade() method?

_____

_____

Step 8: Adding Comments

Be sure to add a complete set of comments.

Step 9: Running the Class

Compile, run, and test the class.

Lab 4.5.6: Switch Statements

Estimated Time: 25 minutes

Learning Objective

- In this lab activity, the student will include the use of the Java language control structure switch in the method definitions.

Description/Scenario

- Switch statements are also known as *branching statements*. They are a special kind of selection control that allows for more than two choices when the condition is evaluated. In the switch statement, the expression must be assignment compatible with an int type. The keyword break ends the sequence of actions and exits from this control structure. Without the break, after a case is evaluated to true, all remaining statements in the switch are executed.

- The switch statement syntax is as follows:

```
switch (expr1) {

case constant1:
statements;
break;
    case constant2:
statements;
break;
    default:
statements;
break;
    }
```

A switch statement must have at least one case or default.

- You must use several keywords and symbols in this control structure. The keyword switch begins the selection, and the braces follow the expression. The keyword case tests whether the condition is equal to the constant. The colon (:) at the end of this statement is required. The keyword break ends the sequence of actions and exits from this control structure. The keyword default specifies the set of actions that will be executed if no match was found between the expression and each constant.

- Build a class Vowel. This class will have a main method with a single char variable, and it will implement program decisions. Vowel's function will be to use the input from args to test whether its first character is a vowel. If it is not a vowel, a message will be displayed using a print() method. This lab will also have students go back to the API and look up one of the String class methods charAt(). This lab demonstrates several new Java features.

File Management

Open BlueJ, click on Project from the BlueJ main menu, and select New. Select C:/ in the New Project window and in the Look In list box. If you double-click the javacourse folder listed in the text window, a different New Project window opens with javacourse in the Look In list box. By double-clicking the chap4 folder listed in the text window, a different New Project window opens with chap4 in the Look In list box. In the File Name text box, type lab4.5.6 to create a lab4.5.6 subfolder in the chap4 folder.

Preparation

- Open BlueJ.

Tasks

Step 1: Creating the Vowel Class

- Create the Vowel class, including a main method.

Step 2: Looking Up the charAt() Method

Go to the API and in the String class, look up the charAt() method. This will be used in the form args[0].charAt(0). Why use args[0]? _____What is the value of args[0].charAt(0)? _____What is the value of args[0].charAt(int index) if the int index is 1 or 2? _____

Step 3: Assigning the Character Value

Assign the resulting character value to a local variable of type char. Compare that value to each of the vowels in the alphabet. Implement this class by using the switch statement.

Step 4: Printing a Message

If the input character is not a vowel, print a message telling the user that.

What is the impact on your output if you do not use break statements in your program and the input character is a vowel? _____

Step 5: Adding Comments/Running the Class

Be sure to add a complete set of comments. Compile, run, and test the new class.

Lab 4.5.8: Do While Statement

Estimated Time: 25 minutes

Learning Objective

- In this lab activity, the student will develop skills in using the iterative control structure do-while loop.

Description/Scenario

- The Java programming language supports three types of loop constructs: for, while, and do loops. The for and while loops test the loop condition before executing the loop body. The do loops check the condition after executing the loop body. The for loop should be used when the loop is executed a predetermined number of times. All loop structures have four elements or actions that occur: 1) Initialization 2) Testing a condition or expression 3) Execution of statements 4) Altering the condition or expression to exit the loop.

  The syntax for the do loop is as follows:

  ```
  do {
      statement or block;
  } while (boolean test);
  ```

- Create a class named MyBalance. The main method will contain two method variables: a double variable balance assigned the value of 2000.00 and a char variable answer. The main method will also display the balance and then ask the user, "Do you want to see your balance again? Y or N". If the answer is "Y," the balance will be displayed again. The program will continue to loop until the answer is "N." Use the System.in.read() method as in the following code example:

  ```
  //answer is a char variable and will hold the value input from the keyboard.
  answer = (char)System.in.read();
  ```

  All data is read and written in bytes. In Java, the reading of input from the console is not an easy task. The Java language API provides the read() method of the System.in object to allow a programmer to obtain input from the user. When the user enters data, the data is read as an int. This int must be cast to a char. The statement

  ```
  answer = (char)System.in.read();
  ```

  reads input of a single character from the keyboard as an int. The (char) expression casts this int value as a char.

File Management

Open BlueJ, click on Project from the BlueJ main menu, and select New. Select C:/ in the New Project window and in the Look In list box. If you double-click the javacourse folder listed in the text window, a different New Project window opens with javacourse in the Look In list box. By double-clicking the chap4 folder listed in the text window, a different New Project window opens with chap4 in the Look In list box. In the File Name text box, type lab4.5.8 to create a lab4.5.8 subfolder in the chap4 folder.

Preparation

- Open BlueJ.

Tasks

Step 1: Creating the MyBalance Class

Create the class MyBalance.

Step 2: Adding Method Variables

Add the method variables balance and answer to the main method.

Step 3: Adding a Prompt Statement and Displaying the Balance

Add to the main method a prompt statement and a do while loop to display the balance.

Step 4: Adding the System.in.read() Statement

Add the System.in.read() statement to get keyboard input.

Step 5: Adding the Main Method

Add a header line throws Exception to the main method to allow the use of the System.in.read() method.

Step 6: Running the Class

Compile and run the class.

Step 7: Question

How would the code be changed to accept either an uppercase or lowercase Y or N?

_____

_____

_____

_____

Code Help

```
/*this throws statement will be explained in a later chapter. For now, it
is required when using System.in.read() */
public static void main(String args[]) throws java.io.IOException
    {
        do
        {
          print the balance using System.out.println()

          print the prompt "Do you want to see your balance again? Y
or N" using System.out.println()

          get the answer from the keyboard using System.in.read()

          use System.in.read() by itself to absorb the enter key

        }while (answer = 'Y');

    }
```

Lab 4.5.9: Use of While Loops

Estimated Time: 15 minutes

Learning Objectives

In this lab activity, the student will develop skills in using the iterative control structure while loop.

Description/Scenario

- The while loop syntax is as follows:

```
while (Boolean)
{
statement or block;
}
```

- Ensure that the loop control variable is appropriately initialized before the loop body begins execution, and ensure that the loop condition is true at the beginning. You must update the control variable appropriately to prevent an infinite loop.

- Create a new class named CountLoop.

- The class named CountLoop will contain a public static int class variable (field) count initialized with a value of 0. The main method will have a while loop that will display "Hello World" and count for every loop. The while loop will continue until count reaches 40.

File Management

Open BlueJ, click on Project from the BlueJ main menu, and select New. In the New Project window and in the Look In list box, select C:\. If you double-click the javacourse folder listed in the text window, a different New Project window opens with javacourse in the Look In list box. By double-clicking the chap4 folder listed in the text window, a different New Project window opens with chap4 in the Look In list box. Next, in the File Name text box, type lab4.5.9 to create a lab4.5.9 subfolder in the chap4 folder.

Preparation

- Open BlueJ.

Tasks

Step 1: Creating the CountLoop Class

Create the class CountLoop.

Step 2: Adding the Class Variable

Add the class variable count of type int. Using this variable initializes its value. Increment this value inside the loop. The value is incremented after the printing activity is completed in the loop. Using this loop print the message "Hello World" 40 times. The class uses the main method and does not have other attributes.

Step 3: Running the Class

Compile and run the class.

Lab 4.5.10: For Loops

Estimated Time: 25 minutes

Learning Objective

- In this lab activity, students will develop skills in using the iterative control structure for loop.

Description/Scenario

- You should use the for loop when the loop is executed a predetermined number of times. All loop structures have four elements or actions that occur: 1) Initialization 2) Testing of a condition or expression 3) Execution of statements 4) Altering the condition or expression to exit the loop.

- The Java programming language allows the comma separator in a for loop structure. For example, for (int i = 0, j = 0; j < 10; i++, j++) { } is legal. It initializes both i and j to 0 and increments both i and j after executing the loop body. In this example, int i is declared and defined within the for block. The variable i is accessible only within the scope of this particular for block.

- In this lab exercise, students will build a new class named EvenOdd. The main method will contain several local variables (variables within the main method) and produce the output for the program. Using two for loops, the main method will print to the console all the even numbers from 1 to 40; in the second for loop, the method will print to the console all the odd numbers from 1 to 40.

File Management

- Open BlueJ, click on Project from the BlueJ main menu, and select New. Select C:/ in the New Project window and in the Look In list box . If you double-click the javacourse folder listed in the text window, a different New Project window opens with javacourse in the Look In list box. By double-clicking the chap4 folder listed in the text window, a different New Project window opens with chap4 in the Look In list box. In the File Name text box, type lab4.5.10 to create a lab4.5.10 subfolder.

Preparation

- Open BlueJ.

Tasks

Step 1: Creating the EvenOdd Class

Create a new class named EvenOdd.

Step 2: Adding the Main Method

Add a main method. Within the main method, create an int variable x (int x;).

Step 3: Adding a for Loop for the Even Numbers

Add a for loop to print the even numbers from 1 to 40.

Hint: You'll need an if statement to check whether x is divisible by 2 without a remainder. Review the modulus operator, %.

Step 4: Adding a for Loop for the Odd Numbers

Add a for loop to print the odd numbers from 1 to 40.

Step 5: Adding Comments

Be sure to add a complete set of comments.

Step 6: Running the Class

Compile and run the class.

Step 7: Explaining the Operations

Explain the ++ and % operators.

_____

_____

_____

_____

Lab 4.6.1.1: The java.lang.System Class

Estimated Time: 45 minutes

Learning Objective

- In this lab activity, the student will use the System class to read input from the keyboard and process it in the program.

Description/Scenario

- Complex activities such as accepting input on GUI screens or printing to the printers requires the use of the Java classes in Swing and AWT API. In Java, data flowing in and out of a program is called a *stream*. The language provides the System class to access properties of the underlying operating system devices to stream data in and out of the program. The System class contains references to three useful objects: in, out, and err. These objects can send and receive data from the default input and output devices. System.in accepts data from the keyboard buffer by using read(). The following sample code illustrates the use of System.in.read(). Note the throws Exception statement:

```
public class GetUserInput
{

    public static void main (String[] args) throws java.io.IOException
    {
        char userInput;
        System.out.println("Please enter a user character");
        userInput = (char) System.in.read();
        System.out.print(" You entered "  + userInput);

    }
}
```

The throws Exception is required because the read() method declares the possibility of sending an error message in case it cannot read data from the input stream. When using any method that throws an exception, users are required to notify the complier about the possibility of such an error message.

- Build a class called MyMenu that will ask the user to enter an M, A, E, N, or Q. When the user types Q, the program will exit. When the user types M, A, E, or N, the program will display the message "Good Morning", "Good Afternoon", "Good Evening", or "Good Night" and then ask for input. If something other than an M, A, E, N, or Q is entered, an error is displayed and input is requested again. The MyMenu class will have one non-static char variable aletter and one non-static Boolean variable done assigned the value false. The main method will contain the while loop, which will contain the menu items. The menu item will be displayed by using System.out.println().

- Use the System.in.read() method to get char input as in this code example. The identifier aletter is a char variable that will hold the value input from the keyboard.

```
aletter = (char)System.in.read();
```

File Management

Open BlueJ, click on Project from the BlueJ main menu, and select New. Select C:\ in the New Project window and in the Look In list box. If you double-click the javacourse folder listed in the text window, a different New Project window opens with javacourse in the Look In list box. Bu double-clicking the chap4 folder listed in the text window, a different New Project window opens with chap4 in the Look In list box. In the File Name text box, type lab4.6.1.1 to create a lab4.6.1.1 subfolder in the chap4 folder.

Preparation

- Open BlueJ.

Tasks

Step 1: Creating the MyMenu Class

Create the class MyMenu.

Step 2: Adding the char Variable

Add the char class variable aletter.

Step 3: Adding the boolean Variable

Add the boolean class variable done.

Step 4: Adding the main Method

Add the main method with the while loop and then add the menu in the while loop. Remember that to access the nonstatic class variables, you must instantiate a MyMenu object and use the dot operator.

Step 5: Adding the System.in.read() Statement

Add the System.in.read() statement in the while loop to get keyboard input.

Step 6: Adding a Header

Add a header line to the main method, throws Exception. This allows the use of the System.in.read() method.

Step 7: Adding an if Statement

Add an if statement to change the Boolean done to true (to exit the loop) if the user inputs a Q.

Step 8: Running the Class

Compile and run the class.

Step 9: Question

Why would the second System.in.read() be needed by itself?

_____

_____

_____

_____

Step 10: Question

Where else could the student put the (done = true) and have the program work the same as with the if statement?

_____

_____

_____

Lab 4.6.1.2: The Console Class

Estimated Time: 15 minutes

Learning Objective

- In this lab activity, the student will explore the code use of the System.in member and its methods using a sample class to obtain user input from the keyboard.

Description/Scenario

- This lab is an introduction to the Console class. The Console class is a custom class that is designed to accept input from the keyboard. This class implements methods to read the data and return the data as int, char, or String. The students will explore this class and its methods so that they can use this class in future labs.

- The Java platform provides the System class to access properties of the underlying operating system devices to stream data in and out of the program. The System class contains references to three useful objects: in, out, and err. These objects can send data and receive data from the default input and output devices. Although quite powerful on their own, these objects require additional coding. The Console class, which is powerful and flexible, has already been created to provide some of the basic input and output methods that are needed.

- Open the Console class with BlueJ and review the available methods. Note what capabilities are available.

File Management

Open BlueJ, click on Project from the BlueJ main menu, and select Open. Select C:\ in the Open Project window and in the Look In list box. If you double-click the javacourse folder listed in the text window, a different New Project window opens with javacourse in the Look In list box. By double-clicking the chap4 folder listed in the text window, a different Open Project window opens with chap4 in the Look In list box. Select the Console file and click Open.

Preparation

- Open BlueJ and get out a paper and pencil.

Tasks

Step 1: Opening the Console Class

Open the Console class.

Step 2: Reviewing the Methods

Review each of the available methods. Note the function of each method, the parameter required by some, and what each returns.

Step 3: Question

How many methods are available? _____

Name all of the types that can be returned. _____

Which one of the methods returns a Boolean value?_____

How many methods potentially throw exceptions? _____

Step 4: Question

Could the Console class be used in one of your previous classes? _____

Give an example code segment showing how this class could be used.

_____
_____
_____
_____

Step 5: Remembering the Location

Remember the location of this class for later use.

Lab 4.7.1: Control Structures

Estimated Time: 15 minutes

Learning Objective

- In this lab activity, the student will practice additional applications of the Java control structures switch, if, and else if.

Description/Scenario

This lab implements the following key points from Chapter 4:

- No matter what procedure or progression of logical actions the computer is to perform, all programming logic can be broken down into one of three control structures: sequence, selection or decision, and repetition. A control structure is a standard progression of logical steps to control the execution sequence of statements. The purpose of these structures is to define the logic flow of the procedure. All of these structures can nest inside each other. A sequence structure can nest inside a selection; a selection and sequence can nest inside a repetition; and so on.

- All loop structures have four elements or actions that occur:
    1. Initialization
    2. Testing a condition or expression
    3. Execution of statements
    4. Altering the condition or expression to exit the loop

- The System class contains references to three useful objects: the static objects in, out, and err. *Static* means that the value is based on the class. That is, no object is needed to use this member. Objects of the type System do not need to be created to access the member object out, in, or err. These objects can send and receive data from default input and output devices.

- Develop a Java program for vehicle leasing business using control structures.

- Problem statement: Create a program that asks two questions to a customer, to which you will reply with a recommendation as to the model of vehicle that would best suit the customer's needs. The first question will be the intended use of the vehicle. To simplify things, the user will enter: C for Carpool, F for Family Use, or S for Sport. The next question will be "How many passengers?" The user will use: A for 1–2, B for 2–3, C for 3–4, D for 4–6, E for 6–8, F for 8–10, and G for 10–16. Your program will then implement the following table to provide the final solution:

Use	Load	Model
Carpool	10–16 passengers	Blue Bird Mini Bus
Carpool	8–10 passengers	Dodge RAM Van
Carpool	6–8 passengers	Ford Windstar
Family	4–6 passengers	Pontiac Grand Prix
Family	3–4 passengers	Ford Thunderbird

Sport	2–3 passengers	Ford Mustang
Sport	1–2 passengers	Dodge Viper

File Management

Open BlueJ, click on Project from the BlueJ main menu, and select New. In the New Project window and in the Look In list box, select C:\. Then double-click the javacourse folder listed in the text window, and a different New Project window opens with javacourse in the Look In list box. If you double-click the chap4 folder listed in the text window, a different New Project window opens with chap4 in the Look In list box. In the File Name text box, type lab4.7.2 to create a lab4.7.2 subfolder in the chap4 folder.

Tasks

Step 1: Creating the VehicleLeasing Class

Create a class called VehicleLeasing. In the main method, use System.out.println() to ask the user for his choice of vehicle type and passenger capacity. Use the System.in.read() method to read user input into char variables called vehicleType and vehicleCapacity.

Sample code:

```
System.out.println("Enter your choice: ");
VehicleType = (char) System.in.read();
```

Note: The System.in.read() methods throws an exception; exceptions will be dealt with in future chapters. For this program, add the throws java.io.IOException clause to the main method to compile successfully.

Step 2: Using if and else Statements

Use if and else if statements to decide on vehicleType. Use switch and case statements to decide on vehicleSeating and print the appropriate vehicle model to the screen.

```
Sample code:
    if (vehicleType == 'C')
    {
        switch (vehicleCapacity)
            case 'E':
                System.out.println("Ford Windstar");
                    break;
            -
            -

    }
```

Step 3: Running the Class

Compile and test the class.

Chapter 5 Labs – Basics of Defining and Using Classes

Lab 5.2.4: Four Steps to Creating Objects

Estimated Time: 30 minutes

Learning Objectives

- In this lab activity, the student will create classes and objects by applying a four-step technique.

Description/Scenario

- The four steps necessary to create objects are as follows:
  1. Design the attributes and behaviors of the class.
  2. Define the object. Create a class definition or blueprint.
  3. Create an object.
  4. Use the object.

- An *attribute* is the data stored in an object. Attributes are declared using variables to identify storage of data. Data can be a reference to any of the eight primitive data types (boolean, char, byte, short, int, long, float, or double). Data can also be a reference for another object.

- Attributes can also be public or private. The private access modifier limits the use of these variables to the class. The public access modifier allows other classes to use the contents of the variables. These keywords precede the data type attributes:

```
public int days;
private String name;
```

- A class definition can include three categories of variables, including instance or object variables, static data or class variables, and local or method variables.

  ⇒ Instance data or instance variables are stored in each object of a class.

  ⇒ Class data or static variables are stored in the class and are available to all objects of a class or objects of other classes if the access is permitted. This is data that can be shared.

  ⇒ Local data or method variables are the data used in a method. This data is temporary and does not exist after the method has completed execution.

- Objects are created when the new operator is used. There are almost no restrictions as to when an object can be created. Objects can be created in methods of other classes, as a part of the attribute definition of another class, and within the definition of the class of the object. The creation of an object is also referred to as *instantiation*. An instance of the class is created.

The creation of an object using two statements is shown next:

```
Student s1;
s1 = new Student(name, grade);
```

The first statement declares a variable to hold the reference to the object, and the second statement uses the new operator to create the object.

- Create a class called Employee. The lab implements the four-step process.

- Create a TestProgram that instantiates the Employee objects.

File Management

Open BlueJ, click on Project from the BlueJ main menu, and select New. In the New Project window and in the Look In list box, select C:\. If you double-click the javacourse folder listed in the text window, a different New Project window opens with javacourse in the Look In list box. Then double-click the chap5 folder listed in the text window, and a different New Project window opens with chap5 in the Look In list box. In the File Name text box, type lab5.2.4 to create a lab5.2.4 subfolder in the chap5 folder.

Tasks

Step 1: Designing the Attributes and Behaviors for the Employee Object

a. Implement the attributes of an Employee object: employeeFirstName, employeeLastName, employeeID, and employeeDepartmentID.

b. Implement the behaviors of an Employee object to set and get: employeeFirstName, employeeLastName, employeeID, and employeeDepartmentID.

Step 2: Creating the Employee Class Definition

a. Using BlueJ, create the Employee class.

b. Define the attributes employeeFirstName and employeeLastName of type String with private access. Define employeeID and employeeDepartmentID of type int with private access. Define a constructor with no arguments.

c.   Define the following set methods:

- setEmployeeFirstName(String first_name) to set the employeeFirstName

- setEmployeeLastName(String last_name) to set the employeeLastName

- setEmployeeID(int id) to set the employeeID

- setEmployeeDepartmentID(int deptid) to set the employeeDepartmentID

d.   Define the following get methods:

- getEmployeeFirstName() to return the employeeFirstName

- getEmployeeLastName() to return the employeeLastName

- getEmployeeID() to return the employeeID

- getEmployeeDepartmentID() to return the employeeDepartmentID

Step 3: Creating the Employee Object

a.   Create the TestEmployee class with a main method.

b.   In the main method, create an instance of the Employee object called employee1 by using the default constructor.

Step 4: Using the Employee Object

a.   Use the set methods to set the firstName, lastName, empID, and departmentID of the Employee object.

b.   Use the get methods to get the firstName, lastName, empID, and departmentID and print them to the screen.

Step 5: Running the Class

Compile and test the class.

Lab 5.3.5: Creating Objects, Encapsulation Concepts, and Attributes

Estimated Time: 60 minutes

Learning Objectives

- In this lab activity, the student will create classes implementing encapsulation, add attributes to the class, use classes to create objects applying a four-step technique, and test the impact of access modifiers and qualifiers.

Description/Scenario

- Create the class Car by using the four steps to creating objects discussed in Lab 5.2 of the curriculum. Use the business rules described here in designing and defining the class.

- Test the use of the access modifiers private, public, protected, and default. Also test the qualifier modifiers static and final.

- Access all the attributes with a test class called StartProgram. This is the entry point of the application.

Business Rules

- A new car dealer would like to sell several models of sports utility vehicles (SUVs).

- The buyer can select from one to five models: model_M with a moon roof, model_MT with a moon roof and tinted windows, model_M2 with a moon roof and two-wheel drive, model_N2 with no moon roof and two-wheel drive, and model_MT4 with a moon roof, tinted windows, and four-wheel drive.

- The car dealer would like to keep track of unit sales by model for a month and be able to print unit sales by model for a month.

File Management

Open BlueJ, click on Project from the BlueJ main menu, and select New. In the New Project window and in the Look In list box, select C:\. If you double-click the javacourse folder listed in the text window, a different New Project window opens with javacourse in the Look In list box. By double-click the chap5 folder listed in the text window, a different New Project window opens with chap5 in the Look In list box. In the File Name text box, type lab5.3.5 to create a lab5.3.5 subfolder in the chap5 folder.

Tasks

Step 1: Identifying Classes, Attributes, and Methods

Look up the Business Rules section and do the following:

- Identify the nouns. The nouns in our problem statement are car dealer, car, model, tinted windows, moon roof, two-wheel drive, four-wheel drive, and unit sale.

- Discover the objects and define the classes. In our case, we can group the car objects into a class called Car. The common attributes for the Car class are model, type of windows, type of roof, type of drive, and so on. The common methods of the Car class are selling the car, knowing the car model, and other car information.

- To keep track of the cars sold, use a class called CarSales. The attributes of the CarSales are keeping track of each model sold. The methods of the CarSales are updating and reporting on cars sold.

Step 2: Creating Car Classes

a. Using BlueJ, create the Car class.

b. To make the model names meaningful, declare the different models as integer variables and give them public access to be accessible by other classes. These values are constant for the entire application, so make them final.

Sample code:

```
public final int model_M = 1;
```

c. Having defined the car model as public final, the model for a car is set when a car object is created. In the no arguments/null constructor, set the model to be of type model_N2.

Sample code:

```
public final int model;
public Car()
{
    model = model_N2;
}
```

d. To keep track of whether a car has tinted windows or a moon roof, define private variables of type boolean. The default values can be set to false.

Sample code:

```
private boolean moonRoof = false;

private boolean tintedWindows = false;
```

e. To keep track of whether a car is two-wheel drive or four-wheel drive, define a variable of type int. This variable can be protected for future use by the subclasses of the Car class.

Sample code:

```
protected int drive;
```

f. In the constructor of the Car class, pass the Car model as an argument.

g. Check the type of car model and assign whether it has tinted windows, whether it has a moon roof, and whether it has two-wheel drive or four-wheel drive.

h. Create the class CarSales to keep track of the model type sold. For example:

```
public static int model_M_count;
```

to keep track of the number of car models sold of type model_M (moon roof, no tinted windows and two-wheel drive).

i. The CarSales class has a static method sold() that takes the model type as an argument and checks the type of model.

j. The CarSales class has a static method printSales() that prints the total number of cars sold.

k. In the Car class, define a method sell(), which calls the static method sold() of the CarSales class.

Step 3: Creating Car Objects and Testing

a. Create the StartProgram class with a main method that will access each attribute with either an instance and dot notation or a class name and dot notation.

b. Create instances of the Car class. Car car = new Car(Car.model_MT);, model_MT is a static final member of the Car class, and you can access it by using the Car class. Call the sell() method of the Car class for each instance created.

c. To print the total number of cars sold, call the printSales() method of the CarSales class. Print out the number of individual cars sold.

Step 4: Review Questions

a. List the four steps for creating objects.

_____

_____

_____

_____

b. Define the method signature.

_____

_____

_____

c. Define encapsulation.

_____

_____

_____

d. Define inheritance.

_____

_____

_____

e. In designing a blueprint for objects, what can lead a programmer to possible data/attributes of the object? What can lead to methods of an object?

_____

_____

_____

f. What is the syntax for a class definition?

_____

_____

_____

g. List the class definition constructs or structures.

_____

_____

_____

h. What is the purpose of a constructor?

_____

_____

_____

i.   Does a constructor have a return value?

_____

j.   How do you declare data of an object to be hidden?

_____

_____

_____

k.   What operator is used to create an object?

_____

l.   What is another name used to refer to the creation of an object?

_____

m.   When a class contains a main method, what is it considered to be?

_____

n.   How is encapsulation implemented?

_____

_____

_____

o.   List the three types of access modifiers. (Remember: Default is not actually typed in code.)

_____

_____

_____

p.   What happens when no access modifier is used?

_____

_____

_____

q.   True or False: You should explicitly specify your class members as public or private rather than omitting the access modifier.

_____

r.   List the eight primitive data types.

_____

_____

_____

_____

s. Where can attributes of a class be defined?

_____

_____

_____

t. What is the coding convention for identifiers or variables?

_____

_____

_____

u. What is the area of RAM that is used for objects?

_____

_____

_____

v. What is the area of RAM that is used for method data?

_____

_____

_____

w. What do you use to reference a variable of an object by another object?

_____

_____

_____

Lab 5.6.4: Constructors and Methods

Estimated Time: 30 minutes

Learning Objective

- In this lab activity, the student will define classes to include default and explicit constructors and create objects using them.

Description/Scenario

- Instantiate objects using the default and explicit constructors.

- Demonstrate the use of object methods.

- Create Customer and Account objects by using default constructors and explicit constructors.

- Invoke methods on Customer and Account objects to set and get data.

- Four types of access modifiers are used to define access to class or object information. In addition to the keywords public, protected, and private, the access modifier can be omitted. When no access modifier is used, the access level is referred to as default. The table that follows reflects the influence of access modifiers.

Keyword	Level of Access
public	All classes and objects of the class
protected	Subclasses, objects of the class, and other classes that are stored in the same directory or package
private	Methods of the object can access
default or no access modifier	Object of the class; classes in the same directory or package

- Calling the new operator results in allocation of space for the new object in this sequence:

  1. Memory allocation: Space for the new object is allocated. Instance variables are initialized to their default values.

  2. Explicit initialization is performed. Variables that are initialized in the attribute declaration will have the default values replaced with this initial value.

  3. A constructor is executed. Variable values can be reset or set in the constructor. Constants should be set in the constructor.

4. A variable assignment is made to reference the object. That is, a reference value for the object is stored in the variable.

```
Student  s1 =  new Student ( 23559, " Mary Martin ");
```

- Students have seen sample code where no constructor is defined. How is an object created? The Java compiler inserts a constructor in the class definition. This constructor will have the same name as the class and will require no arguments or specialized instructions. This type of a constructor is also referred to as the *null constructor*. It does nothing. An object created using the null constructor will have all the member data initialized to its default values or to the initialization values that are explicitly assigned in the declaration section of the class or an initializer block.

- When a class definition includes an explicit constructor, the compiler will use the constructor. The compiler will not insert a null constructor in the class definition.

File Management

Open BlueJ, click on Project from the BlueJ main menu, and select New. In the New Project window and in the Look In list box, select C:\. If you double-click the javacourse folder listed in the text window, a different New Project window opens with javacourse in the Look In list box. Then double-click the chap5 folder listed in the text window, and a different New Project window opens with chap5 in the Look In list box. Next, in the File Name text box, type lab5.6.4 to create a lab5.6.4 subfolder in the chap5 folder.

Import the JBANK classes from lab3.7.1.

Tasks

Step 1: Creating Objects

a. In this lab, we will include the default constructor and overloaded constructors.

b. Take a look at the UML diagram. In the Customer class, include a default constructor and a constructor that takes the customer's first name, last name, and date of birth. Similarly, in the Account class, include a default constructor and a constructor that takes the account type and amount as arguments. Include the Teller default constructor. A class definition can include one or more constructor methods. The purpose of the constructor method, which must share the same name as the class in which it is located, is to define the specifics for object creation. Objects are created when the constructor is called. The creation of an object is also referred to as *instantiation*. Zero, one, or many constructors can be defined for a class. Constructors do not have a return value and are executed only for object creation.

c. In the Teller class main method, customer1 is created using the default constructor.

d.   Create another instance of the Customer class called customer2 using the constructor, which takes the customer's fname, lname, and dob as parameters. Use the set methods to set the customer's address, e-mail, and phone number. Display the customer information by using the appropriate get methods.

e.   In the Teller main method, create an instance of the Account class called account2 by using the constructor that takes an account type and balance. (Pass an account type of 'S' and balance of 3456.) Display the account type and balance by using the corresponding get methods.

Can a method return more than one value? _____

How many arguments can be passed in a method definition? _____

Using the document "How to Use UMLTestTool," follow the instructions to verify that your JBANK classes match the JBANK UML diagram shown in Figure 5-6-4-1.

Step 2: Documentation

Write javadoc comments for the constructor introduced in this lab.

Figure 5-6-4-1: JBANK Application—Phase I

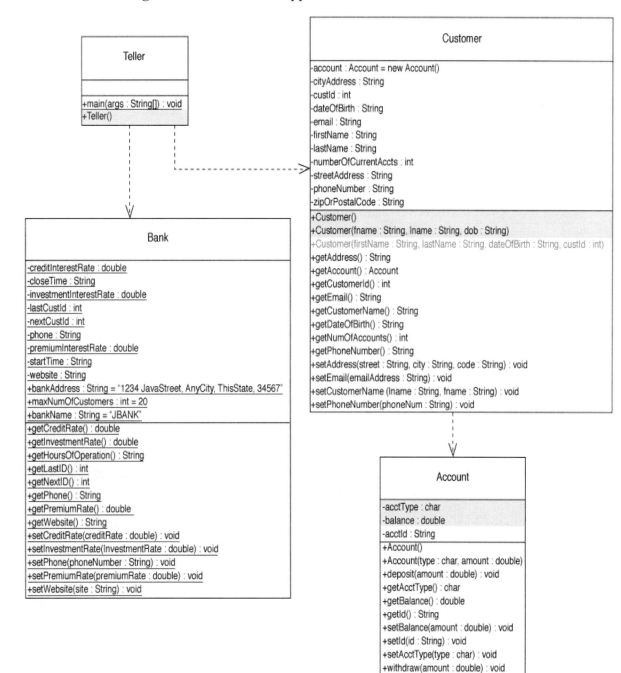

Lab 5.9.2: Overloaded Methods and Constructors

Estimated Time: 20 minutes

Learning Objectives

- In this lab activity, the student will create and use overloaded methods and constructors.

Description/Scenario

- Two or more methods that are in the same class can have the same name. This is called *method overloading*. Typically, methods are overloaded because different versions of a method are desired to accept different input, but they have the same name because they have the same functionality. Both methods and constructors can be overloaded.

- Use the Employee class from lab 5.2.4 and add overloaded constructors that take the employee's firstName and lastName. Define another method to set the empID that takes an argument of type String.

- Use the overloaded constructors to create the employee objects. Use the overloaded method to set the employee ID.

File Management

Open BlueJ, click on Project from the BlueJ main menu, and select New. In the New Project window and in the Look In list box, select C:\. If you double-click the javacourse folder listed in the text window, a different New Project window opens with javacourse in the Look In list box. Then by double-clicking the chap5 folder listed in the text window, a different New Project window opens with chap5 in the Look In list box. Next, in the File Name text box, type lab5.9.2 to create a lab5.9.2 subfolder in the chap5 folder. Import the Employee class and the TestProgram class from lab5.2.4.

Tasks

Step 1: Defining an Overloaded Constructor

a. The rules for overloading methods or constructors are as follows:

The method names or constructor names must be the same.

The arguments must be different (in number).

If the number of arguments is the same, at least one argument must have a different data type.

The return type does not need to be different.

b. In the Employee class, define another constructor that takes two arguments: firstName and lastName of type String.

    Note: Use the this variable if the instance variable name and the argument variable names are the same.

c. Assign the corresponding values of the argument to firstName and lastName.

Step 2: Defining Overloaded Methods

a. In the previous lab, if setID(int empID) was used to set the employee ID, define another method setID(String empID). This is method overloading. To convert a String to an int, use the Integer.parseInt() method, which will be explored in future chapters.

Step 3: Using Overloaded Methods and Constructors

a. In the TestProgram class, create an instance of the Employee class called employee2 using a constructor, which takes the firstName and lastName as arguments. Display the information of employee2 in the output screen.

Lab 5.10.3: Scope of Variables

Estimated Time: 50 minutes

Description/Scenario

- When several objects of a class are created, each object has its own copy of the instance variables. However, only one copy of the class methods is loaded in memory and shared by all the objects. How does a method keep track of which object is using the method currently? Every instance method has a variable with the name this, which refers to the current object for which the method is applied. Each time an instance method is called, the this variable is set to the reference for the particular class object.

- The compiler prefixes the variable this for every instance variable in the class. Some programmers manually insert the this reference for every use of the instance variable. Students do not need to do this. Students do, however, need to use the this reference in many situations. If the instance variable name and the argument variable names are the same, for example, the use of the this variable clarifies which variable the method should work on. A common use of the this reference is in constructors. If students find it confusing, they can create different names for the argument variables. Following is a simple class using the this keyword:

```
public class simple {

    private int aNumber;

    // Constructor

    public Simple(int aNumber)

    {

        this.aNumber = aNumber;

        // here the this clarifies the difference between the
        // variable aNumber that is the method argument from the
        // member variable aNumber defined in the first line of
        // the class definition.

    }

}
```

- In this lab activity, the student will use the variable this to reference objects that will exist at runtime.
- You cannot initialize all things with a single statement. If a large number of variables are to be initialized with some calculated value or be based on testing some condition, then you need to create a code block. This code block has no name, it is not a method, and it is executed before an object is created. This is also known as an *initialization block*.
- There are two types of initialization blocks: static and nonstatic. A static block is used to initialize static variables of a class. This block is executed only once when the class is loaded at runtime. The static block is defined using the keyword static. This block can only initialize static variables of the class. A nonstatic initialization block is

- executed for each object that is created and can initialize instance variables in a class. Nonstatic initialization blocks can initialize both static and instance variables. Object data is always initialized when an object is created.

- The student will include code for initializing static and nonstatic attributes by using initializer code blocks.

Learning Objectives

- Use the variable this to initialize like name variables in the constructors.

- Implement initialization blocks.

- Test the scope of variables.

- Implement an immutable object.

- Set objects ready for garbage collection in a dispose method.

- Create the class TreeLandscape to display tree packages for the customers. Each instance of this class is a tree package someone could purchase.

- Choose between three types of trees: shade, desert, and fruit. The only packages available are P1–three trees, P2–two trees, and P3–one tree. Create the StartProgram2 class to display the three available packages.

File Management

Open BlueJ, click on Project from the BlueJ main menu, and select New. In the New Project window and in the Look In list box, select C:\. If you double-click the javacourse folder listed in the text window, a different New Project window opens with javacourse in the Look In list box. Then double-click the chap5 folder listed in the text window, and a different New Project window opens with chap5 in the Look In list box. Next, in the File Name text box, type lab5.10.3 to create a lab5.10.3 subfolder in the chap5 folder.

Tasks

Step 1: Designing Classes

    a.   Discover the class to be defined.

    b.   Design the attributes and behaviors of the object.

Step 2: Creating the TreeLandscape Class

a. Create the TreeLandscape class.

b. Add the following attributes:

```
private final String coName = "Joe's Landscaping";
private String address;
private String city;
private String state;
private String phone;
public String tree1;
public String tree2;
public String tree3;
```

c. Add overloaded constructors to initialize attributes with one tree, two trees, and three trees. Use the variable this to initialize like name variables in the constructors. Because the instance variable name and the argument variable names are the same, the use of the variable this clarifies which variable the method should work on. A common use of the this reference is in constructors.

d. Add a nonstatic initialization block to initialize company data. A nonstatic initialization block is executed for each object that is created and can initialize instance variables in a class.

e. Add the get and set method for each attribute to access the members in the TreeLandScape class.

Step 3: Creating TreeLandScape Objects and Testing

a. Create the StartProgram2 class with a main method that will create three objects of the class TreeLandScape by using three different constructors:

```
TreeLandScape("Shade");
TreeLandScape("Shade","Desert");
TreeLandScape("Shade","Desert","Fruit");
```

Then create a dispose method that sets each object created to null. Make the main method call it as the last task before exiting.

b. Compile the TreeLandScape and StartProgram2 classes.

c. Run the StartProgram class to verify the output.

Step 4: Review Questions

a.   When several objects of a class are created, how many copies of the instance methods are loaded into memory?

_____

b.   Every instance method has a variable with what name?

_____

c.   What will the statement "return this;" return?

_____

_____

d.   What are the four potential sources of data available when writing code for a method?

_____

_____

_____

_____

e.   True or False: Encapsulation occurs in methods naturally.

f.   True or False: Hidden instance data of an object can be accessed or changed using getter and setter or accessor and mutator methods.

g.   What is it called when two or more methods exist in the same class with the same name?

_____

h.   List the four rules for overloading methods or constructors.

_____

_____

_____

_____

i.   What is the reason for overloading?

_____

_____

j.   True or False: The compiler uses a process called name mangling to generate distinct internal names for methods.

k.   True or False: Constructors have a return value.

l.   True or False: Static variables of a class are initialized before an object is created.

m.   Define an intialization block.

_____

_____

n.   What are the two types of initialization blocks?

_____

_____

o.   When are parameter variables initialized?

_____

p.   True or False: Local variables can be used before initialization.

q.   What is the scope of an instance variable?

_____

r.   True or False: Class variables are available as long as the class is loaded in memory.

s.   True or False: Variables of a method are known as automatic, temporary, and local.

t.   True or False: Parameters or variables defined inside a method are automatically created in the heap.

u.   True or False: In general, the lifetime of a variable (object or method) is for the duration of the application.

v.   What is the lifetime of an object?

_____

w.   True or False: If an object is declared to be immutable, all the values of its member variable are changeable.

x.   The String class is declared as immutable with the keyword _____ in the class definition.

y.   What happens when the reference variable of an object is set to null?

_____

z.   True or False: Garbage collection must be coded within a program for it to do its job.

aa.   What happens when the count of a reference reaches 0?

_____

bb.   When does the count reach 0?

_____

cc.   When does garbage collection occur?

_____

dd.   True or False: Finalizers should be used sparingly.

ee.   What is an alternative to finalizer methods?

_____

ff.   True or False: Every class inherits from the superclass Object. _____

Lab 5.11.1: Completing the JBANK Phase1 Application

Learning Objective

- In this lab activity, the student will complete all the classes for Phase I of the JBANK application.

- The student will apply the concepts of overloaded constructors, variable this, all access modifiers, create, use, and destroy objects.

Description/Scenario

- Demonstrate overloading of constructors.

- Use the variable this to clarify a method variable from the object variable.

- Use private, public, static, and final keywords in JBANK classes.

- Create, use, and destroy objects.

- Complete all the JBANK Phase I classes as per the UML diagram specified.

- Implement overloaded constructors and instantiate objects by using overloaded constructors.

- Apply static final fields to the Bank class so that any other class can use it.

File Management

Open BlueJ, click on Project from the BlueJ main menu, and select New. In the New Project window and in the Look In list box, select C:\. If you double-click the javacourse folder listed in the text window, a different New Project window opens with javacourse in the Look In list box. By double-clicking the chap5 folder listed in the text window, a different New Project window opens with chap5 in the Look In list box. In the File Name text box, type **lab5.11.1** to create a lab5.11.1 subfolder in the chap5 folder.

Import the JBANK classes from lab5.6.4.

Tasks

Step 1: Using static and final Keywords

a. Make the Bank fields Name, Address, and maxNumberOfCustomers static final. In the Java language, the keyword final qualifies a class attribute or method as final. Class attributes that are qualified as final are also referred to as *constants*. The use of the final keyword instructs the compiler to assign a value to the object attribute. After the object is created and this attribute has a value, it cannot be changed. Each instance of the class will have its own copy of the attribute.

b. In the Customer class, make the customer fields custId and dateOfBirth final. Remove the setCustomerId() method and setDateOfBirth() method because the attributes/fields are final. In the default Customer constructor, initialize the dateOfBirth to null and custId to zero. In the Constructor, which takes the fname, lname, and dob as arguments, initialize the custId to zero.

c. In the Teller class, display the bank's Name, Address and MaxNumberOfCustomers using the static methods defined in the Bank class. A static method can be called by referencing class-name.method().

d. What is the difference between instance methods and class methods?

_____

e. How does making the Name field "static final" in the Bank class change its accessibility?

_____

Step 2: Using the Overloaded Constructor and the This Variable

a. In the Customer class, insert a constructor Customer(firstName, lastName, dateOfBirth, custId). Because the instance variable names and the argument variable names are the same, use the variable this to clarify a method variable from the class variable. The variable this refers to the current object for which the method is applied.

b. In the teller class main method, create an instance of the customer called customer3 by using the constructor Customer(firstName, lastName, dateOfBirth, custId).

c. Set the address, phone number, and e-mail address of the customer by using the set methods. Methods that can only be accessed through an object of a class are known as *instance methods*.

d. Display the customer information by using the get methods.

Step 3: Creating, Using, and Destroying Objects

a. Create an instance of Account class account3 and set the balance to a value of 2750.00 by using the setBalance() method.

b. Withdraw $400.00 from the account.

c. Display the balance by using the getBalance() method.

d. Destroy the object account3. (*Note:* Reset the value of the reference variable to null.)

Step 4: Documentation

Using the document "How to Use UMLTestTool," follow the instructions to verify that your JBANK classes match the JBANK UML diagram shown in Figure 5-11-1-1.

No documentation is required here.

Figure 5-11-1-1: JBANK Application—Phase I

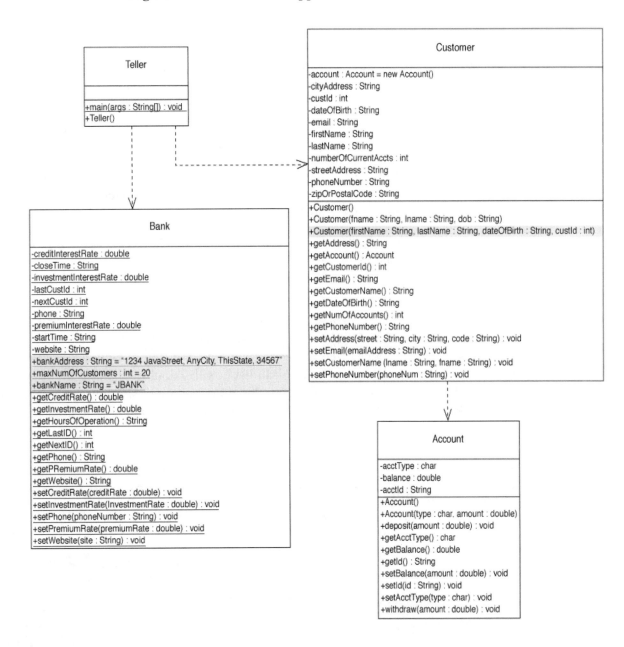

Chapter 6 Labs – System, String, StringBuffer, Math, and Wrapper Classes

Lab 6.1.2: Reading Input Using System.in

Estimated Time: 20 minutes

Learning Objectives

- In this lab activity, the student will expand the use of the System class and character input techniques.

Description/Scenario

- The System class has three objects that you can use to input and output data from a program. This lab uses the methods of the object in to read data from the keyboard.

- The System.in object can be used to read one character at a time. The in object has several methods for reading data. The data returned from the read() method has an int datatype. The int needs to be converted to (cast as) a char.

- To store more than one set of keyboard characters as one value in a variable, include repetition of the simple System.in.read() instruction until the user has typed all of the information and pressed the Enter key.

- Create a class called MyPassword that accepts a five-character password from the keyboard by using a System.in.read() method.

File Management

Open BlueJ, click on Project from the BlueJ main menu, and select New. In the New Project window and in the Look In list box, select C:\. If you double-click the javacourse folder listed in the text window, a different New Project window opens with javacourse in the Look In list box. By double-clicking the chap6 folder listed in the text window, a different New Project window opens with chap6 in the Look In list box. Next, in the File Name text box, type lab6.1.2 to create a lab6.1.2 subfolder in the chap6 folder.

Tasks

Step 1: Accepting Input from the Keyboard by Using System.in.read()

a. Define a class called MyPassword. In the main method, define five char variables: c1, c2, c3, c4, and c5.

b. Use the System.in.read() method to accept one character at a time from the keyboard. Because the System.in.read() method throws an exception, you need to add the clause throws Exception to the main method.

Sample code:

```
c1 = (char)System.in.read();
```

c.   The in object has several methods for reading data. The data returned from the read() method has an int datatype. The int needs to be converted to (cast as) a char. Even if the user types in a number, the int value is the byte translation of the symbol for the number, not the value of the number. For example, if the user types a 7, the int would not be a 7 but the byte translation of the symbol 7, which is 55.

d.   Test all five characters. If the characters spell c i s c o, then issue the message that the password is valid; otherwise, issue a message that the password is not valid.

e.   Use System.out.println() to print the password.

Step 2: Running the Class

Compile and test the class.

Lab 6.2.2: String Methods

Estimated Time: 20 minutes

Learning Objectives

- In this lab activity, the student will make use of the String class and its methods.

Description/Scenario

- The String class is defined as final. This means that any objects created of this class are considered immutable or unchangeable.

- When a String is created using a literal assignment, the String is stored in a memory space that can be shared by all String objects that were created by using a literal assignment. This is often referred to as the *string pool*.

- When a new operator is used to create a String, the variable references a String object that will be created in heap memory, not in the string pool.

- Strings can be operated on by using the + operator. Testing the equality of Strings by using the == operator will only test the equality of the references. To compare Strings, several methods are defined in the String class, such as equals() and equalsIgnoreCase().

- Any String method that makes changes to the String actually results in a copy of the String being created with the change.

- Create a class called StringDemo. The StringDemo class uses String variables to hold the objects and demonstrate the usage of String class methods such as equals(), equalsIgnoreCase(), compareTo(), charAt(), and length().

File Management

Open BlueJ, click on Project from the BlueJ main menu, and select New. In the New Project window and in the Look In list box, select C:\. If you double-click the javacourse folder listed in the text window, a different New Project window opens with javacourse in the Look In list box. By double clicking the chap6 folder listed in the text window, a different New Project window opens with chap6 in the Look In list box. Next, in the File Name text box, type lab6.2.2 to create a lab6.2.2 subfolder in the chap6 folder.

Tasks

Step 1: Using the String Class and Its Methods

a. Define a class called StringDemo and define the following statements:

```
String s1 = new String("Jones"); // s1 references a String object
created in heap

String s2 = new String("James"); // s2 references a String object
created in heap

String s3 = s1; // s3 and s1 reference the same object in the heap

String s4 = s3; // s4 and s3 reference the same object in the heap

String s5 = "Tom"; // s5 references a String object in the String
pool

String s6 = "Jones"; // s6 references a String object in the
String pool

String s7 =new String("James"); // s7 references String object
created in heap

String s8 = "Tom";

String s9 = new String("jones");
```

b. Verify the following statements for true or false and state the reason.

Statement	True or False	Why?
s1.equals(s2) ;		
s4.equals(s1) ;		
s2.equals(s7) ;		.
s1.equals(s6);		
s4 == s1;		
s2 == s7;		
s8 == s5;		
s1.equalsIgnoreCase(s9);		

c. What is the output of the following statements?

s1.compareTo(s9);	
s6.length();	
s5.charAt(2);	
s7.substring(3);	

Step 2: Running the Class

Compile and test the class.

Lab 6.2.3: Casting and Conversion

Estimated Time: 20 minutes

Learning Objectives

- In this lab activity, the student will apply concepts of type casting and data conversion.

Description/Scenario

- The Java programming language provides wrapper classes to manipulate primitive data elements as objects. Such data elements are "wrapped" in an object that is created around them. Each Java primitive data type has a corresponding wrapper class in the java.lang package.

- Wrapper classes implement immutable objects. This means that after the primitive value is initialized in the wrapper object, you can't change that value. Wrapper classes are useful when you're converting primitive data types because of the many wrapper class methods that are available. For example, to convert a numeric value stored as a String, use the Integer class method to extract an int from a String.

- Create a class called ReadNum to read numbers from the console into an int variable. You read these numbers one character at a time to build a number String. You use the Interger.parseInt() method to parse the String to int type.

File Management

Open BlueJ, click on Project from the BlueJ main menu, and select New. In the New Project window and in the Look In list box, select C:\. If you double-click the javacourse folder listed in the text window, a different New Project window opens with javacourse in the Look In list box. By double-clicking the chap6 folder listed in the text window, a different New Project window opens with chap6 in the Look In list box. Next, in the File Name text box, type lab6.2.3 to create a lab6.2.3 subfolder in the chap6 folder.

Tasks

Step 1: Reading Numbers from the Keyboard

    a.   Create a class called ReadNum. In the main method, use System.in.read() in a while loop to read character by character. Break the while loop when the Enter key is read—that is, if the character read is a '\n' (newline) character. Concatenate each character read into a variable numString of type String. Add a throws Exception clause to the main method. (Or, more specific to the exception that can be thrown by the System.in.read() method, you could add a throws java.io.IOException clause to the main method.)

    b.   Use Integer.parseInt(numString) to parse a String to int type. The Java platform provides wrapper classes such as Integer, Double, and Character to manipulate primitive data elements as objects. Such data elements are "wrapped" in an object created around them. Each primitive Java data type has a corresponding wrapper class in the java.lang package. Each wrapper class object encapsulates a single primitive value.

Step 2: Running the Class

    Compile and test the class.

Lab 6.6.1: Using the Math Class

Estimated Time: 20 minutes

Learning Objectives

- In this lab activity, the student will use several methods of the Math class to perform mathematical calculations on numeric values.

Description/Scenario

- Create a class called NumberPlay to use various Math class methods on int and double numbers.

File Management

Open BlueJ, click on Project from the BlueJ main menu, and select New. In the New Project window and in the Look In list box, select C:\. If you double-click the javacourse folder listed in the text window, a different New Project window opens with javacourse in the Look In list box. By double-clicking the chap6 folder listed in the text window, a different New Project window opens with chap6 in the Look In list box. Next, in the File Name text box, type lab6.6.1 to create a lab6.6.1 subfolder in the chap6 folder.

Tasks

Step 1: Using the Various Math Class Methods

    a.   Define a class called NumberPlay. In the main method, define a double variable num1 and initialize it to 34.7889.

    b.   Define an int variable num2 and initialize it to 36. The Math class has static methods defined; an instance of this class is not needed to use its methods.

    c.   Use the Math.sqrt(num2) to find the square root of num2. Use Math.round(num1) to round num1 to the closest integer.

    d.   Use max(num1, num2) to find the largest of two numbers.

Step 2: Running the Class

Compile and test the class.

Lab 6.7.1: Using the Math Package

Estimated Time: 20 minutes

Learning Objectives

- In this lab activity, the student will use the classes BigDecimal and BigInteger from the Math package to store and operate on arbitrarily sized numeric data.

Description/Scenario

- BigDecimal and BigInteger classes are for manipulating numbers with an arbitrarily long sequence of digits. The documentation for these classes can be found in the section on the java.math package in the Java API documentation.

- BigDecimal objects can perform calculations that might result in numbers larger than a 64-bit storage number, such as a double. BigDecimal objects hold signed decimal numbers that are accurate to an arbitrary level of precision and are useful for currency operations. This class gives programmers control over rounding and scaling behavior and provides methods for performing basic operations.

- BigInteger can perform calculations that might result in numbers larger than a 64-bit storage number.

- Create a class called BigNumberPlay to add and multiply long sequence of digits using BigDecimal and BigInteger class methods.

File Management

Open BlueJ, click on Project from the BlueJ main menu, and select New. In the New Project window and in the Look In list box, select C:\. If you double-click the javacourse folder listed in the text window, a different New Project window opens with javacourse in the Look In list box. By double-clicking the chap6 folder listed in the text window, a different New Project window opens with chap6 in the Look In list box. Next, in the File Name text box, type lab6.7.1 to create a lab6.7.1 subfolder in the chap6 folder.

Tasks

Step 1: Defining the BigInteger and BigDecimal Classes

a. Create a class called BigNumberPlay. In the main method, create a BigInteger object using the following syntax:

```
import java.math.*// first line in the source file

BigInteger bigInteger = new
BigInteger("1240321448912348724793249872498723");
```

The constructor converts a long sequence of digits into a BigInteger.

b.   Similarly, create a BigDecimal object of a long sequence of digits using the following syntax:

```
BigDecimal  bigDecimal = new
BigDecimal("13241234123413242134213421342.13421");
```

Step 2: Operating on BigInteger and BigDecimal Objects

a.   The add() method of the BigInteger class requires an argument of type BigInteger. To add an ordinary number (number of type int) to a BigInteger, convert the number to a BigInteger using the valueOf() method. For example, to add 100 to bigInteger, use the following syntax:

```
bigInteger = bigInteger.add(BigInteger.valueOf(100));
```

b.   To multiply 5000.234f to a BigDecimal, use the following syntax:

```
bigDecimal =
bigDecimal.multiply(BigDecimal.valueOf((long)5000.234f)));
```

To print bigInteger, use the following syntax:

```
System.out.println(bigInteger);
```

Step 3: Running the Class

Compile and test the class.

Lab 6.8.3: Working with Dates

Estimated Time: 20 minutes

Learning Objectives:

- In this lab activity, the student will work with the Date class, the Calendar class, and the DateFormat class to operate on date values.

Description/Scenario

- Dates are used to document many events, such as date of birth, date hired, completed course date, and date started.

- Three classes in the Java API documentation are concerned with dates. The Date class creates a Date object, and the Calendar class sets or changes the date for a Date object. The DateFormat class displays the date in different formats. The Date and Calendar classes are located in the java.util package, whereas the DateFormat class is part of the java.text package. When you use these classes, specify their location by using the following statements before the class header.

```
import java.util.*;
import java.text.* ;
```

- Create a class called DateDemo. In this class, students will create Date objects, use the DateFormat class to parse different date formats, and use the Calendar class to set the date of a Date object.

File Management

Open BlueJ, click on Project from the BlueJ main menu, and select New. In the New Project window and in the Look In list box, select C:\. If you double-click the javacourse folder listed in the text window, a different New Project window opens with javacourse in the Look In list box. By double-clicking the chap6 folder listed in the text window, a different New Project window opens with chap6 in the Look In list box. Next, in the File Name text box, type lab6.8.3 to create a lab6.8.3 subfolder in the chap6 folder.

Tasks

Step 1: Creating, Setting, and Displaying Dates

a. Create a class called DateDemo in the main method. To display the current date of your computer in full format, use the following sample code:

```
Date today = new Date();

DateFormat df = DateFormat.getDateInstance(DateFormat.FULL,
   Locale.US);

String date = df.format(today);

        System.out.println("Current date on this computer is:
   " + date);
```

b. To set a Date variable with a Date object from a full format String "Tuesday, May 23, 2002" and display it in short format "mm/dd/yy", use the following sample code:

```
Date newday;

DateFormat newdf = DateFormat.getDateInstance(DateFormat.SHORT,
   Locale.US);

newday = df.parse("Tuesday, May 23, 2002");

date = newdf.format(newday);

System.out.println("Date in short format: "  + date);
```

c. To calculate the calendar date after seven weeks from today using the Calendar class, use the following sample code:

```
GregorianCalendar calendar = new GregorianCalendar();

calendar.add(GregorianCalendar.DATE, 49);

newday = calendar.getTime();

date = df.format(newday);

        System.out.println("Date after 7 weeks is: " + date);
```

Step 2: Running the Class

Compile and test the class.

Lab 6.9.1.1: System, String, StringBuffer, and Use of the Console Class

Estimated Time: 45 minutes

Description/Scenario

- Use the System class for input and output.

- Use the String and StringBuffer classes.

- Read Customer data from standard input using System.in.

- Output Customer data to standard output using System.out.

- Use String and StringBuffer classes to store, retrieve, and manipulate data.

- Use the Console class provided in the Resource folder to read Customer data. You can use the Console class to display any prompt to the user and collect input from the user. The methods of the Console class are static.

- String and StringBuffer are independent classes, with many different methods and fields. Use the StringBuffer class as the working space for manipulating the characters and the String class as the place where the final result will be placed.

File Management

Open BlueJ, click on Project from the BlueJ main menu, and select New. In the New Project window and in the Look In list box, select C:\. If you double-click the javacourse folder listed in the text window, a different New Project window opens with javacourse in the Look In list box. By double-clicking the chap6 folder listed in the text window, a different New Project window opens with chap6 in the Look In list box. Next, in the File Name text box, type lab6.9.1.1 to create a lab6.9.1.1 subfolder in the chap6 folder. Import the JBANK classes from lab5.11.1.

Tasks

Step 1: Reading Data from the Console

a. In the main method of the Teller class, declare a StringBuffer called greeting and initialize it to "Hello".

b. Using the StringBuffer insert() method, insert "Mr" at the seventh position in the StringBuffer greeting.

c. Use System.in.read() to read a customer's name from the console (refer to page 6.1.2 of the curriculum Figure 4 MoreThanOneCharInput.java example. *Hint:* Use a while loop to check until the Enter key or a carriage return is pressed.) You can use the System.in object to read one character at a time. The in object has several methods for reading data. The data returned from the read() method has an int datatype. The int needs to be converted to (cast as) a char. Include a throws Exception in the main method. (Exceptions will be covered in detail in later chapters.)

d. Append the customer's name to the StringBuffer greeting by using the append() method. Use System.out.println() to display the greeting. The out object is an object of the class PrintStream. This class has overloaded methods print() and println(). These are particularly useful for console output.

Step 2: Using String and StringBuffer Methods to Manipulate and Display Customer Data

a. In the Customer class, implement the toString() method to return a String object. In this method, declare a StringBuffer called customerData and use the append() method to append Customer fields to customerData. Use the toString() method of the StringBuffer class to return the String object from customerData.

b. In the Teller class main method, use the System.out.println() method to display the customer data in customer3.toString().

c. Use the System.out.println(customer3) to display Customer data. What is the difference between b and c?

Step 3: Using the Console Class to Read Customer Data

a. Import the Console class from the Resource folder. The Console class is provided to obtain input from the keyboard. The methods of the Console class are static. The following is sample code for using the Console class:

```
double price = Console.readDouble("Enter the balance amount");
```

b. In the Teller class main method, create an instance of Customer called customer4 using the constructor Customer(firstName, lastName, dateOfBirth, custId). Use readline() and readInt() methods of the Console class to read Customer data such as Customer streetAddress, cityAddress, zipOrPostalCode, phoneNumber, and e-mail address. Use the set methods to set the values.

c. Use the toString() method of the Customer class in the System.out.println() method to print the customer data.

118

Step 4: Review Questions

    a.   What is the advantage of StringBuffer over String? (*Hint:* Immutability.)

_____

    b.   Using StringBuffer() what is the limit to the number of input characters?

_____

Step 5: Documentation

Using the Document "How to use UMLTestTool," follow the instructions to verify that your JBANK classes match the JBANK UML diagram shown in Figure 6-9-1-1.

Write javadoc comments for the methods introduced in this lab.

Figure 6-9-1-1: JBANK Application—Phase II

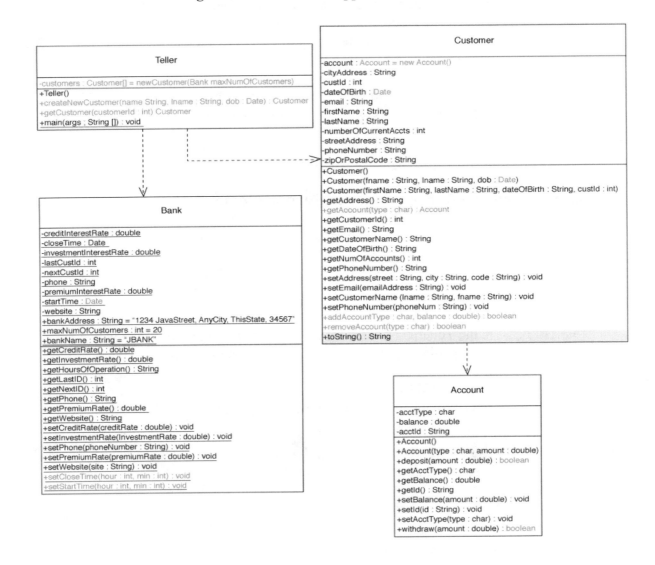

Lab 6.9.1.2: Wrapper Classes, Math Class, Date Class

Estimated Time: 40 minutes

Learning Objective

- In this lab activity, the student will use wrapper classes to convert String data to primitives and use methods of the Date, BigDecimal, and BigInteger classes.

Description/Scenario

- Wrapper classes manipulate primitive data types. Every primitive data type has a corresponding wrapper class. This class is also useful for converting String data to primitives.

- BigDecimal and BigInteger classes are useful for manipulating numbers with an arbitrarily long sequence of digits. The documentation for these classes can be found in the section on the java.math package in the Java API Documentation.

- There are three classes in the Java API documentation concerned with dates. The Date class creates a Date object. The Calendar class sets or changes the date for a Date object. The DateFormat class displays the date in different formats. The Date and Calendar classes are located in the java.util package. The DateFormat class is part of the java.text package.

- Use the Date class to set the hours of operation for the Bank and customers DOB field.

- Use BigDecimal and BigInteger for manipulating numbers with an arbitrarily long sequence of digits to calculate the interest on the Account balance.

- Use wrapper classes to convert String data to primitive data types.

File Management

Open BlueJ, Click on Project from the BlueJ main menu and select New. In the New Project window and in the Look in: list box select C:\. Now, double click the javacourse folder listed in the text window and a different New Project window opens with javacourse in the Look in: list box. Now, double click the chap6 folder listed in the text window and a different New Project window opens with chap6 in the Look in: list box. Next, in the File name text box type lab6.9.1.2 to create a lab6.9.1.2 sub-folder in the chap6 folder. Import classes from lab6.9.1.1.

Tasks

Step 1: Using the Date Type for Customer DOB and Bank's Hours of Operation

a. In the Customer class, replace the dateOfBirth field of type String by the Date type.

b. Modify the Customer constructors that take dateOfBirth of type String to accept a date. Modify the getDateOfBirth() method to return a date.

c. Similarly in the Bank class, replace the startTime and closeTime fields of type String with the Date type. The Date class is found in the java.util package. Include the statement import java.util.* in the Teller, Bank, and Customer classes.

d. In the Bank class, add the method public static void setStartTime(int hour, int min) to set the startTime.

Sample code:

```
setStartTime(int hour, int min)
{
        GregorianCalendar sTime = new GregorianCalendar();
        int year = sTime.get(GregorianCalendar.YEAR);
        int month = sTime.get(GregorianCalendar.MONTH);
        int date = sTime.get(GregorianCalendar.DATE);
        sTime = new GregorianCalendar(year, month, date, hour, min);
        startTime = sTime.getTime();

}
```

e. Use the preceding template for the setCloseTime method.

f. Modify the getHoursOfOperation() method to return a String (startTime to closeTime).

g. Remove the code in the Teller class main method, which exists from the previous lab. In the Teller class main method, using the Bank class' static method setStartTime(), set the start time to 8:30. The setStartTime() takes hour and min as arguments. Set the hour to 8 and minutes to 30. Similarly, set the close time to 5:30.

h. Display the hours of operation by calling the getHoursOfOperation() method defined in the Bank class.

Step 2: Using the Date and Date Format Method

a. In the Teller class main method, read the Customer's firstName, lastName, dateOfBirth, and custId using the Console class. Use the DateFormat class to convert the String dateOfBirth to a date. (Include the statement import java.text.*; .) The students must review the API and find the methods to convert the String to a date. Create an instance of the Customer called customer5 using the constructor that takes firstName, lastName, dateOfBirth, and custId. Pass the values read from the Console into the constructor.

Suggested Data:

Customer firstName: John

Customer lastName: Doe

Customer Date Of Birth: 7/8/70

Customer ID: 1001

b. Use the Console class to read the Street Address, City Address, Zip or Postal Code, Phone Number, and E-Mail Address. Use the set methods to set the values.

Suggested Data:

Customer Street Address: 123 N. Java Street

Customer City Address: Java City

Customer Zip Or Postal code: 99999

Customer Phone Number: 778-888-9999

Customer E-Mail: javaStudent@email.com

c. To deposit an amount of $2000 into the account of customer5, use the getAccount() method defined in the Customer class that returns an Account object. Call the deposit() method defined in the Account class by passing an amount of $2000. Similarly, withdraw an amount of $780 from the account of customer5. Modify the toString() method of the Customer class to display the account balance.

d. Display the customer5 information.

Step 3: Using BigDecimal and BigInteger to Calculate the Interest Rate and Use of Wrapper Classes

To compute long-term investment, use the Console class to read the invested amount into a String variable investAmount and the investment period into an int variable term. Set the investment rate to 5% by calling the setInvestmentRate() method of the Bank class. Call the getInvestmentRate() method of the Bank class to return an investmentRate into a variable of type double called interestRate. Declare a variable called futureValue of type BigDecimal, and in the BigDecimal constructor, pass the investAmount. Use BigDecimal to calculate the interest earned. (*Hint:* Review the API and use multiply() and add() methods of the BigDecimal method to calculate the interest earned.) To use the BigDecimal class, include the statement import java.math.*;. Use wrapper classes to convert a double to a String. Students might have to review the API for this lab. To learn more about BigDecimal and BigInteger, refer to the site http://www.javaworld.com/javaworld/jw-06-2001/jw-0601-cents_p.html.

Step 4: Review Questions

a. Name two wrapper classes.

_____

_____

_____

b. What must be imported to use the Date class?

_____

_____

_____

Step 5: Documentation

Using the Document "How to Use UMLTestTool," follow the instructions to verify that your JBANK classes match the JBANK UML diagram shown in Figure 6-9-1-2.

Write javadoc comments for the methods introduced in this lab.

Figure 6-9-1-2: JBANK Application—Phase II

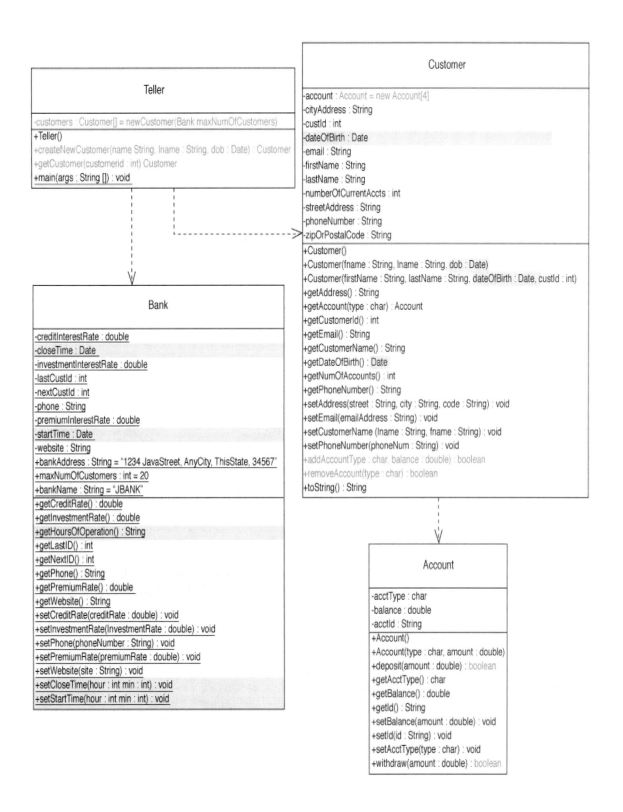

Chapter 7 Labs – Arrays

Lab 7.4.2: Passing an Array to a Method

Estimated Time: 20 minutes

Learning Objectives

- In this lab activity, the student will create and use array objects as part of the class definition.

- The student will demonstrate the use of array references in the method calls.

Description/Scenario

- The syntax for declaring and populating an array of object references is as follows:

```
JavaStudent studentsInACourse[] = new JavaStudent[10];
```

This statement creates a reference variable identified by studentsInACourse to reference an array object that will hold an array of references to JavaStudent objects. When this statement is executed, a reference variable and an array object with 10 reference variables will be created. The length of the array is 10. Each element of the array referenced by studentsInACourse will contain a null value because no JavaStudent objects have been created.

```
StudentsInACourse[0] = new JavaStudent();
```

This statement creates a JavaStudent object and stores the reference to the object in the first element of the array studentsInACourse.

- An array element can be passed to a method that requests a single value. A method with the signature averageStudentPerc(JavaStudent astudent){} will accept the following argument:

```
averageStudentPerc(studentsInACourse[0]);
```

Here the argument is a reference to the student object referenced in the array element [0]. This is no different from using a single reference variable. This method will now have access to the non-private data and methods of the JavaStudent object. In this example, the method requires a single JavaStudent object.

- A reference to an array object can be passed to a method:

```
averageClassPerc(JavaStudent[] students, int testnumber);
```

```
In this example, the method requires a reference to an array object of
JavaStudent references as its first argument, and a test number (int) for its
second argument.
```

```
averageClassPerc(studentsInACourse, 0);
```

- Create a class called ArrayDemo. In this class, define a method that takes an array reference, an array index, and a value as arguments and changes the corresponding array index element to the new value.

File Management

Open BlueJ, click on Project from the BlueJ main menu, and select New. In the New Project window and in the Look In list box, select C:\. If you double-click the javacourse folder listed in the text window, a different New Project window opens with javacourse in the Look In list box. When you double-click the chap7 folder listed in the text window, a different New Project window opens with chap7 in the Look In list box. Next, in the File Name text box, type lab7.4.2 to create a lab7.4.2 subfolder in the chap7 folder.

Tasks

Step 1: Using an Array Reference in a Method Call

a. Create a class called ArrayDemo. Define a public static method called replaceArrayElement() that takes names (a reference to an array object of String), index (of type int) and value (a String object reference) as arguments.

b. In the main method, define a String array called names and initialize it with some values.

Sample code:

```
String names[] = {"Joe", "Ben", "Tom", "John");
```

c. Using a for loop, iterate through the array elements and print the array elements to the output screen:

d. Using the Console class, accept a number that represents an array index and a String to replace the array element corresponding to the index. Use the replaceArrayElement(names, index, value) statement to replace an array element and display the modified array elements. In the replaceArrayElement() method, use the index to identify the array element to be replaced and assign the String to this element.

Sample code:

```
public static replaceArrayElement( String[] names, int index, String
value) {..}
```

e. Using a for loop, iterate through the updated array elements and print the array elements to the output screen.

Step 2: Running the Class

Compile and test the class.

Lab 7.4.3: Creating and Traversing Through Arrays

Estimated Time: 20 minutes

Learning Objectives

- In this lab activity, the student will use parallel arrays to store data and apply iterative loop structures for traversing (scanning) through the arrays.

Description/Scenario

- In the JavaStudent class, you can think of each of the arrays as a parallel array. That is, the value in one element of the array has a corresponding meaning for the value of the same element in another array.

  For example:

  testDate[0], testName[0], maxPoints[0] all hold different information about the first test.

  testScore[0] and percentage[0] contain the scores and percentages of a specific student for the first test.

- You can use this parallel relationship between the arrays to process and handle these arrays in the same loop construct, the same if statement, or any other method or statement. You can use a single int variable to access the parallel elements of the array. It is important to note that declaration of similar arrays does not make them parallel. It is the deliberate storing of corresponding meaningful values that makes arrays parallel. The test[0] should store the score for the first test, and the maxPoints[0] should store the corresponding value for the maximum points for the first test. It is the programmer's responsibility to understand the data and ensure its validity.

- Create and traverse through arrays.

- Use arrays to store student IDs and student names. The value of a Student ID in the Student array corresponds to a student name in the student name array.

- Use the Console class to accept a student ID and display the corresponding student name.

File Management

Open BlueJ, click on Project from the BlueJ main menu, and select New. In the New Project window and in the Look In list box, select C:\. When you double-click the javacourse folder listed in the text window, a different New Project window opens with javacourse in the Look In list box. Double-clicking the chap7 folder listed in the text window causes a different New Project window to open with chap7 in the Look In list box. Next, in the File Name text box, type lab7.4.3 to create a lab7.4.3 subfolder in the chap7 folder.

Tasks

Step 1: Creating and Initializing Arrays

a. Create the class called StudentIdName. In this class, define and initialize an array of type int called studentID and define and initialize another array of type String called studentName. An array object creates and stores data in a sequential set of storage locations. Make sure that the studentID and studentName arrays are initialized with the same number of elements.

Code sample:

```
private int[] studentID = {101,102,104,105,106}
```

b. Define a set method to change a studentID in the studentID array. The set method takes two arguments. The first argument is of type int and represents an index of the array, and the second argument is of type int and represents a student ID. Use a similar approach to define a set method to change a student name in the studentName array.

c. Define a get method that takes an argument of type int that represents an index of the studentID array and returns the studentID of the corresponding index. Similarly, define a get method to get a student name from the studentName array by an index.

Step 2: Traversing Through the Arrays

a. Define a main method that uses the Console class to accept a studentID. Using the student ID, traverse through the studentID array to find the index to get the corresponding student name from the studentName array.

b. Compile and run the class.

c. Do the student IDs have to be in sequence to work here?

_____

d. Update the array objects at the second and fifth index for the IDs and names. Then, as in step 1, display all the IDs and names in both arrays.

e. Is it possible to change the array size dynamically?

_____

f. What comparison operator would be needed to check the name? Could we use "==" ?

_____

_____

_____

_____

g. What would happen if in the set or get methods, the index argument was greater to or equal to the size of the arrays? What if the index was a negative number? What if the index pointed to a null value for a studentName?

_____

_____

_____

_____

_____

_____

_____

_____

_____

_____

Lab 7.4.4: Searching and Sorting an Array

Estimated Time: 20 minutes

Learning Objectives

- In this lab activity, the student will implement methods to sort arrays in ascending and descending order.

Description/Scenario

- *Sorting* is the process of arranging a series of objects in some logical order. When objects are placed in an order beginning with the lowest value and ending at the highest value, they are being sorted in *ascending order*. The case of a character can influence the data sort. When objects are placed in an order beginning with the highest value and ending with the lowest value, they are being sorted in *descending order*. In the examples used so far in this chapter, the array elements have been manipulated in the sequence in which they were created.

- A commonly used programming/sorting technique is called a *bubble sort*. This particular technique relies on being able to compare pairs of values, assuming that there is some order in which the values can be organized. In this technique, two values are compared. If the values are out of order, then they are swapped. Sorting a large number of values without the use of arrays can be a difficult task. You can use the simple swap technique to process an array several times until the values are in the necessary order. The technique to do this is called a bubble sort. In this technique, the array is processed until the largest or the smallest number is assigned to the first element. The lowest or highest value bubbles to the start of the array. Each processing of the array includes the comparison of pairs of values and swapping the values if needed. Before values are swapped, one of the pair of values is stored in a temp variable.

For example:

```
int x = 20 , y = 10, temp;


// swapping
if (y < x )
{
        temp = x;
        x = y;
        y = temp;
}
```

- Sorting objects is not much different from sorting primitives. Objects are generally sorted based on the value of some data in the object. For example, if the teacher wanted to sort the students in the class by ID, the JavaStudent array would be processed comparing the ID for each of the students. The only difference here is that the temp variable is of the type JavaStudent, and the comparison for swapping uses the method getId() to compare the ID for each student.

- Define a class called SortArray, which contains references to arrays of char and int. Implement methods to sort character arrays in ascending order and integer arrays in descending order. Instantiate an object of the class and invoke the methods to display a sorted order of char and int.

File Management

Open BlueJ, click on Project from the Bluej main menu, and select New. In the New Project window and in the Look In list box, select C:\. By double-clicking the javacourse folder listed in the text window, a different New Project window opens with javacourse in the Look In list box. If you double-click the chap7 folder listed in the text window, a different New Project window opens with chap7 in the Look In list box. Next, in the File Name text box, type lab7.4.4 to create a lab7.4.4 subfolder in the chap7 folder.

Tasks

Step 1: Sorting Character and Integer Arrays

a. Define a class called SortArray.

b. Define a public static void charSortArray() method that takes a char array reference and the length of the array as arguments. In the charSortArray() method, two for loops are needed to sort the array and each must execute a number of times that is one less than the length of the array. The second loop checks whether the first element is greater than the second element in the array and swaps the values if the first element is greater than the second element; it does this by storing one element in a temp variable.

c. Similarly define a public static void intSortArray() method that takes an int array reference and sorts the numbers in descending order.

d. In the main method, define an array of type char called charArray and initialize the array with character values. Similarly, define an array of type int called intArray and initialize the array with integer values. Use a for loop to print the elements in the arrays before the sorts. Invoke the charSortArray(charArray) method and print the result after the sort. Invoke the intSortArray(intArray) method and print the results after the sort.

Step 2: Running the Class

Compile and test the class.

Lab 7.4.5: Extended Use of Arrays

Estimated Time: 15 minutes

Learning Objectives

- In this lab activity, the student will create an array of Strings and retrieve elements based on specific index values provided using the Math.random() method.

Description/Scenario

- Create a class called PickADay with an array of Strings initialized with the seven days of the week.

- Utilize a class constructor to create a random number to index a day in the array. The random() method of the java.lang.Math class is a static method that returns a random number as a double, where the following is true:

  $0.0 <= $ returned double $ < 1.0$

File Management

Open BlueJ, click on Project from the Bluej main menu, and select New. In the New Project window and in the Look In list box, select C:\. By double-clicking the javacourse folder listed in the text window, a different New Project window opens with javacourse in the Look In list box. If you double-click the chap7 folder listed in the text window, a different New Project window opens with chap7 in the Look In list box. Next, in the File Name text box, type lab7.4.5 to create a lab7.4.5 subfolder in the chap7 folder.

Tasks

Step 1: Create an Array of Strings and Retrieve Elements Using the Math.random() Method

a. Create the class PickADay. This class has a static array object named weekday as a class attribute. The array object weekDay is of the type String.

b. Use a static initializer block to load the weekday array object with the seven days of the week.

c. Create an instance variable index of the type int and make it private static.

d. In the PickADay constructor, use the random method in the Math class to set the value of the index and make sure that it is an int that is between 0 and 6.

e. In the main method, create an instance of PickADay. Using a single println() statement, display the day of the week that was randomly selected.

f. Compile and run the class.

g. What would happen if the index was larger than 6? _____

h. Modify the main method println() statement to say "sorry" if the day that was randomly selected is already a normal day off (Saturday or Sunday).

Lab 7.5.2: Traversing a Multidimensional Array

Estimated Time: 20 minutes

Learning Objectives

- In this lab activity, the student will implement code to traverse a multidimensional array.

Description/Scenario

- The syntax for declaring and storing data in a multidimensional array is as follows:

```
int [] []  aTableofNumbers;
```

Here, the statement creates a 3-row and 3-column array to store int:

```
aTableofNumbers = new int[3][3];
```

Alternatively, each row of the array can have a different number of elements. This syntax will result in each element of the array holding the default int value 0.

```
aTableofNumbers = new int[3][];
aTableofNumbers[0] = new int[3];
aTableofNumbers [1] = new int[5];
aTableofNumbers[2] =new int[7];
```

Here, each row is different and has data stored in each element:

```
int [][] aTableofNumbers ={ {3,4,5,6},
                            {2,3,4},
                          {1,2,3,4,5}};
```

- To reference a single element of a multidimensional array, reference the index value for each dimension. For example, aTableofNumbers[1][3] will reference the element in the second row and fourth column.

- To access more than one element of a multidimensional array, nested for loops can be used. Each loop processes elements of one dimension.

- Create a class called EmployeeData. This class stores the employee names and employee titles in a two-dimensional array and stores the employees' salaries in a single-dimensional array. Students will traverse through the arrays to display employees who earn more than $2000.

File Management

Open BlueJ, click on Project from the Bluej main menu, and select New. In the New Project window and in the Look In list box, select C:\. If you double-click the javacourse folder listed in the text window, a different New Project window opens with javacourse in the Look In list box. By double-clicking the chap7 folder listed in the text window, a different New Project window opens with chap7 in the Look In list box. Next, in the File Name text box, type lab7.5.2 to create a lab7.5.2 subfolder in the chap7 folder.

Tasks

Step 1: Creating Multidimensional Arrays

a. Define a class called EmployeeData. In the main method, define a multidimensional String array called employeeInfo, which stores the employee name and title.

b. Define a second array called salary of type double, which stores the employee's salary. Traverse through the multidimensional array and display the employee name and title for those who earn a salary greater than $2000. Display the results.

Sample code for initializing Multidimensional arrays:

```
String[][] employeeInfo = { {"Alex", "Joe", "James", "Tom"},
        {"Manager", "Clerk", "Analyst", "Manager"} };
```

Step 2: Running the Class

Compile and test the class.

Lab 7.6.1: Implementing Arrays in the JBANK Application

Estimated Time: 60 minutes

Learning Objectives

- In this lab activity, the student will incorporate array objects to store Customer and Account data.

Description/Scenario

- Use arrays to store objects.

- Traverse through an array using loops.

- Use arrays to store 20 customers' objects.

- Use arrays to hold a maximum of four accounts for every customer.

- Traverse through the arrays to perform deposits and withdrawals for a particular customer.

File Management

Open BlueJ, click on Project from the BlueJ main menu, and select New. In the New Project window and in the Look In list box, select C:\. If you double-click the javacourse folder listed in the text window, a different New Project window opens with javacourse in the Look In list box. By double-clicking the chap7 folder listed in the text window, a different New Project window opens with chap7 in the Look In list box. Next, in the File Name text box, type lab7.6.1 to create a lab7.6.1 subfolder in the chap7 folder. Import JBANK classes from lab6.9.1.2.

Tasks

Step 1: Creating an Array of 20 Customers

a. In the Teller class, define an array of Customer objects called customers as a private field. The size of the array is determined by the Bank attribute maxNumberOfCustomers, which is assigned a value of 20. The data in the array object is a sequence of references to the actual objects. Both the array object and the objects it references are created on the heap.

b. In the Teller class, define a public method createNewCustomer(String fname, String lname, Date dob), which returns a Customer object. In this method, using a for loop, create Customer objects by using the Customer constructor, which takes firstName, lastName, dateOfBirth and custId. The custId is generated by the Bank attributes lastCustId and nextCustId. In the Bank class, initialize the lastCustId to 1000 and the nextCustId to 1001. Modify the getNextID() method, which assigns nextCustId to lastCustId to increment nextCustId by 1 and return the lastCustId. Call the getNextID() method in the createNewCustomer() method of the Teller class to generate custId.

    c.   In the Teller class, define a public method getCustomer (int customerId), which takes customerId as an argument and returns a Customer object. In this method using a loop, go through the customer array object and check for the Customer with the particular customerId and return the Customer object.

Step 2: Modifying the Customer Class to Add an Account, Get an Account, or Remove an Account

    a.   In the Customer class, modify the account attribute, which takes an array of four Account objects.

    b.   Define a method addAccount() in the Customer class, which takes a type (an Account type) and balance as arguments. Use a for loop to check that the number of accounts does not exceed four.

    c.   Create a new account by checking for a null position in the array object. Increment the attribute numberOfCurrentAccts by 1. The method returns a Boolean value, which is true if the account is created and false if the account is not created.

    d.   Define a removeAccount() method that takes a type (Account type) as an argument. This method goes through the Account array and checks for the account with that particular account type and assigns null to the reference at that position. Decrement the numberOfCurrentAccts attribute by 1. This method returns a Boolean value, which is true if the account is removed and returns false if it's not removed.

    e.   Modify the getAccount() method to take a type (account type) as argument. This method goes through the account array and checks for the account with that particular account type. The method then returns that particular Account object.

    f.   Modify the toString() method to display an account type.

Step 3: Modifying the Account Class' Deposit and Withdraw Methods

    a.   In the Account class, modify the deposit() method to return a Boolean. The method checks whether the deposit was successful. If it was, the method returns true; otherwise, it returns false.

    b.   Modify the withdraw() method to return a Boolean. The withdraw() method checks that the Account has a minimum balance of $10 even after withdrawal.

Step 4: Testing the Program

a. Create a list of three customers with the suggested data provided next.

Suggested customer data:

Customer 1

FirstName: John

LastName: Doe

City Address: Phoenix

Street Address: 4128 W. Van Buren Street

E-Mail: Rman@theriver.com

Phone Number: 111-111-1111

zipOrPostalCode 67777

DOB 2/1/50

Account SAVINGS, 3000

Customer 2

FirstName: Betsy

LastName: Smith

City Address: Glendale

Street Address: 123 E. Elm Street

E-Mail: betsy@aol.com

Phone Number: 222-222-2222

zipOrPostalCode 9999

DOB 5/7/70

Account LINEOFCREDIT, 5000

Customer 3

FirstName: Joe

LastName: Smith

City Address: Mesa

Street Address: 890 W. Pine Street

E-Mail: joe@java.com

Phone Number: 333-333-3333

zipOrPostalCode 9999

DOB 2/8/80

Account SAVINGS, 4500

b.   Display all the customer information.

c.   Deposit an amount of $1000 into the savings account for Customer1.

d.   Withdraw an amount of $500 from the savings account for Customer3.

Step 5: Documentation

a.   Using the UMLTestTool, verify that your JBANK classes match the JBANK UML diagram shown in Figure 7-6-1-1.

b.   Write javadoc comments for the methods introduced in this lab.

139

Figure 7-6-1-1: JBANK Application—Phase II

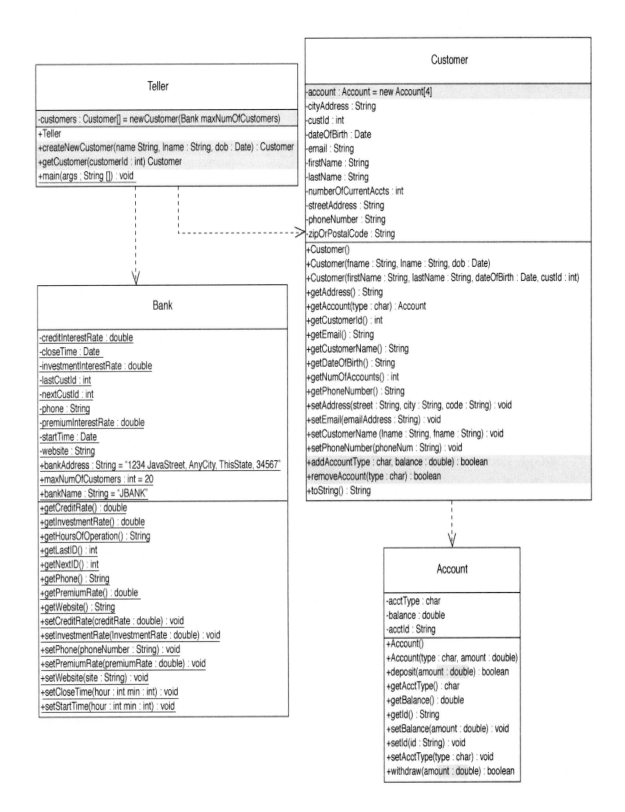

Chapter 8 Labs – Classes and Inheritance

Lab 8.7.1: Implement Abstraction in the Banking Application

Estimated Time: 15 minutes

Learning Objectives

- In this lab activity, the student will discover the common fields and behaviors for different types of Account classes.

- The student will use these generalizations to define abstract classes.

Description/Scenario

- As the programmer moves up the inheritance hierarchy, classes become more general and probably more abstract. At some point, the ancestor class becomes so general that it is regarded as a guideline for other classes, rather than as a definition for an object that can be used. When the class in a hierarchy serves as a framework or guideline for other classes, the class is defined as abstract. In this case, the class is not expected to be used to create objects that store data and do work. The class is used to set boundaries for definitions of other subclasses. The abstract class is viewed as a common framework for a set of related subclasses.

- The ultimate goal of object-oriented design (OOD) is to factor out the common operations and data to a higher level in the inheritance hierarchy. As the common operations are factored out, it might become apparent that the details of how the operations are implemented cannot be specified in the higher-level class. An abstract method is declared using the following syntax:

```
<modifiers> abstract <return-type> method-name (arguments);
```

The keyword abstract is one of the method's modifiers/

- An abstract method does not have a body of code. A class that has an abstract method must be declared abstract using this syntax:

```
<modifier> abstract class ClassName { }
```

The keyword abstract is one of the class' modifiers.

- Define abstraction by discovering common attributes and behaviors among classes.

- Define the Account class as an abstract class. The Account class will be the superclass for different types of Account classes.

File Management

Open BlueJ, click on Project from the BlueJ main menu, and select New. In the New Project window and in the Look In list box, select C:\. Then double-click the javacourse folder listed in the text window, and a different New Project window opens with javacourse in the Look In list box. If you double-click the chap8 folder listed in the text window, a different New Project window opens with chap8 in the Look In list box. In the File Name text box, type lab8.7.1 to create a lab8.7.1 subfolder in the chap8 folder. Import JBANK classes from lab7.6.1.

Tasks

Step 1: Identifying General Attributes and Behaviors of Different Types of Account Classes

a. When you're designing classes, common fields and behaviors lead to generalizations about the classes. You can implement this generalization through the design of a parent class also known as superclass. In the JBANK application, we have various types of accounts such as savings, investment, line of credit, and overdraft protection. Each account type has common attributes and methods. In the Account class, the acctId and balance are the common attributes, and getBalance(), setBalance(), deposit(), and withdraw() are the common methods. The Account class will become the parent class for different types of accounts. Make the Account class abstract because it's useless to create an Account object without a type.

Sample code:

```
public abstract class Account
```

b. Do not change the method implementation of the getBalance(), setBalance(), and deposit() methods. Note that the implementation of the withdraw() and getAcctType() methods are different for different account types; make these methods abstract and remove their implementation. Making a method abstract forces the user to implement the method in child classes.

Sample code:

```
public abstract double withdraw(double amount);
```

c.   Modify the constructor of the Account class, which previously took a type and amount as arguments, to take a custId of type int, type, and balance as arguments. Remove the default constructor. The attribute acctType is not required because the getAcctType() method is made abstract and each of the child classes implements the getAcctType() to return an account type such as 'S' if it is a savings account or 'I' if it is an investment account. Remove the setAcctType(). The method setId(String id) is no longer used because the Account constructor now takes a custId, and the acctId is assigned a value by concatenating custId + type.

d.   In the Teller class main method, create an instance of the Account class. Can the program be compiled?

Step 2: Documentation

Using the document "How to Use UMLTestTool," follow the instructions to verify that your JBANK classes match the JBANK UML diagram shown in Figure 8-7-1-1.

Write javadoc comments to match the changes made to the Account class.

Figure 8-7-1-1: JBANK Application—Phase III

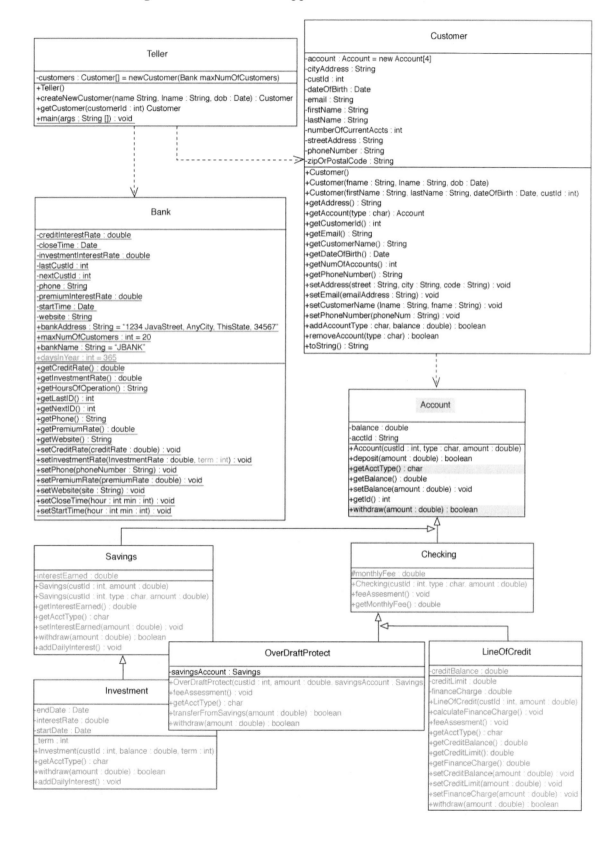

Lab 8.7.2.1: Implement Inheritance, Extending from Abstract and Concrete Classes

Estimated Time: 60 minutes

Learning Objectives

- In this lab activity, the student will apply inheritance principles to extend concrete classes from abstract superclasses.

Description/Scenario

- Extend concrete classes from abstract classes.

- Use the keywords this and super.

- Overload and override methods in child classes.

- Create a concrete Savings class from the abstract Account class.

- Extend the Investment class as a concrete class from the Savings class.

- Programmers arrive at abstract and concrete designs of classes in one of two ways:

  ⇒ *Generalization*, or discovery of general behaviors among classes

  ⇒ *Specialization*, or identification of specific adaptation of general behaviors or adoption of new behaviors in an inherited class

- When you design classes, common fields and behaviors lead to generalizations about the classes. You can implement these generalizations through the design of parent classes, also known as *superclasses*. Superclasses can then be designed to describe required and optional fields and behaviors. A superclass can be an abstract representation of common behaviors and data.

- The term *abstract* is applied to classes from which no objects are expected to be created.

- Generalizations of classes into a superclass can be either concrete or abstract.

Business Rules

- Savings accounts require a minimum balance of $10. When a new customer joins the bank, he is assigned a savings account and must deposit at least $10. Customers will be allowed to withdraw from the savings account at any time. Customers cannot withdraw amounts exceeding the amount in their account. The savings interest rates are calculated on a daily basis depending on the premium interest rates set in the Bank class.

- Account ID is given by "CustomerID + Account identifier." For example, if the CustomerId is 1001 and the account type is a savings account, the Account ID is '1001S'.

- Investment accounts are used to save money for an extended period of time. This account provides the customer with a higher interest rate based on how long he invests money in the account. The longer the customer keeps the money in the account, the higher the interest rate earned. Investment accounts require a minimum amount of $100 to open the account, and a minimum investment term of six months. An *investment term* is how long the money has to remain in the account without withdrawals. Investment interest rates are 6 months at 5% and 12 months at 7%, both compounded monthly. The penalty for early withdraw is 20%.

File Management

Open BlueJ, click on Project from the BlueJ main menu, and select New. In the New Project window and in the Look In list box, select C:\. If you double-click the javacourse folder listed in the text window, a different New Project window opens with javacourse in the Look In list box. By double-clicking the chap8 folder listed in the text window, a different New Project window opens with chap8 in the Look In list box. In the File Name text box, type lab8.7.2.1 to create a lab8.7.2.1 subfolder in the chap8 folder. Import JBANK classes from the lab8.7.1 Resource folder.

Tasks

Step 1: Extending the Savings Class from the Account Class

    a.   Create the Savings class, which extends from the abstract Account class. The Savings class is a concrete class. In object-oriented programming, the term *concrete* means a class from which an object can be created and used. To keep track of the interest earned, define a private attribute of type double called interestEarned.

    b.   Add a Savings constructor that takes a custId of type int and amount of type double as arguments. Call the parent constructor by using the keyword super and passing the custID character 'S' for savings and balance as arguments. Each constructor in the subclass must include a call to the parent constructor. The call to a parent constructor happens through the use of the keyword super, and it must be the first call in the subclass' constructor.

Code sample:

```
super(custId, 'S', balance);
```

    c.   In the Savings class, define one more constructor that takes a custID of type int, an account of type char, and an amount of type double. The subclasses of the Savings class require this constructor.

d. Define the method setInterestEarned(), which takes an amount as argument and sets the interestEarned to the amount passed. Define the getInterestEarned() method, which returns the interestEarned.

e. To calculate daily interest earned and then add this amount to the interestEarned attribute, define a method addDailyInterest() by using the sample code shown next:

```
public void addDailyInterest(){
        setInterestEarned(interestEarned + (getBalance() *
        Bank.getPremiumRate()/Bank.daysInYear));
}
```

Define a public static attribute daysInYear in the Bank class, which is assigned a value of 365.

f. Also implement the getAcctType() method to return a character 'S' for savings account.

g. Implement the withdraw() method specific to the savings account. Check for the savings account to maintain a minimum balance of $10.

Step 2: Extending an Investment Account from the Savings Account Class

a. Create an Investment class that extends from Savings. The Investment account is a savings account that provides a user with higher interest rates. Define one private attribute of type Date to hold the startDate of the investment and another private attribute of type Date to hold the endDate. Define a private attribute of type int to hold the term (how long money is invested). Define a private attribute of type double to calculate the interestRate.

b. The constructor for the Investment account takes the custID, balance, and term as arguments. The constructor for the Investment account takes one more argument of type int used to set the term, which demonstrates the overloading concept. In the constructor, make a call to parent class Constructor by using the keyword super, which takes custId, account type, and balance as arguments. In the constructor, set the interestRate by calling the getInvestmentRate() method of the Bank class. Set the startDate to today's date and set the endDate by adding the term to today's date.

    c.   The withdraw() method makes a call to the superclass withdraw() method.

    d.   Implement the getAcctType() method to return I (for investment account).

    e.   Define the method addDailyInterest(), which sets the interestEarned. To calculate the interestEarned, modify the Bank class setInvestmentRate(), which takes the rate and term as arguments. The getInvestment() method is modified to take term as an argument and return the investmentRate. You will be creating a static initializer block in the Bank class to set the investment rate.

Step 3: Testing the Program

In the Teller class main method, create a customer with a savings account and an investment account. Deposit an amount of $1000 into the savings account. Withdraw an amount of $500 from the investment account. Print the results.

Step 4: Documentation

Using the document "How to Use UMLTestTool," follow the instructions to verify that your JBANK classes match the JBANK UML diagram shown in Figure 8-7-2-1.

Write javadoc comments to the Savings and Investment classes.

Figure 8-7-2-1: JBANK Application—Phase III

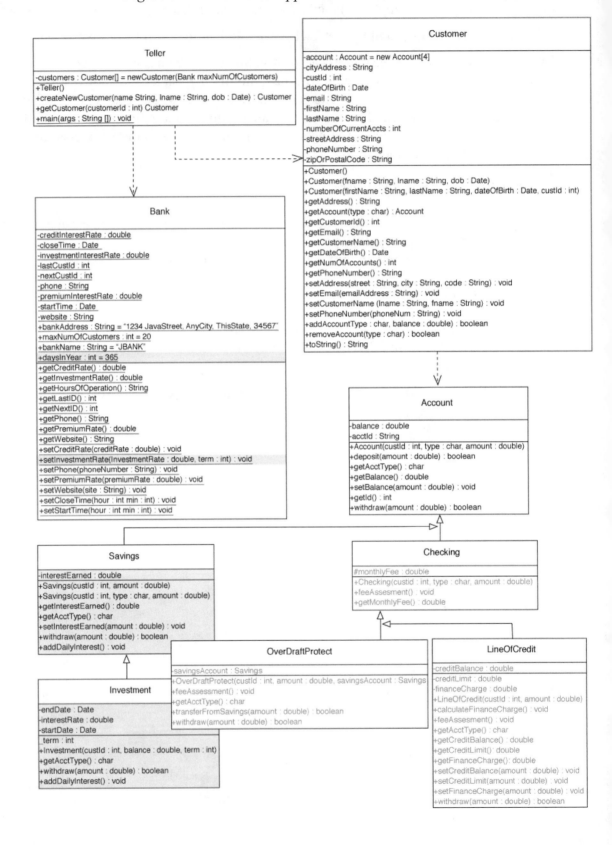

Lab 8.7.2.2: Abstraction at Several Levels – Checking Account

Estimated Time: 30 minutes

Learning Objectives

- In this lab activity, the student will apply inheritance principles for continuing the abstraction into a child class.

Description/Scenario

- Inherit an abstract class from an abstract superclass.

- Overload and override.

- Use the keyword super.

- Create an abstract Checking class that extends the Account class.

- Create concrete classes such as LineOfCredit and OverDraftProtect from the abstract Checking Account class.

Business Rules

- Checking accounts must have overdraft protection links to the savings account. What is an overdraft? When you try to withdraw money from your checking account and the amount you want to withdraw is more than the amount of money in your checking account (balance), you are *overdrafting* your checking account. JBANK provides all its customers with overdraft protection by linking the customer's checking account balance to their savings account balance. This type of bank account allows the customer to deposit any amount of money and withdraw any amount as long as there is adequate money in the checking account, in the savings account, or a combination of both. For example, if a customer has $40 in her checking account and $100 in her savings account, then she can withdraw a maximum of $140. A withdrawal of this amount will cause the savings account and checking account balance to become zero. A transaction fee is assessed to the overdraft account for ordering checks, bouncing checks, overdrafts, and so on.

- Line of credit (LOC) accounts are tied to a credit card and have a fixed maximum credit limit of $500. In this type of checking account, overdraft protection is provided by allowing a negative balance limited to the established $500 maximum. This type of account charges the customer a finance charge when the balance in the account drops below zero. The customer can only withdraw amounts equal to the sum of the available LOC checking balance and the credit limit. The amount withdrawn from the credit limit will be the first paid back by a customer deposit. The LOC interest is 18% per-annum calculated daily. A transaction fee is assessed to LOC for credits, new credit cards, and so on.

File Management

Open BlueJ, click on Project from the BlueJ main menu, and select New. In the New Project window and in the Look In list box, select C:\. If you double-click the javacourse folder listed in the text window, a different New Project window opens with javacourse in the Look In list box. By double-clicking the chap8 folder listed in the text window, a different New Project window opens with chap8 in the Look In list box. In the File Name text box, type lab8.7.2.2 to create a lab8.7.2.2 subfolder in the chap8 folder. Import JBANK classes from the lab8.7.2.1 Resource folder.

Tasks

Step 1: Implementing an Abstract Checking Account Class

a. According to business rules, a checking account should be of type LineOfCredit and OverDraftProtection; it's not necessary to create instances of the Checking account type. Create the Checking account class as an abstract class that extends the Account class.

b. Identify the common attributes and behaviors of the two types of checking accounts—LineOfCredit and OverDraftProtection—and define them in the Checking class.

c. Both types of checking accounts are required to keep track of the fee assessed on the transactions on a monthly basis. Define a protected attribute called monthlyFee of type double. Each of the checking accounts has its own rules for feeAssessment(), so define an abstract feeAssessment() method signature.

Sample code:

```
public abstract void feeAssessment();
```

The constructor of the Checking Account class takes a custId, type, and amount as arguments. The constructor calls the superclass constructor, which takes custId, type, and amount as arguments. Define the getMonthlyFee() method to return the monthlyFee.

Step 2: Extending OverDraftProtect and LineOfCredit from the Abstract Checking Class

a. Define an OverDraftProtect account, which extends from the Checking class. This class is a concrete class from which objects can be created and used. Define a private attribute savingsAccount of type Savings. The constructor of the OverDraftProtect class takes a custId, an amount, and a reference to the savings account. In the constructor call, the superclass constructor takes the custId and passes the acctType O and an amount. Override the getAcctType() to return a O (for OverDraftProtect).

b. Define a transferFromSavings() account that takes an amount as argument. This method withdraws an amount from the savings account.

c. The withdraw() method checks whether there are sufficient funds in the OverDraftProtect account; if there are insufficient funds, the withdraw() method gets an amount from the savings account by calling the transferFromSavings() method. Implement the feeAssessment() method.

d. Define a LineOfCredit class, which extends from the abstract Checking class. This class is a concrete class from which objects can be created and used. Declare the attributes private double creditBalance, private double creditLimit initialized to 500, and private double financeCharge.

e. In the constructor, call the superclass constructor and pass an L for the account type. Implement the getAcctType() to return L (for LineOfCredit).

f. Define the setter methods setCreditBalance(double amount) method to set the creditBalance, setCreditLimit(double amount) method to set the creditLimit, and setFinanceCharge(double amount) method to set the financeCharge. Define getter methods to getCreditBalance(), getCreditLimit(), and getFinanceCharge().

g. Implement the withdraw() method that checks the creditLimit, calculates the creditBalance, and sets the balance.

Step 3: Testing the Program

a. Test your program by creating a customer with an OverDraftProtect account, savings account, and LineOfCredit account. Deposit $1500 into the LineOfCredit account and withdraw $2000 from the LineOfCredit account.

b. Deposit $3000 into the LineOfCredit account and withdraw $1500 from the LineOfCredit account.

c. Deposit $1500 into the savings account and $2500 into the OverDraftProtection account. Withdraw $3000 from the OverDraftProtection account and check the balance in both accounts. Now withdraw another $1500 from the OverDraftProtection account.

Step 4: Documentation

Using the document "How to Use UMLTestTool," follow the instructions to verify that your JBANK classes match the JBANK UML diagram shown in Figure 8-7-2-2.

Write javadoc comments to the Checking, LineOfCredit, and OverDraftProtect classes.

Figure 8-7-2-2: JBANK Application—Phase III

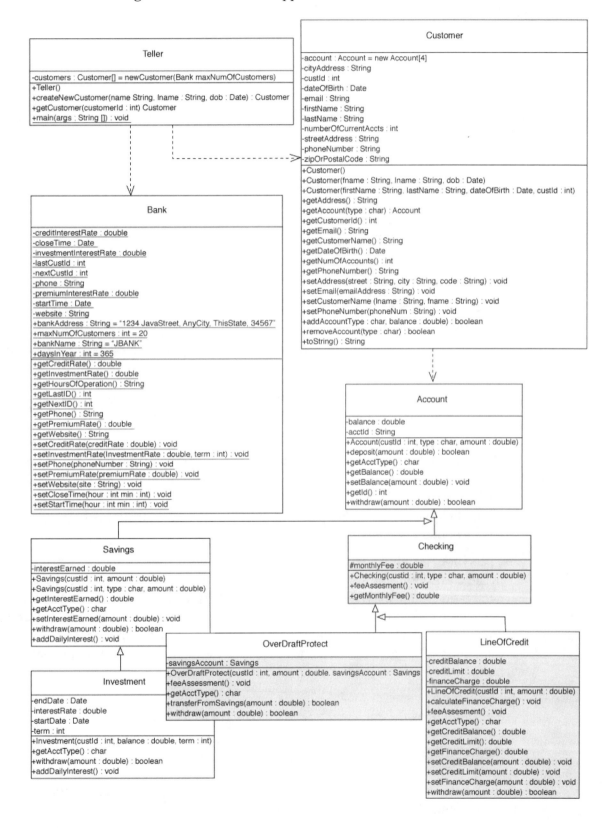

Lab 8.8.2: Interface and Abstract Class

Estimated Time: 60 minutes

Learning Objective

• In this lab activity, the student will learn about abstraction by using interfaces.

Description/Scenario

• Create an abstract class with data and methods that can be inherited and methods that must be implemented by the subclass.

• Create interface methods that must have behavior designed by each class that implements the interface.

• Create several subclasses that extend the abstract class and implement the interface.

• Define an abstract class called Animal that has two boolean attributes, one nonabstract method, and two abstract methods.

• Create two interfaces—Flying and NonFlying—that have three abstract methods each.

• Java does not allow for multiple inheritance. However, the Java language provides interfaces for implementing inheritance from two unrelated sources.

Interfaces are similar to abstract classes that define abstract methods and constants. However, unlike the inheritance restriction on extending from a single parent, a class can implement one or more interfaces. The purpose of an interface is to serve as a design document for external features of a class. All the methods in an interface must be public. Interfaces provide a mechanism for a subclass to define behaviors from sources other than the direct and indirect superclasses.

The syntax for implementing an interface includes the use of the keyword implements in the class definition statement. However, implementing interfaces is more than the declaration in the class definition statement. This declaration is viewed as a contract between the class that implements the interface and the interface itself. The compiler enforces this contract by ensuring that all methods declared in the interface are also implemented in the class. In some cases, this might include a null implementation. A *null implementation* is an implementation of a method definition without procedural code.

The guidelines for implementing interfaces are as follows:

⇒ A *public interface* is a contract between the client code (that is, the code in the interface class) and the class that implements the interface.

⇒ A *Java interface* is a formal declaration of a contract in which no methods contain implementation. That is, all methods are abstract.

$\Rightarrow$ Many unrelated classes can implement the same interface.

$\Rightarrow$ A class can implement many interfaces.

$\Rightarrow$ A class that implements an interface is an instance of the interface class. This relationship that exists between super and subclasses also applies to classes that implement interfaces.

$\Rightarrow$ All methods of an interface are declared public and are automatically abstract. The keyword abstract is not required to define the methods as such.

$\Rightarrow$ An interface cannot include methods with qualifiers such as native, static, synchronized, or final. These keywords imply implementation code, and methods cannot be implemented in an interface.

$\Rightarrow$ An interface can also declare constants, and they are public, static, and final. If the qualifiers are omitted, the Java compiler provides them.

$\Rightarrow$ Interfaces can extend other interfaces.

- Create classes named Bat and Hawk that extend Animal and implement Flying.

- Create classes named Snake and Monkey that extend Animal and implement NonFlying.

- All methods will print a statement that describes the Animal in some way or print its name.

File Management

Open BlueJ, click on Project from the BlueJ main menu, and select New. In the New Project window and in the Look In list box, select C:\. If you double-click the javacourse folder listed in the text window, a different New Project window opens with javacourse in the Look In list box. By double-clicking the chap8 folder listed in the text window, a different New Project window opens with chap8 in the Look In list box. Next, in the File Name text box, type lab8.8.2 to create a lab8.8.2 subfolder in the chap8 folder.

Tasks

Step 1: Creating the Abstract Class

a. Create the abstract class called Animal with two Boolean attributes— wings and legs—set to false; a constructor that accepts two Boolean arguments—wings and legs; two abstract methods—eat() and hair(); and one concrete method—sound()—that prints the sound the animal makes.

b.   The abstract class Animal will provide some data and methods that a subclass can inherit and will have two methods that the subclass must override. Each subclass that extends the Animal class will inherit a sound() method and two attributes (wings and legs). The abstract methods hair() and eat() must be implemented specific to each animal.

Step 2: Creating the Flying Interface

a.   Create the interface Flying with abstract methods setName(), getName(), and takeOff().

b.   Create the interface NonFlying with the abstract methods setName(), getName(), and movement(). These interfaces are created to define what methods are needed but have the methods execute different behavior for each class that implements the interface.

Step 3: Creating the Snake and Monkey Classes

a.   Create the Snake and Monkey classes that extend Animal and implement NonFlying.

b.   Create the Bat and Hawk classes that extend Animal and implement Flying.

c.   In this lab, Snake and Monkey must provide different behaviors for the super abstract methods hair() and eat() because Snake objectss do not have hair but Monkey objects do. Snake and Monkey also must implement specific behaviors for setName(), getName() and movement() from the interface NonFlying because Snake objects and Monkey objects have different names and different ways to move. Bat and Hawk are created with the same logic as Monkey and Snake.

Step 4: Creating a Test Class

a.   Create a test class named AnimalTest that will demonstrate calling super methods, different implementations of the interfaces, and the use of extended methods.

b.   Use this data: monkey = "spider," hawk = "redtail," snake = "cobra," bat = "fox"

In the main method of AnimalTest, include the following:

```
Snake s = new Snake("cobra");
Bat b = new Bat("fox");
Hawk h = new Hawk("redtail");
Monkey m = new Monkey("spider");
Animal a = new Animal(true,false)
Animal z = new Hawk();
NonFlying f = new Monkey();
s.movement();
System.out.println("Snakes have legs? "+s.legs+" Snakes have
wings? "+s.wings);
b.takeoff();
z.eat();
z.hair();
z.sound();
f.movement();
```

What happens if you try to instantiate an abstract class or an interface?

_____
_____
_____
_____
_____
_____
_____
_____
_____
_____
_____

Step 5: Documentation

Using the document "How to Use UMLTestTool," follow the instructions to verify that your classes match the UML diagram shown in Figure 8-8-2-1.

Figure 8-8-2-1: Animal—Abstraction Using Interfaces

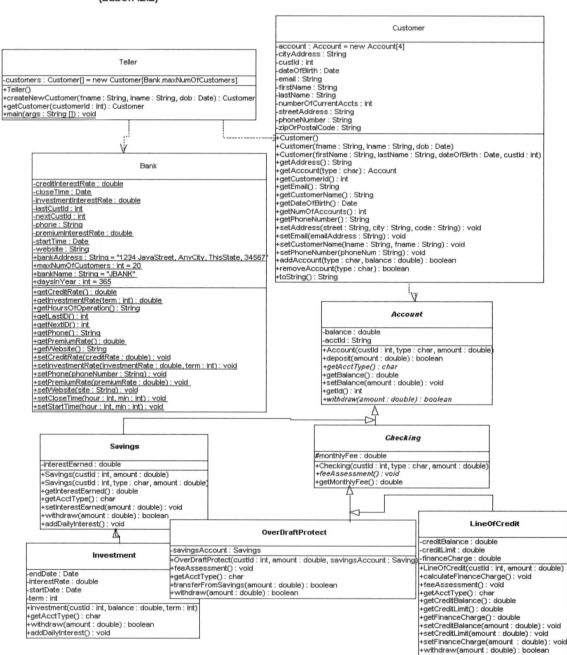

Lab 8.10.1: Polymorphism in the Banking Application

Estimated Time: 30 minutes

Learning Objectives

- In this lab activity, the student will create objects from classes with inherited attributes and demonstrate the application of polymorphic behaviors and dynamic binding.

Description/Scenario

- *Polymorphism* literally means "many forms." Polymorphism is a mechanism in the Java language that adds enormous flexibility to programs. In general terms, polymorphism allows the same code to have different effects at runtime depending on the context. Polymorphism takes advantage of inheritance and interface implementations.

- Inheritance only works in one direction: from superclass to subclass. A method that receives an object of a type can be called with objects that are subclasses of that type, but not more general or superclasses of the type. This is also true for variables. Variables that have been declared to hold a reference to an object of a type can be assigned a reference to objects that are subclasses of that type.

- The technique of resolving the behaviors of the object at runtime is known as *dynamic method binding*, or *virtual method invocation*. This is a key feature of polymorphism.

- Dynamic binding resolves which method to call at runtime when more than one class in an inheritance hierarchy has implemented the method. The JVM looks at the type of object for which the call is made, not the type of object reference in the calling statement.

- Dynamic binding also resolves the handling of the arguments being passed to a method. Again, the JVM looks at the type of object being passed by value as an argument, not the reference type of the variable being passed as an argument to the method.

- Create objects of inherited classes.

- Demonstrate polymorphism and dynamic binding.

- Modify the addAccount() method of the customer to demonstrate polymorphism.

Business Rules

- Each customer will be provided with a basic savings account. A customer cannot have more than four accounts or more than one of each type of account.

- The AccountID for an account is assigned as "CustomerID + account type identifier." For example, if the CustomerID is 1001 and the account type is a savings account, then the account ID is 1001S.

File Management

Open BlueJ, click on Project from the BlueJ main menu, and select New. In the New Project window and in the Look In list box, select C:\. If you double-click the javacourse folder listed in the text window, a different New Project window opens with javacourse in the Look In list box. Then double-click the chap8 folder listed in the text window, and a different New Project window opens with chap8 in the Look In list box. Next, in the File Name text box, type lab8.10.1 to create a lab8.10.1 subfolder in the chap8 folder. Import JBANK classes from lab8.7.2.2.

Tasks

Step 1: Adding Accounts to the Customer

a. In the addAccount() method of the Customer class, traverse through the accounts array and make sure the account type of the new account to be added doesn't already exist. While traversing through the accounts array, use the getAcctType() method of the array object to know its account type. This demonstrates polymorphism. In our case, the accounts array is an array of account objects of different account types, and each has its own version of the getAcctType() method. During runtime, the getAcctType() of the corresponding Account class is executed. For example, if the account is of type Savings, then the getAcctType() of the Savings class is executed.

b. If the type of the account to be created does not already exist, create an instance of the corresponding Account class and assign it to the Accounts array.

Step 2: Testing the Program by Using Suggested Data

    a.   Compile ran the code. Using the suggested data, create a customer with multiple accounts and print the results. Try to add a previously existing account to the customer and note the results.

Suggested Data:

FirstName: John

LastName: Doe

City Address: Phoenix

Street Address: 4128 West Van Buren

E-mail: Rman@theriver.com

Phone Number: 111-111-1111

zipOrPostalCode: 67777

DOB: 2/1/50

Account SAVINGS: 3000

Customer 2

FirstName: Betsy

LastName: Smith

City Address: Glendale

Street Address: 123 East Pine Street

E-mail: betsy@aol.com

Phone Number: 222-222-2222

zipOrPostalCode: 9999

DOB: 5/7/70

Account SAVINGS: 3210

Account LINEOFCREDIT: 5000

Customer 3

FirstName: Joe

LastName: Smith

City Address: Mesa

Street Address: 890 West Elm Street

E-mail: joe@java.com

Phone Number: 333-333-3333

zipOrPostalCode: 9999

DOB: 2/8/80

Account SAVINGS: 4500

Account OVERDRAFTPROTECT: 3500

Account LINEOFCREDIT: 2000

Step 3: Documentation

Using the document "How to Use UMLTestTool," follow the instructions to verify that your JBANK classes match the JBANK UML diagram shown in Figure 8-10-1-1.

Write javadoc comments to the methods introduced in this lab.

Figure 8-10-1-1: JBANK Application—Phase III

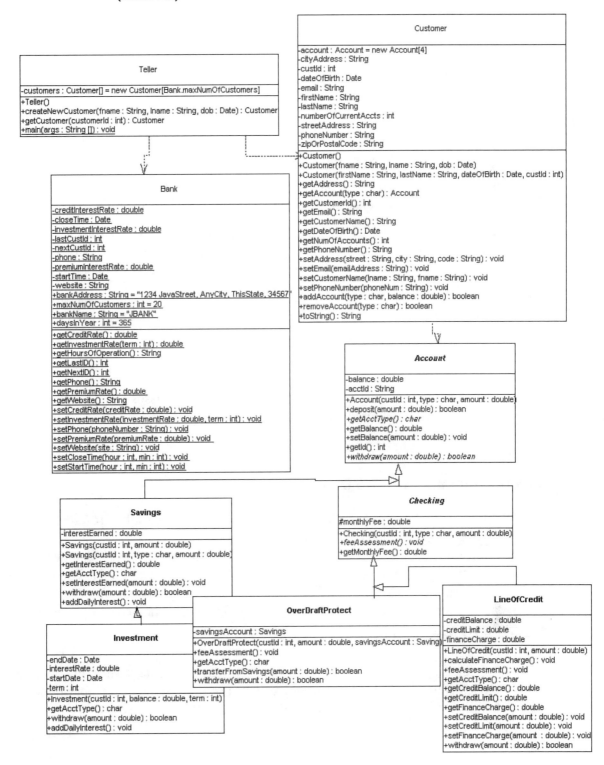

Chapter 9 Labs – Understanding Packages

Lab 9.4.1: Exploring the API Packages

> **Estimated Time:** 20 minutes

Learning Objectives

- In this lab activity, the student will investigate the Java core package structures and their classes.

Description/Scenario

- A *package* is a collection of classes. The Java platform uses packages to manage and group classes that share a common function.

- Classes are packaged based on their commonality of use. Inheritance does not affect the ability to package classes that have different inheritances in the same package.

- Classes that belong to the same package will inherit all default, protected, and public attributes and methods of the super/parent class. Classes that are in a different package will only inherit the public and protected attributes of the parent class.

- Access to attributes of a class is also influenced by packages. Classes can access public and default attributes of other classes in the same package.

- Explore the Java core API packages structure.

- Locate classes.

- Investigate the Java core package structures and their classes. This will help the student locate the required classes.

Tasks

Step 1: Finding the Java Docs API

> Find a local copy of the Java Docs API and open it with the browser. Alternatively, you can open the browser to http://java.sun.com/j2se/1.3/docs/api/index.html. After the API is open, you should become familiar with the different sections. Go to the Packages frame and look at the available packages. Understanding the package structure and the classes in the packages will help you quickly locate the necessary classes.

Step 2: Understanding the Package Structure

> Click on the java.awt package and go through the package structure. Classes are packaged based on their commonality of use. Inheritance does not affect the ability to package classes with different inheritance hierarchies in the same package.

Step 3: Inheritance in the Same Package

a. Selecting a specific package such as java.awt narrows the listing of the classes to that particular package. In the package java.awt, select the class Button. The class definition shows both the package location and the inheritance. The Button class is a subclass of the Component class. The Button and the Component classes are in the same package: java.awt.

b. Which attributes do classes that belong to the same package inherit?

_____

Step 4: Inheritance in Different Packages

a. The Applet class is in the java.applet package, and it inherits from or is a subclass of the Panel class in the java.awt package. Here the classes have been grouped for commonality of use and might be subclasses of packages in other classes.

b. Which attributes do classes that belong to a different package inherit?

_____

c. Go through the java.io package and become familiar with the various classes.

Lab 9.4.2: Build a Banking Package

Estimated Time: 20 minutes

Learning Objectives

- In this lab activity, the student will create directory structures to store packaged classes.

- The student will implement packaging to organize classes and include import statements to access classes in packages.

Description/Scenario

- Create directory structures.

- Use the keyword package to organize Java classes.

- Use classes from other packages by import statements.

- Archive packages in jar files.

- Create a directory structure that helps students organize their classes into a Banking package.

- Organize the classes by phase into separate subdirectories under the JBANK directory.

- Use package statements and import statements to access the classes in those packages.

- Create a jar file for archiving Phase I classes of the JBANK application.

- Java packaging is the management of classes in a group. The package statement defines a class as part of a collection, and the import statement defines the namespace to locate the class.

- There are two main reasons for creating Java packages. The primary reason is that the Java interpreter locates and loads the classes for the program by using namespaces. The second reason to consider organizing classes into packages is to manage the program as a collection of classes.

- The package statement in the Java language allows these collections of classes to be identified as belonging with each other.

- The import statement in Java ensures that the interpreter knows where the classes that are referenced are located. It declares the unique namespaces for the classes.

- For the Java run-time environment, the two variables that affect access to JDK programs and class files are the PATH variable and the CLASSPATH variable.

- The PATH variable is an operating system variable that will contain the names of directories where many programs are located. The operating system on a machine uses these paths to locate programs that need to be launched.

- The Java compiler and the interpreter use the variable CLASSPATH to locate classes and packages. The CLASSPATH variable can contain paths to many directories that contain packages.

- The CLASSPATH variable can be overridden by the use of the -classpath option when you're using the compiler and the use of the -cp option when you're using the interpreter.

- All the files in a package can be combined into a single compressed file by using the jar (Java Archive) utility. The jar utility will take all the class files in the directory and the directories and compress (pack) them into one file. This file is known as an archive file. When using jar files, note that the CLASSPATH variable must reference the jar file, not just the directory in which the jar file is located.

Tasks

Step 1: Creating the Directory Structure

a. In BlueJ, when the programs are compiled, the class files are created in the same directory as that of the source files. Because students need to build packages from a directory with class files only, they will be making use of a DOS command-line window and jdk utilities for this lab.

b. There are two main reasons for creating Java packages. First, the Java interpreter locates and loads the classes for the program by using namespaces. Namespaces are identifiers of a class and its methods. Second, you create Java packages so that you can manage the program as a collection of classes.

c. Using Explorer, create a new folder called JBANK under the c:\javacourse directory.

d. Create a folder inside JBANK called phase1, as illustrated in Figure 9-4-2-1.

Figure 9-4-2-1: Exploring JavaCourse

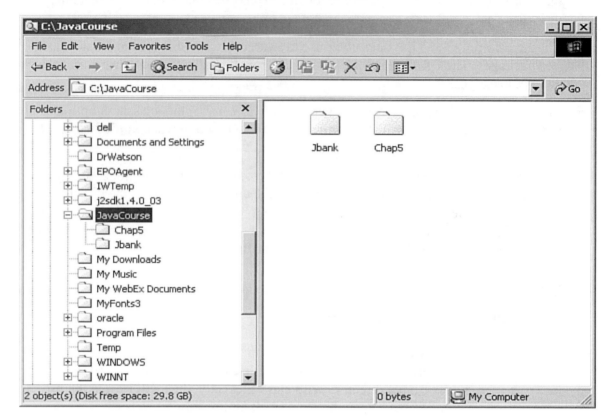

Step 2: Creating the Subdirectory

Create a phase1 subdirectory under Chap5 and copy all of the classes in the
JBANK Application created in lab 5.11.1 to the phase1 subdirectory, as illustrated
in Figure 9-4-2-2.

Figure 9-4-2-2: Exploring Phase 1

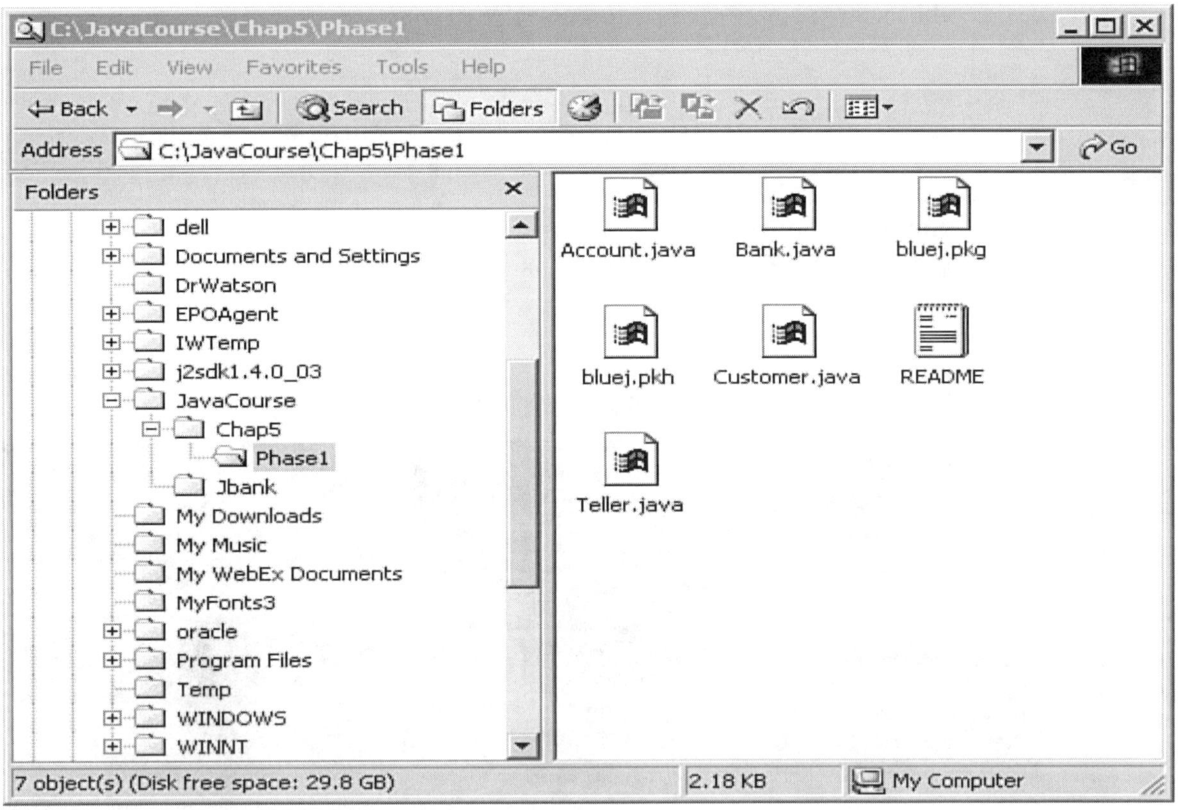

Step 3: Opening the DOS Command-Line Window

At the C: prompt, enter the following:

```
cd \javacourse\chap5\phase1
```

Step 4: Including the Statement Package

a. To package the classes so that you can identify each class as a member of the package, you must include the statement package <packagename> as the first statement of the source file. This statement causes the compiler to insert the package reference in the class byte code. Insert the package statement package phase1; for the Teller class.

b. If the classes that are needed for the program are located in a specific directory and have been identified as part of package, then you can identify the location of these classes by using import statements. Alternatively, you can identify the package name in each use of the classes in the package. The Teller class references the Date class, which is located in the package java.util. These packages of classes are generally located in the jdk1.3.1/jre/lib directories. Similarly, Teller class references BigDecimal and BigInteger are located in the package java.math. The import statements have already been inserted in the previous labs, as shown here, to access these packages:

```
package phase1;

import java.math.*;

import java.util.*;
```

a. Similarly, update the Account.java, Customer.java, and Bank.java with package and import statements, as shown in Figures 9-4-2-3 and 9-4-2-4.

Figure 9-4-2-3: MSDOS Prompt

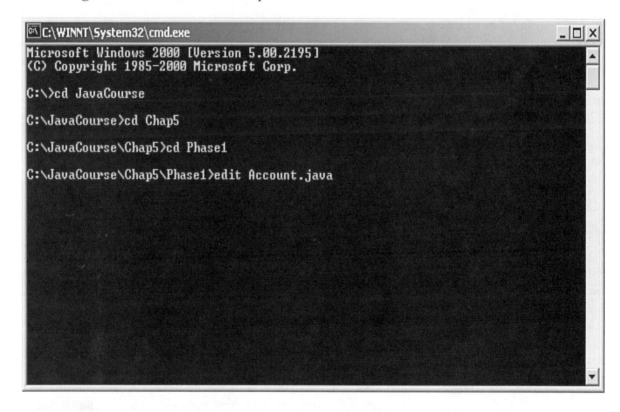

Figure 9-4-2-4: MS-DOS Prompt- EDIT

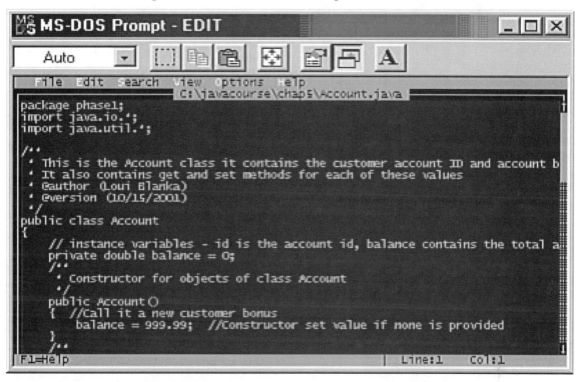

Step 5: Displaying the Directory Structure

Go to the directory c:\javacourse. At the prompt, enter dir/p, which will display the directory structure, as shown in Figure 9-4-2-5.

Figure 9-4-2-5: MSDOS Prompt

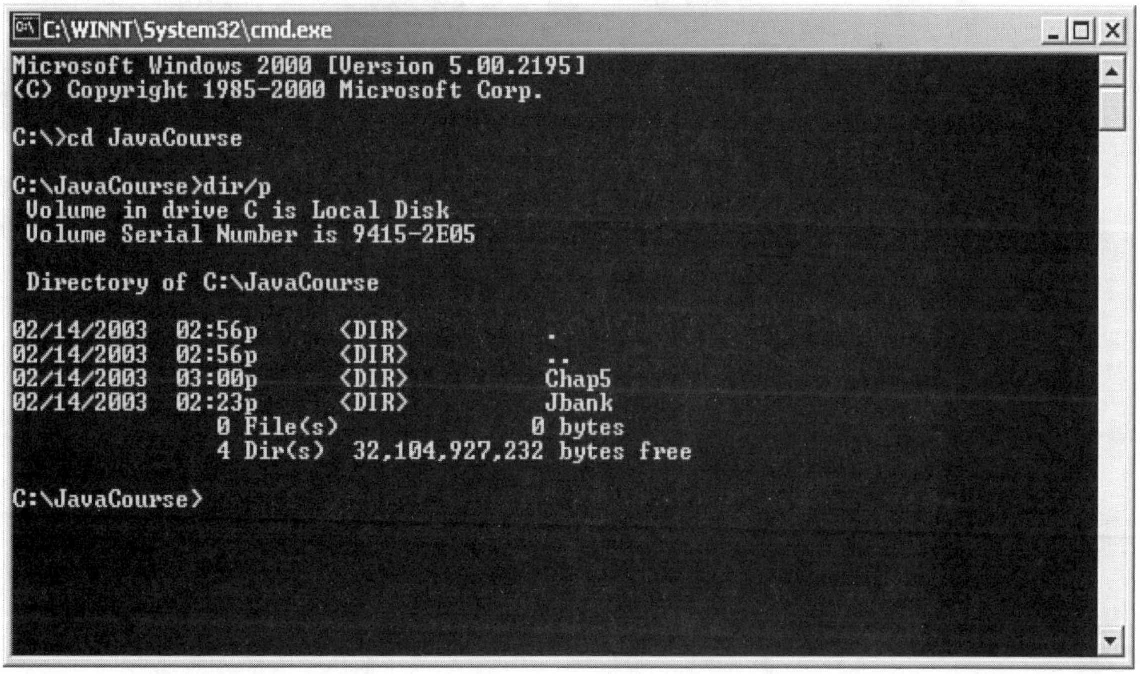

```
C:\WINNT\System32\cmd.exe

Microsoft Windows 2000 [Version 5.00.2195]
(C) Copyright 1985-2000 Microsoft Corp.

C:\>cd JavaCourse

C:\JavaCourse>dir/p
 Volume in drive C is Local Disk
 Volume Serial Number is 9415-2E05

 Directory of C:\JavaCourse

02/14/2003  02:56p       <DIR>          .
02/14/2003  02:56p       <DIR>          ..
02/14/2003  03:00p       <DIR>          Chap5
02/14/2003  02:23p       <DIR>          Jbank
               0 File(s)              0 bytes
               4 Dir(s)  32,104,927,232 bytes free

C:\JavaCourse>
```

Step 6: Creating the Class Files

To create the class files using the –d option, change directories to the JBANK directory. Then enter the following command, as shown in Figure 9-4-2-6:

```
javac -d . c:\javacourse\chap5\phase1\*.java
```

- javac is the compile command.

- The third argument tells the javac command where to locate the files to be compiled. In this case, the files are at c:\javacourse\chap5\phase1*.java, and the *.java restricts the selection only to files that end in .java.

- The –d option informs the compiler that the next argument is the directory in which to place the compiled class files.

- The resulting compiled byte code is placed into the file location described by the first argument—in this case ' . ', which is the current directory c:\javacourse\jbank.

Figure 9-4-2-6: MSDOS Prompt

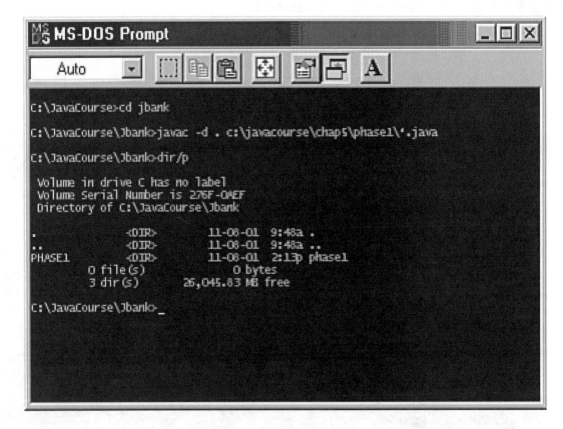

Look for the class files under the c:\javacourse\jbank\phase1 folder, as shown in Figure 9-4-2-7.

Figure 9-4-2-7: MS-DOS Prompt

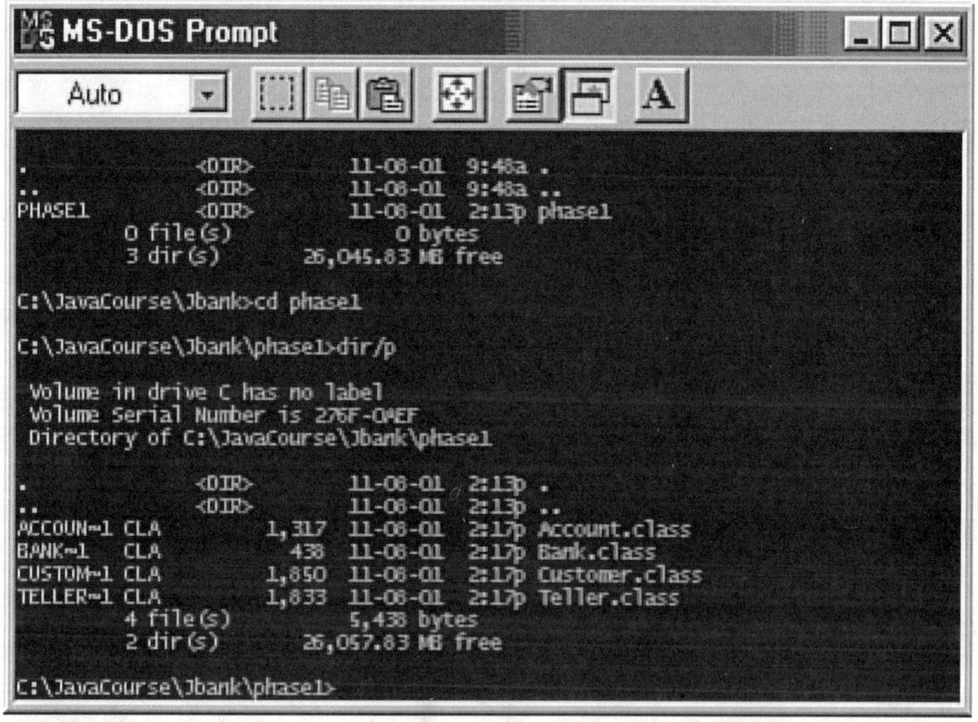

Step 7: Creating the Jar File

To create a jar file containing the JBANK\phase1 directory, return to the \JavaCourse\jbank directory, and at the prompt enter this code:

```
jar cvf jbank.jar phase1
```

c   Creates a new, empty jar file

v   Produces verbose output while the jar file is being built, indicating the name of each file being added to the jar file

f   Indicates the jar filename named in the jar file command

Refer to Figure 9-4-2-8.

Figure 9-4-2-8 MS-DOS Prompt

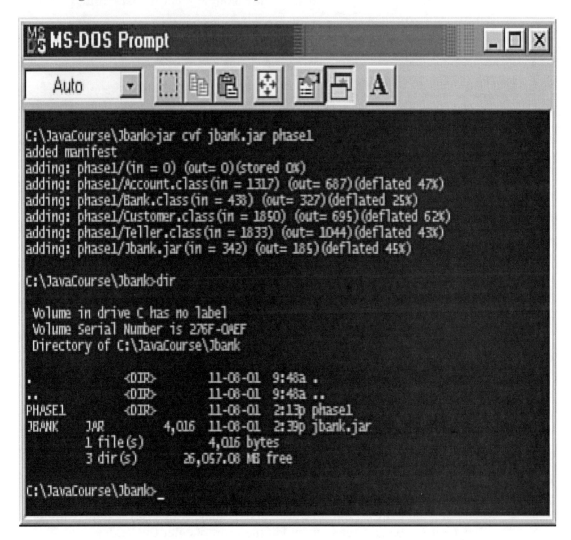

Step 8: Listing the Contents

To list the contents of the jar file, enter the following at the prompt:

```
jar tf jbank.jar
```

t   Type a list of contents of an existing jar file

f   The jar filename named in the jar file command

Refer to Figure 9-4-2-9.

Figure 9-4-2-9: MS-DOS Prompt

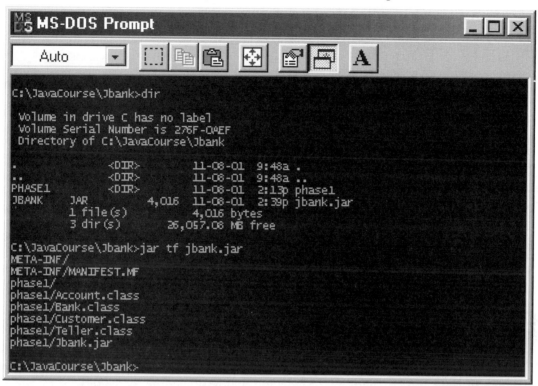

Step 9: Repeating the Process

Repeat steps 1 through 8 for Phase II (Lab7.6.1 is the end of Phase II) and Phase III (Lab8.10.1 is the end of Phase III) of the JBANK application.

Lab 9.6.1.1: Designing the GUI to Represent an ATM for Customers

Estimated Time: 15 minutes

Learning Objective

- In this lab activity, the student will explore the API and locate references for classes in the Abstract Windowing ToolKit package.

- The student will apply appropriate design principles to design a GUI based on the provided specifications.

Description/Scenario

- In this lab, students are provided with a design specification for designing a GUI. Use the specification to select the components and the layout, and design a GUI that meets the specification.

- To design the GUI, students should research the classes that are available in the java.awt package. This package represents the classes that form the Abstract Windowing Toolkit. The package lists the components alphabetically. Many of the components include visual examples of the object displayed.

  Using only paper and pen or pencil, students will select all of the components that they will need and lay them out in a design that will become their GUI.

  This lab prepares students for designing a GUI for the Banking application JBANK. The object is to create a display that serves as an Automated Teller Machine (ATM). This is just a simulation; students will not actually be concerned with the retrieval of money.

  Step 1 of the lab describes the requirements for the ATM GUI.

Tasks

Step 1: Understanding the Requirements

- The student's ATM will interact with only one customer at a time and will use the following:

  ⇒ Customer input for the following information.

    Customer ID: This will be used to retrieve the Customer Name Account ID to use for the transaction.

    Account type: This will allow the user to make selections from four radio buttons (one for each type of account including Savings, Investment, Line of Credit, and Overdraft Protection).

⇒ Amount to use for the transaction

⇒ Buttons to invoke transaction activities such as deposit, withdrawal, and exit.

- In addition to input from the user, the ATM window will display the following information:

⇒ Customer's full name

⇒ Transaction details such as Withdrawing $1000 or Depositing $1000, and the balance as a result of the transaction

Note: In this lab, students are not concerned about how the activity will be transacted or displayed; they are only concerned with organizing the screen to accomplish these tasks.

Study the Java AWT API and determine what objects can help when considering the preceding specifications.

- Review the functions of each of the components.

- Note the available constructors and methods for the components selected.

Step 2: Making the Inventory

a. Make an inventory of all the components that will be used.

b. Lay out the components on a paper in the final design layout.

c. When the layout is complete, review it against the sample that the teacher provided.

Lab 9.6.1.2: Designing the GUI Interfaces

Estimated Time: 15 minutes

Learning Objective

- In this lab activity, the student will identify the appropriate methods and constructors to use to manage the properties of GUI components.

Description/Scenario

Use the GUI created in the previous lab and the API docs for java.awt.

Tasks

Step 1 Questions

Using the GUI designed in the previous lab (9.6.1.1), explore the API docs to locate the answers to the questions provided:

a. Which constructor for the Button class was used to create each of the buttons? What is the syntax for using this constructor?

Button	Constructor Syntax
deposit	
withdraw	
exit	

b. To change the label on the button, which method of the button class could be used? What is the syntax for changing the button label 'exit' to 'end'?

_____

_____

_____

c. This GUI uses the following labels. Which method is used to change the text of the label?

_____

_____

_____

d.   The longest ID for the customer is 10 digits, and the longest ID for the account is 15. How could the size of the TextField be set so that it does not exceed these limits?

_____
_____
_____

e.   Which of these provides a scrollbar: TextArea or TextField?

_____

f.   Which method can be used to set the scrollbars?

_____
_____
_____

g.   What is the inheritance hierarchy for the following? Provide a complete list on a separate sheet of paper.

TextArea

MenuBar

CheckboxGroup

Checkbox

Chapter 10 Labs – Creating GUIs Using AWT

Lab 10.2.2.1: Creating the Components (TellerView Class)

Estimated Time: 15 minutes

Learning Objective

- In this lab activity, the student will identify the components used in the TellerView.

Description/Scenario

- Identify and use components.

    The definition of a GUI class begins with the creation of references for all of the component objects. Some of the components available include the Button class, Label class, and the subclasses of TextComponent. Some of the methods have been identified in this description, but the student will obtain the most accurate and complete information about each of these classes from the API docs.

- The Button class provides two constructors and several methods. The Button class also has several methods that are useful for programming event handling. These methods include setLabel(String label), which changes text that displays as the label on a button, and setActionCommand(String command), which sets a specific String that represents an action on the button. If the action command on a button is not set, the label of the button is used as the action command.

- The Label class is used to display text as labels on the screen. Labels can be changed using the setText(String text) method.

- The TextComponent class is subclassed into a TextField and TextArea.

- A TextField is a single line of text. The size of this field can be set either upon construction of the object or after the object is created using setColumns(int column). The TextField(String text, int columns) constructor can create a TextField object with text initialized for display and wide enough to hold the specified number of columns. The columns argument refers to the number of characters to be displayed. Alternatively, you could use the TextField(int columns) constructor and the setColumns(int column) method to achieve a similar result.

- The *TextArea* is an area in which the user can enter several lines of text. TextAreas can be set to have a certain length of rows and width of characters. Several constructors are available for the creation of TextArea objects. The syntax that follows is a constructor that includes initial text, rows, and columns for the TextArea. Columns reference the number of characters on a line:

```
public TextArea(String text, int rows, int columns)
```

- In addition to the methods in the class, these classes inherit from the Component class. Review the section on inherited methods for each component selected.

File Management

File management is not required for this class. This is a workbook lab. Use the forms provided to complete the analysis of the GUIs provided.

Tasks

Step 1: Reviewing the GUIs

Review the screen display for a TellerView and a Customer GUI shown in Figure 10-2-2-1-1 and Figure 10-2-2-1-2. These GUIs were designed to provide interfaces for a bank teller to input data into a customer account and to create or edit customer information.

Figure 10-2-2-1-1: TellerView GUI

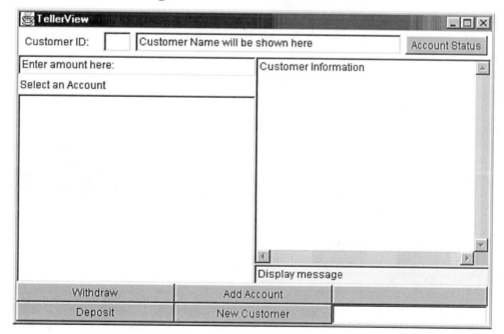

Figure 10-2-2-1-2: Customer GUI

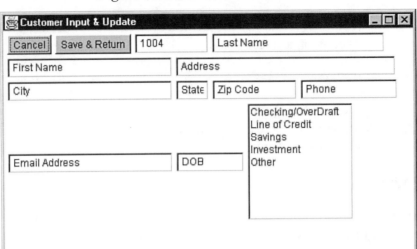

Step 2: Answering the Following Questions by Using the TellerView and Customer GUI

a.   Which components are used to accept text data from the user? Identify the specific Component class that is used.

For the TellerView:

_____
_____
_____
_____
_____

For the Customer GUI:

_____
_____
_____
_____
_____

b.   Which components are used to display information but not input information? Which method in the component allows for such features? Are scrollbars used in any components? What caused the scrollbars to display?

For the TellerView:

_____
_____
_____
_____
_____

For the Customer GUI:

_____

_____

_____

_____

_____

c. The TellerView displays a "Thank you" message. What is being used to do this? Include the name of the component and any methods that might be called.

_____

_____

_____

d. How will the user interact with the GUI to have a specific banking transaction performed or to update and create customer accounts?

In the TellerView:

_____

_____

_____

_____

e. How will the user notify that input for the customer data has been completed and should be saved or cancelled?

_____

_____

_____

_____

_____

Step 3: Identifying the Steps for Creating a GUI

The code for the TellerView class is shown next. Identify the steps (2 through 6) for creating a GUI in the code provided. Use a comment line that labels each step. These are the steps for creating a GUI:

1. Design the GUI. (This is completed and provided in the form of the sample output.)

2. Create the components.

3. Select the containers.

4. Lay out managers for containers.

5. Size components and containers.

6.   Display the GUI.

```java
import java.awt.*;
import java.awt.event.*;
/**
 * The class TellerView extends from a Panel. It is
 * a GUI that provides interfaces for a bank Teller to
 * input data into a customer's Account and to create new
 * Customer objects or edit Customer information.
 * @author (your name)
 * @version (a version number or a date)
 */
public class TellerView extends Panel
{
        Button accountStatusButton, withdrawButton, depositButton;
        Button addAccountButton, newCustomerButton,
        futureUseButton;
        TextField custIdTextField, customerNameTextField,
        amountTextField;
        TextField dateDisplayTextField, messageTextField;
        TextArea customerInformation;
        List accountInformation;
        Label customerIdLabel, accountSelectionLabel;
        Panel topPanel, buttonPanel, messagePanel,
        customerDisplayPanel;
        Panel displayPanel,accountPanel, listPanel;

    /** Default constructor which calls the buildTellerPanel */
        public TellerView()
        {
                buildTellerPanel();
        }

    /** buildTellerPanel method builds the TellerView GUI */
        public void buildTellerPanel()
        {

                accountStatusButton = new Button("Account Status");
                withdrawButton = new Button("Withdraw");
                depositButton = new Button("Deposit");
                addAccountButton = new Button("Add Account");
                newCustomerButton = new Button("New Customer");
                futureUseButton = new Button(" ");

                customerNameTextField =
                        new TextField("Customer Name will be shown
                        here",
                        40);
                messageTextField = new TextField("Display message",
                 20);
                amountTextField = new TextField("Enter amount here:",
                 20);
                custIdTextField = new TextField(" ");
                dateDisplayTextField = new TextField(" ");

                customerIdLabel = new Label("Customer ID:");
                accountSelectionLabel = new Label("Select an
                 Account");

                customerInformation = new TextArea("Customer
                Information",
                15,20);
                accountInformation = new List(8);
```

185

```java
        /* Creating the top Panel */
                topPanel = new Panel();
                topPanel.setLayout(new FlowLayout(FlowLayout.LEFT));
                topPanel.add(customerIdLabel);
                topPanel.add(custIdTextField);
                topPanel.add(customerNameTextField);
                topPanel.add(accountStatusButton);
        /* Building the Button panel */
                buttonPanel = new Panel();
                buttonPanel.setLayout(new GridLayout(2, 6));
                buttonPanel.add(withdrawButton);
                buttonPanel.add(addAccountButton);
                buttonPanel.add(futureUseButton);
                buttonPanel.add(depositButton);
                buttonPanel.add(newCustomerButton);
                buttonPanel.add(dateDisplayTextField);

        /* Building the Panel to hold Customer information */
                customerDisplayPanel = new Panel();
                customerDisplayPanel.setLayout(new BorderLayout());
                customerDisplayPanel.add(messageTextField, "South");
                messageTextField.setBackground(Color.yellow);
                customerDisplayPanel.add(customerInformation,
                 "Center");

                displayPanel = new Panel();
                displayPanel.setLayout(new GridLayout(1,2));
        /* Building the listPanel to display Account information */
                listPanel = new Panel();
                listPanel.setLayout(new BorderLayout());
                listPanel.add(accountInformation, "Center");
                listPanel.add(accountSelectionLabel, "North");
        /* Building the accountPanel to accept account details */
                accountPanel = new Panel();
                accountPanel.setLayout(new BorderLayout());
                accountPanel.add(amountTextField, "North");
                accountPanel.add(listPanel, "Center");
        /* Building the TellerView Panel by adding the Panels to the
           Teller View */
                setLayout(new BorderLayout());
                add(topPanel, "North");
                add(buttonPanel, "South");
                displayPanel.add(accountPanel);
                displayPanel.add(customerDisplayPanel);
                add(displayPanel, "Center");
                setSize(500, 300);

        }
        public static void main(String[] args)
        {
                TellerView tellerView = new TellerView();
                Frame frame = new Frame("TellerView");
                frame.add(tellerView);
                frame.pack();
                frame.setVisible(true);
        }

}
```

Lab 10.2.2.2: Creating the Components (ATMGUI Class)

Estimated Time: 30 minutes

Learning Objective

- In this lab activity, the student will learn to correctly select and apply components to a GUI.

Description/Scenario

- Apply the components that have been selected to a GUI.

- The definition of a GUI class begins with the creation of references for all of the component objects. Some of the components available are the Button class, the Label class, and the Text component. The Button class provides two constructors and several methods. The Button class also has several methods that are useful for programming event handling. These methods include setLabel(String s), which changes text that displays as the label on a button, and setActionCommand(String s), which sets a specific String that represents an action on the button.

- In addition, there are methods to add and remove a listener from the component.

- The Label class is used to display text as a label on the screen. Labels can be changed using the setText method.

- The TextComponent class is subclassed into TextField and TextArea.

- A TextField is a single line of text. The length of this field can be set.

- The TextArea is an area where the user can enter several lines of text. TextAreas can be set to have a length of rows and width of characters.

File Management

Open BlueJ, click on Project from the BlueJ main menu, and select New. In the New Project window and in the Look In list box, select C:\. If you double-click the javacourse folder listed in the text window, a different New Project window opens with javacourse in the Look In list box. Then double-click the chap10 folder listed in the text window, and a different New Project window opens with chap10 in the Look In list box. Next, in the File Name text box, type Lab10.2.2.2 to create a Lab10.2.2.2 subfolder in the chap10 folder. Then create a class named ATMGUI, which will be reused for several labs in this chapter. Save work from this lab in a folder named chap10. Import the JBANK classes from Lab8.10.1.

Tasks

Step 1: Reviewing the ATMGUI Components

The final version of the ATMGUI is shown in Figure 10-2-2-2-1. The components required to create this GUI are identified below:

a.   Label: "Enter customer id", "Enter amount here:"

b.   TextField: box next to the labels. You should limit the size of these fields to the number of digits that needs to be displayed. The highest account number will be a value of 9999999999, and the highest dollar amount will be a value of $999.99. (The decimal point is included in figuring the size.)

c.   CheckBox: Defaulting to Savings, with all the others shown below it.

d.   CheckBoxGroup: The collection object that holds references to the checkboxes.

e.   TextArea: The area displaying "Welcome".

f.   Button: Deposit, withdraw, exit.

g.   Frame: The window displaying the GUI.

h.   The four panels are not visible. The first is used to display all the buttons, and the second is used to group the account types (check boxes). The third is used to display the account information (account ID and amount), and the fourth is used to display the TextArea.

Figure 10-2-2-2-1: ATMGUI Layout

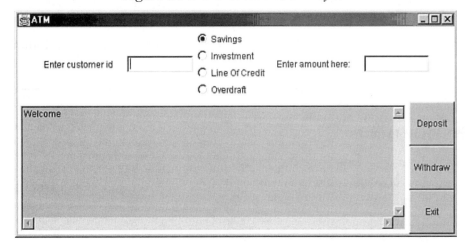

188

Step 2: Adding import Statements

Include the proper import statements that will allow the classes in the awt package to be accessed.

Step 3: Creating GUI Component Objects and Their References

a. In the appropriate section of the class ATMGUI, create the references for the components and create the component objects.

b. The components can be instantiated as the references are created. Alternatively, the references can be created first and then the components can be instantiated in a buildGUI method or in the constructor.

c. If the components are created in the buildGUI() method, then this method must be invoked in the constructor so that the GUI can be built and displayed.

d. This class extends from Panel. Note that the ATMGUI cannot be instantiated by itself.

e. Ensure that the class compiles. Subsequent lab instructions will continue to utilize this class.

f. When you're declaring or creating the components, group the statements by component type. For example, create and perform all of the activities related to a button together.

g. Remember to use the appropriate constructors.

Step 4: Review Questions

Consider these features in the code:

a. The TextArea is currently writeable. (That is, the user can enter several lines of text.) What method would prevent this? (See the java.awt API.)

_____

b. What would be the necessary size in terms of rows and columns needed for the TextField and TextArea?

_____

_____

Step 5: Documentation

Write all needed javadoc comments and document elements for the lab. Then, using BlueJ, select **Tools** and create the javadocs by selecting **Project Documentation**.

Lab 10.2.3.1: Selecting Containers (TellerGUI Class)

Estimated Time: 10 minutes

Learning Objective

- In this lab activity, the student will identify the containers used in a GUI.

Description/Scenario

- Identify the containers used in a GUI.

- Use AWT containers. The two main types of containers are Window and Panel. A container can hold not only components, but also other containers. A Window is a freestanding native window on the display that is independent of other containers. The two important types of Window are Frame and Dialog. Frame is a Window with a title, border and resizing. A Panel is contained within another container. A Panel identifies a rectangular area into which other components can be placed. A Panel must be placed into a Window to be displayed.

File Management

- None

Tasks

Step 1: Identifying Containers

a. Using the hard copy of the TellerGUI source code, identify the containers used in this GUI. *Note*: A class can extend a panel.

b. Add line comments to the sheet indicating each of the components and its use.

Step 2: Review Questions

a. Were these the same components that were chosen?

_____

b. Which components are placed on which containers?

_____

c. Which containers are placed on which containers?

_____

d. Will the close window icon work on the TellerGUI class window?

_____

e. Does the resize icon work on the TellerGUI class window?

_____

Lab 10.2.3.2: Selecting Containers (ATMGUI Class)

Estimated Time: 10 minutes

Learning Objective

- In this lab activity, the student will identify and create the Panel objects that are required for displaying visible components of the ATMGUI.

Description/Scenario

- Select and use the correct panels for the ATMGUI class.

- Learn how panels work and how to apply them to a GUI to achieve any desired arrangement.

- The two main types of containers are Window and Panel. A *container* is a component that can hold other components as well as containers. A *Window* is a freestanding native window on the display that is independent of other containers. A Window can either be a Frame or a Dialog type. The two important types of Window are Frame and Dialog.

- A Frame is a Window with a title and resizing. A Panel is contained within another container.

- A Panel identifies a rectangular area into which other components can be placed. A Panel must be placed into a Window (Frame or Applet) to be displayed.

File Management

- Retrieve the previous lab, Lab10.2.2.2, for use here and in the remainder of the Chapter 10 labs. Continue to save your work in the same chap10 folder. Use Save As and title it Lab10.2.3.2.

Tasks

Step 1: GUI Panels

a. The ATMGUI is a Panel. Use the inheritance model to extend from Panel.

b. Four Panels are required for this GUI:

- One to display all of the buttons

- Another to display the checkboxes

- A third to display the account information (account ID and amount) and the Checkbox panel

- The fourth to display the TextArea

  Note: This GUI is built using the four panels described in the preceding list that are then added to the base Panel, which is the ATMGUI class (extends from Panel).

c. Do not add the components to the Panel yet. You will add these after the layout managers have been selected.

Step 2: Compiling

Compile the class and save the file. (See the file management instructions.)

Step 3: Documentation

Write all needed javadoc comments and document elements for the lab. Then, using BlueJ, select **Tools** and create the javadocs by selecting **Project Documentation**.

Lab 10.2.5.1: Layout Managers (TellerGUI Class)

Estimated Time: 10 minutes

Learning Objective

- In this lab activity, the student will correctly identify layout managers and use them to control the layout of components in containers.

Description/Scenario

- Understand the use and the application of layout managers. Each container object will add other components or containers when both the add() method of the container is called and a component object reference is passed to it. Each container has a default layout manager object that sets the position for displaying each component. The default layout manager for Panel is the FlowLayout manager. For Frames, it is the BorderLayout.

File Management

Continue saving the work in the same chap10 folder. You will use this file again in the next lab.

Tasks

Step 1: Identifying Layout Managers

a. Using the hard copy of the TellerGUI source code and the screen display for the TellerView shown in Figure 10-2-5-1-1, identify the layout managers that are used for this GUI.

b. Add line comments to the sheet, indicating what each one is and how it is used.

Figure 10-2-5-1-1: TellerView

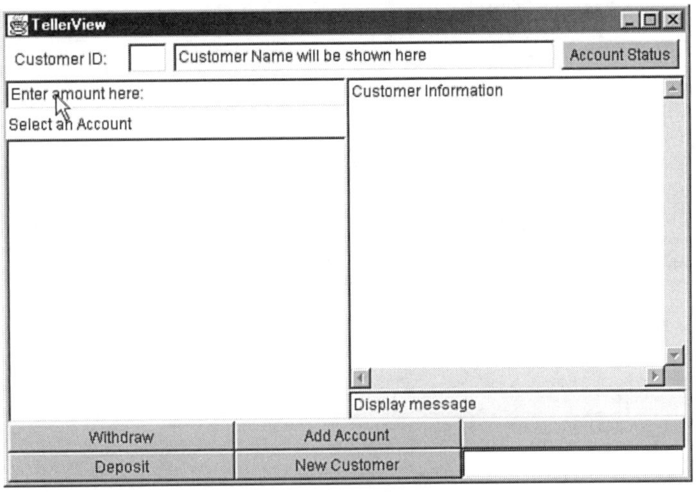

Step 2: Review Questions

a. What are the regions of the BorderLayout?

_____

b. If only one region of BorderLayout is to be used, which one should be selected?

_____

c. What syntax does GridLayout use?

_____

d. Name four layout managers.

_____

e. Can a layout manager be created?

_____

```java
import java.awt.*;
import java.awt.event.*;
/**
 * The class TellerView extends from a Panel. It
 * is a GUI that provides interfaces for a bank Teller
 * to input data into a customer's Account and to create
 * new Customer objects or edit Customer information.
 * @author (your name)
 * @version (a version number or a date)
 */
public class TellerView extends Panel
{
    Button accountStatusButton, withdrawButton,
        depositButton;
    Button addAccountButton, newCustomerButton,
        futureUseButton;
    TextField custIdTextField, customerNameTextField,
        amountTextField;
```

```
        TextField dateDisplayTextField, messageTextField;
        TextArea customerInformation;
        List accountInformation;
        Label customerIdLabel, accountSelectionLabel;
        Panel topPanel, buttonPanel, messagePanel,
          customerDisplayPanel;
        Panel displayPanel,accountPanel, listPanel;

/** Default constructor which calls the buildTellerPanel
*/
        public TellerView()
        {
                buildTellerPanel();
        }

/** buildTellerPanel method builds the TellerView GUI */
        public void buildTellerPanel()
        {

                accountStatusButton = new Button("Account
                  Status");
                withdrawButton = new Button("Withdraw");
                depositButton = new Button("Deposit");
                addAccountButton = new Button("Add Account");
                newCustomerButton = new Button("New
                  Customer");
                futureUseButton = new Button(" ");

                customerNameTextField =
                        new TextField("Customer Name will be
                          shown here", 40);
                messageTextField = new TextField("Display
                  message", 20);
                amountTextField = new TextField("Enter amount
                  here:", 20);
                custIdTextField = new TextField(" ");
                dateDisplayTextField = new TextField(" ");

                customerIdLabel = new Label("Customer ID:");
                accountSelectionLabel = new Label("Select an
                  Account");

                customerInformation = new TextArea("Customer
                  Information", 15,20);

                accountInformation = new List(8);
/* Creating the top Panel */
                topPanel = new Panel();
                topPanel.setLayout(new
                  FlowLayout(FlowLayout.LEFT));
                topPanel.add(customerIdLabel);
                topPanel.add(custIdTextField);
                topPanel.add(customerNameTextField);
                topPanel.add(accountStatusButton);
/* Building the Button panel */
                buttonPanel = new Panel();
                buttonPanel.setLayout(new GridLayout(2, 6));
                buttonPanel.add(withdrawButton);
                buttonPanel.add(addAccountButton);
                buttonPanel.add(futureUseButton);
                buttonPanel.add(depositButton);
                buttonPanel.add(newCustomerButton);
                buttonPanel.add(dateDisplayTextField);
```

```
/* Building the Panel to hold Customer information */
            customerDisplayPanel = new Panel();
            customerDisplayPanel.setLayout(new
              BorderLayout());
            customerDisplayPanel.add(messageTextField,
              "South");
            messageTextField.setBackground(Color.yellow);
            customerDisplayPanel.add(customerInformation,
              "Center");


            displayPanel = new Panel();
            displayPanel.setLayout(new GridLayout(1,2));
/* Building the listPanel to display Account information*/
            listPanel = new Panel();
            listPanel.setLayout(new BorderLayout());
            listPanel.add(accountInformation, "Center");
            listPanel.add(accountSelectionLabel, "North");
/* Building the accountPanel to accept account details */

            accountPanel = new Panel();
            accountPanel.setLayout(new BorderLayout());
            accountPanel.add(amountTextField, "North");
            accountPanel.add(listPanel, "Center");
/* Building the TellerView Panel by add the Panels to the
   Teller View */
            setLayout(new BorderLayout());
            add(topPanel, "North");
            add(buttonPanel, "South");
            displayPanel.add(accountPanel);
            displayPanel.add(customerDisplayPanel);
            add(displayPanel, "Center");
            setSize(500, 300);


    }

    public static void main(String[] args)
    {
            TellerView tellerView = new TellerView();
            Frame frame = new Frame("TellerView");
            frame.add(tellerView);
            frame.pack();
            frame.setVisible(true);

    }

}
```

Lab 10.2.5.2: Layout Managers and Adding Components (ATMGUI Class)

Estimated Time: 10 minutes

Learning Objective

- In this lab activity, the student will use layout managers and methods of the Container class to display and set the size for visible components.

Description/Scenario

- Learn how to identify the correct layout managers to use and how to apply them.

- Learn how to display a GUI and allow it to be resized.

- Understand the uses and applications of layout managers. Each container object adds other components or containers when the add() method of the container is called and a component object reference is passed to it. Each container has a default layout manager object that sets the position for displaying each component. The default layout manager for Panel is the FlowLayout manager, and for Frames it is BorderLayout. The BorderLayout manager breaks up the area into five regions: North, South, East, West, and Center.The setLayout(new BorderLayout()); call created a new instance of the BorderLayout object for the specific container. The add(component, Region); statement adds a specific component in the region. The region can be specified by using the syntax BorderLayout.NORTH, or "North". When you select regions, make sure that the CENTER region is always used in that container.

- Display components by using the setVisible() method. It is best to display the GUI after all the components have been built and added to the Panels, Frames, and Windows. The method setVisible() is used to display components. The last container (the base for the display) is the container whose setVisible() method is called. This method accepts the Boolean value true to make the components visible and false to hide them.

- You can use the setVisible() method on a specific component other than the base container that contains all other components.

- Use the setSize() method. Because the layout manager is responsible for the size and position of components on its container, the programmer should normally not attempt to set the size or the position of components manually. The layout manager could override manual decisions. In addition to the setSize() method, the pack() method sizes the Window based on the preferred sizes of the subcomponents.

File Management

Retrieve the previous lab, Lab10.2.3.2, which will be used here and in the remainder of the Chapter 10 labs. Use Save As to save this lab in the same chap10 folder, and name it Lab10.2.5.2.

Tasks

Step 1: Creating the Panel

a. To create the ATMGUI layout to match the screen shot shown in Figure 10-2-5-2-1, apply the correct layout manager. The class uses Panel containers. The default layout manager for a Panel is the FlowLayout, which places objects from left to right and retains the size of the objects.

b. List the Panel references that were created in the class:

_____

_____

_____

_____

c. The buttons need to be placed on a Panel where the button sizes do not change and where each button occupies the same space on the Panel. Which layout manager is used for the panel that is displaying the buttons?

_____

d. Which layout manager is used to place the check boxes on the panel displaying the CheckBox(es)? _____

e. A Panel will be used to display the Checkbox Panel and the labels and textFields for account ID and amount. Which layout manager is appropriate for this panel?

_____

f. Which layout manager is used to place the TextArea on a panel?

_____

g. Which layout manager is used to manage the containers that will be placed on the base Panel (the ATMGUI)?

Figure 10-2-5-2-1: ATMGUI Layout

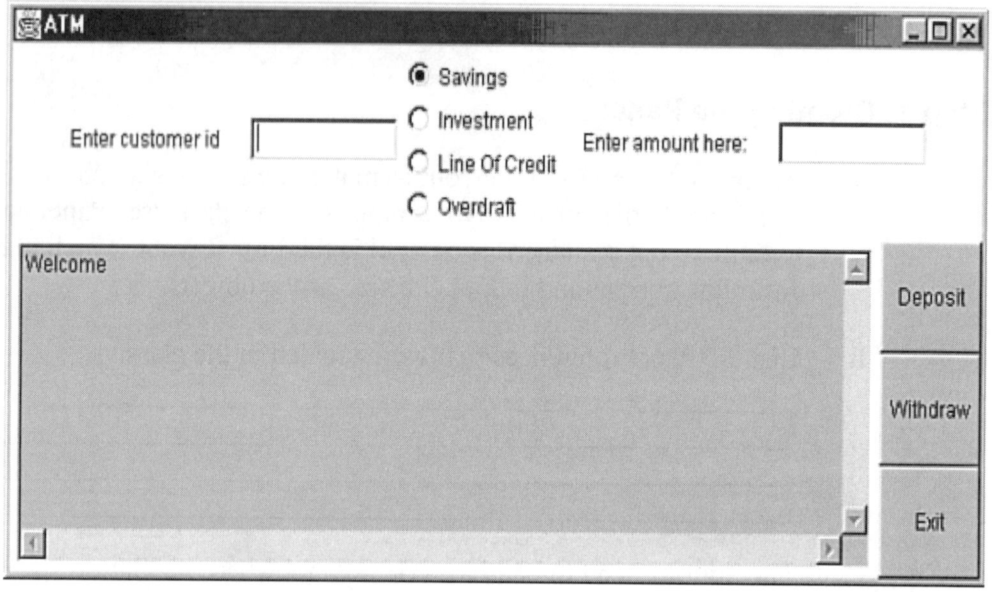

Step 2: Setting Layout Managers

a. Set the layout managers for each of the panels using the selections that were made in the previous step. Place the code for setting the layout manager below each Panel creation statement.

Step 3: Adding Components to Panels

a. Add the components to each of the Panels. At this stage, the code statements used should be in the sequence in which the components need to be displayed with a Panel. Which method is used to add components to a Panel or add a Panel to another Panel?

b. Add the buttons to the panel in the order in which they are to be displayed. (Deposit is the first button.)

c. Add checkboxes to the Panel in the order in which they are to be displayed. (The first is Savings.)

    d.   Add the TextFields, labels, and the CheckBox panel to their base panel.

    e.   Add the TextArea to its panel.

    f.   Build the Base panel, adding each of the other panels in the proper region.

Step 4: Positioning a Component

    a.   The layout manager determines the position and size of a component in a container. When the container needs to position a component, it invokes the layout manager to do so. The same delegation occurs when deciding on the size of a component. The layout manager generally is responsible for the size and positions on its container. What method will be used to set the size of the Panel?

    b.   Set the size of the Base Panel so that it displays a GUI that is approximately 3 inches in height and 5 inches in width. Assume that 100 pixels can be displayed in an inch, and set the size by using pixels.

Step 5: Displaying the GUI

    a.   The GUI is now ready for display. Remember that a *Panel* is a free-floating container that requires a Frame or Window object to be visible. Because this Panel will be used for both an application and an applet (see Chapter 11), this class does not actually display the GUI. The Teller class (Lab10.2.3.2) will be used to launch the ATMGUI in a Frame.

    b.   In the Teller class, instantiate the ATMGUI object and a Frame object. In the constructor of the Teller class, add the ATMGUI to the Frame. Set the size of the Frame by using pack().

    c.   Make the Frame visible. Which method is called and what argument is passed to this method?_____

Step 6: Documentation

    a.   Write all needed javadoc comments and document elements for the lab. Then, while using BlueJ, select **Tools** and create the javadocs by selecting **Project Documentation**.

Lab 10.3.2.1: Identifying Event Handler Features in the TellerGUI Class

Estimated Time: 10 minutes

Learning Objective

- In this lab activity, the student will implement interfaces that apply the Event delegation model for handling user interactions with a GUI.

Description/Scenario

- The student will learn about event sources and components and how to create an event handler.

- What are events and how are they handled?

  An *event* is an action that a user initiates. Some common events are buttons being clicked and text changing. Events are objects that describe what has happened. Many different types of event classes exist to describe different categories of user action. The event delegation model uses the following objects:

  ⇒ A *source* of an event is an object that can generate an event object.

  ⇒ The event is an Event object that encapsulates information about an event.

  ⇒ The *handler* is the object that can handle the event that is performing some task.

- Each of the component classes can generate specific event objects. Button objects generate Action events. TextComponents generate TextEvent objects. The Frame object is a Window that generates a WindowEvent object.

File Management

Continue saving all work because you will use it again in the next lab.

Tasks

Step 1: Review Questions

    a.   Using the hard copy of the TellerGUI source code, identify the sources of the events in this GUI.

_____

    b.   Where and how are these events registered?

_____

    c.   How are these events handled?

_____

    d.   What is the handler access path to the ATMGUI display (TextArea)?

_____

Step 2: Documentation

Write all needed javadoc comments and document elements for the lab. Then, using BlueJ, select **Tools** and create the javadocs by selecting **Project Documentation**.

Lab 10.3.2.2: Implement Event Handling for the ATMGUI Class

Estimated Time: 45 minutes

Learning Objective

- In this lab activity, the student will implement interfaces that apply the event delegation model for handling user interactions with a GUI. The student will apply these principles to the JBANK GUI programs.

Description/Scenario

- Learn how to register and handle events in a GUI.

- Each of the component classes can generate specific event objects. Button objects generate Action events, TextComponents generate TextEvent objects, and the Frame object generates a WindowEvent object.

- The handler is any class that implements a Listener interface that is appropriate for the type of event object generated by the component. Components generate event objects when a Listener object is registered with the component. The method of the component that accomplishes this is the addxxxListener method. The xxx represents the name of a specific listener.

- The listener interface specifies the methods by which the event object can be handled. Listener interfaces are part of the java.awt.event package.

- To handle window events such as window closing, the WindowListener interface is implemented. Although only the window closing event is used, all seven methods must be implemented.

- Also note that the statement import java.awt.event.* must be inserted at the start of the source file. The code that implements the window handler then calls the System.exit(0); method. This will end the program, release all the resources, and close the window. The Button handler checks the source of the event and performs a different action for each source.

File Management

Retrieve the previous lab, Lab10.2.5.2, which will be used here and in the remainder of the Chapter 10 labs. Continue saving your completed work in the same chap10 folder by using Save As and titling the file Lab10.3.2.

Tasks

Step 1: Classes to Listen for Event Objects

a. Create an ATMController class that will listen for event objects that are generated by the Buttons and the Frame (window). Which listener interfaces should be selected for this requirement?

_____

b. In the ATMController class, implement the interfaces that are selected. Ensure that all the methods of the interfaces are implemented. Begin by including code blocks that identify the method signature. Make these code blocks empty:

```
method( ) { }
```

c. Use the appropriate method for closing windows and insert a call to the exit() method of the System class. This method will close the application, which in turn closes the window.

d. Compile the ATMController class.

e. Modify the Teller class to include a reference to an instance of the ATMGUI object.

f. Create a reference for a Frame object. In the constructor of the Teller class, instantiate the ATMGUI and Frame objects.

g. Register an instance of the ATMController class with the Frame object. Which method is used to do this? What is the syntax of this statement?

_____

_____

h. Compile and run the Teller class to test the closing of windows.

Step 2: Implementing User Interactions

a. In this step, you will implement event handling for user interactions with the buttons of the ATMGUI. Some additional logic is required in the JBANK application to accomplish this. The scope of the Button object is only known to the ATMGUI. Define a getExitButton() method to return the exit button. Then define the getDepositButton() and getWithdrawButton() methods, which returns the Deposit and Withdraw buttons. The Button object generates an actionEvent object if a handler is registered with it. Register an instance of the same ATMController object with each of the buttons in the GUI class. The purpose of having an ATMController class is to provide a useful response to a user's interaction.

The ATMController class must respond to the buttons launched in the ATMGUI by the Teller object. The Teller class must register the ATMController object with the Frame and the buttons of the ATMGUI. Create an instance of the ATMController class, and use this reference as the argument to the addXXXListener methods. Accessing the addXXXListener methods as members of the ATMController class references the buttons on the ATMGUI. The following is an example of code from the Teller class:

```
ATMGUI atmg = new ATMGUI();
ATMController atmc = new ATMController(atmg);

//Register a button by referencing it through atmgui
atmg.btnExit.addXXXListener(atmc);
```

Although the ATMController class knows about the button, it does not know about the other objects in the GUI. If the purpose of the ATMController is to respond to a button action by making changes to other components of the GUI, it needs to have a way to reference the GUI. The only way this can occur is if the ATMController object also knows the reference to the ATMGUI object.

b.   In the ATMController class, add an attribute that will hold a reference to an object of the type ATMGUI. Add a constructor to this class that accepts a reference to an object of the type ATMGUI. Assign this reference to the attribute.

c.   In the ATMGUI class, register an instance of the ATMController with each button. The argument for the ATMController constructor will be a reference to the ATMGUI class (using the this variable).

d.   Compile all the classes, but do not run them yet.

Step 3: Handling the Button and Window Activity

a.   In this lab, the complex business logic that is required to deposit, withdraw, or display account information is not implemented. This step covers the complex connections that must occur to handle the button and window activity in a Model View Controller design pattern. The response of the handler will be demonstrated by changing the label of the button and setting a message in the text area.

b. In the ATMController class, implement code in the actionPerformed() method that does the following:

   1. Create a reference for a Button object. This will be used to store the reference for the button that generated the event object. A reference to the Button object is needed so that the label of the object can be changed.

   2. Retrieve the source of the event object using the getSource() method. This method returns an object.

   3. Cast this object to a Button. See the following code example.

```
Button thisButton = (Button) e.getSource();
```

   4. Using the reference to the object, change the label of the button to "Ouch!"

       Which method in the button class is used?

       _____

c. Compile and run the classes. Test the buttons and the window closing features.

d. The task of displaying data in the TextArea is more complex than changing the button properties. This is because the ATMController knows the Button object. To display data in the Text area, obtain the reference to the GUI that contains the TextArea component. Recall that this is the attribute that was assigned a value in the constructor call (see Step b2). Use this attribute to access the TextArea of the GUI.

   See the following code example:

```
ATMGUI   atmgui;
//constructor method
ATMController(ATMGUI atmgui)
{ this.atmgui = atmgui;}
```

   The TextArea is accessed using the reference atmgui.txtDisplay, where txtDisplay is the reference to the TextArea Component in the ATMGUI.

e. Which method is used to change the text displayed in a TextArea?

    _____

f. Which method of the button class would retrieve the label of the button?

    _____

g.   Display a continuous stream of messages that states "The button pressed is" + the name of button in the TextArea. This might require some additional review of the methods of the StringBuffer class and the TextArea class. In the ATM control class, insert the code to retrieve the current text in the TextArea and append a new line that states the button that was currently pressed. (*Hint:* Use a StringBuffer object to hold the current text and add new text.)

h.   Compile and test the classes. Does the TextArea display any new information?

Step 4: UML Tool

Using the document "How to Use UMLTestTool," follow the instructions to verify that the JBANK classes created in this lab match the JBANK UML diagram shown in Figure 10-3-2-2.

Step 5: Documentation

a.   Write all needed javadoc comments and document elements for the lab and then, using BlueJ, select **Tools** and create the javadocs by selecting **Project Documentation**.

Figure 10-3-2-2: JBANK Application—Phase IV

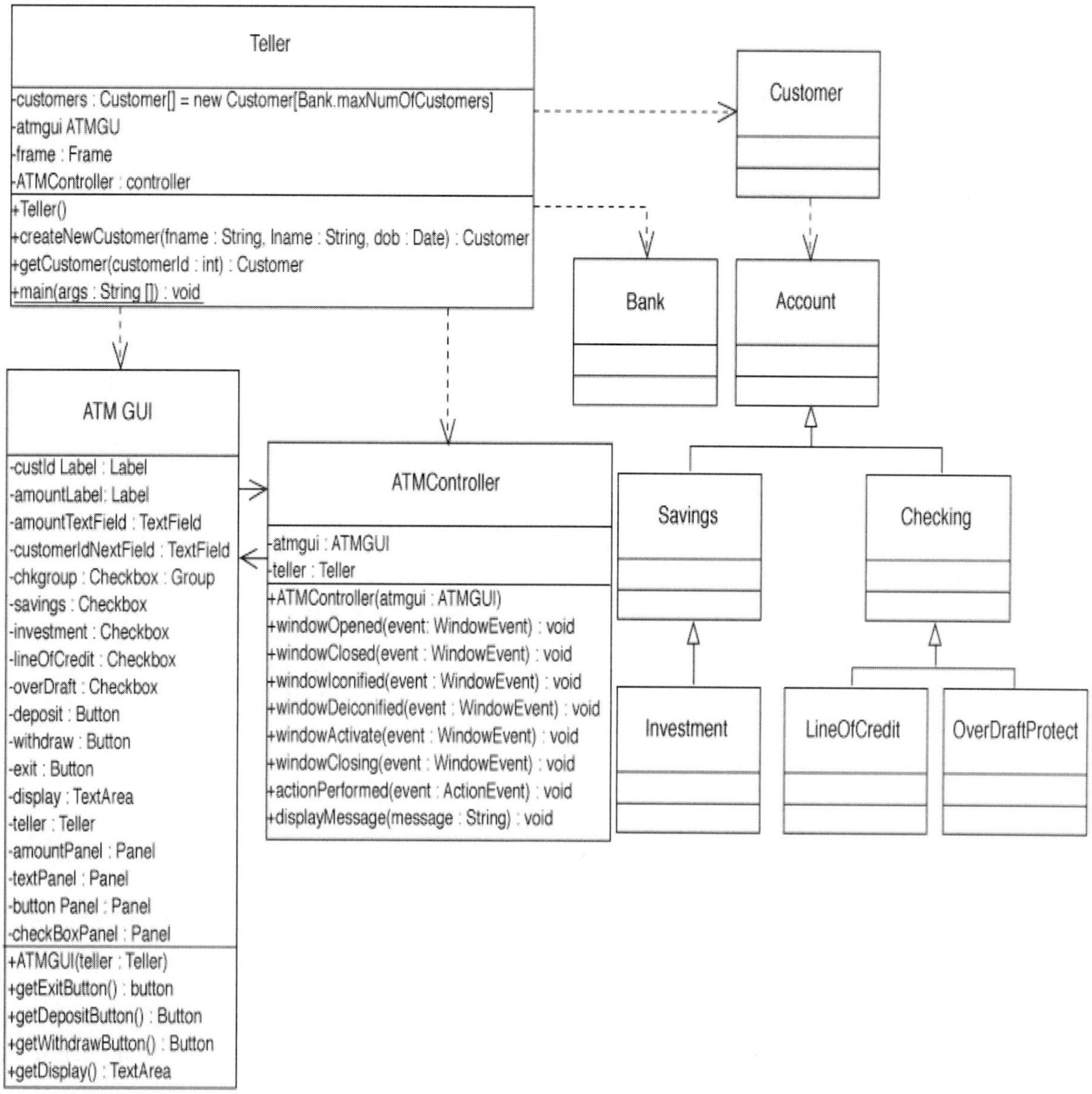

Lab 10.3.4: Implement the Model for the ATMGUI Class

Estimated Time: 10 minutes

Learning Objective

- In this lab activity, the student will use adapter classes to implement listener interfaces and event handling.

Description/Scenario

- Create an adapter class and an interface class, and use them with the ATMGUI.

- Using the interface class allows the implementation of the Model View Controller pattern for the ATMGUI.

- With the adapter class, the programmer only needs to implement the method(s) that are used.

- What are adapter classes and how are they used?

  The Java platform provides adapter classes. These classes are abstract classes that implement the Window Listener interface methods. The programmer can create a handler class that extends from one of these adapter classes. The adapter classes have the name of the Listener interface with the word "Adapter" replacing the word "Listener." In some cases, the student will not be able to extend from the adapter class because you can only extended from one class. The Applet is such a case.

- What are interface classes and how are they used?

  Java does not allow multiple inheritances, so a class cannot extend from two classes. Interfaces are similar to abstract classes that define abstract methods and constants. However, unlike the inheritance restriction on extending from a single parent, a class can implement one or more interfaces. Interfaces provide a way for a subclass to define behaviors from sources other than the direct and indirect super classes.

File Management

Retrieve the previous lab, Lab10.3.2.2. You will use this lab here and in the remainder of the Chapter 10 labs. Continue saving your work in the same chap10 folder. Use Save As and title the file Lab10.3.4.

Tasks

Step 1: Modifying ATMWindowHandler

a.   Create an Adapter class by modifying the ATMWindowHandler class to extend WindowAdapter.

b.   The additional methods in the ATMWindowHandler class are no longer needed. Only the windowClosing event is implemented.

Step 2: Creating a Controller Class

a.   Create the ATMButtonHandler, which implements the ActionListener. Copy the code used in the ATMController for the actionPerformed events. In the ATMButtonHandler class, add an attribute that will hold a reference to an object of the ATMGUI and an attribute that will hold a reference to an object of the Teller. Add a constructor to this class that accepts a reference to an object of the type ATMGUI, and then assign this reference to the attribute. In the ATMGUI class, define a method getTeller() that returns teller, and then register the buttons with the ATMButtonHandler reference. In the ATMButtonHandler Constructor, call the getTeller() method of the ATMGUI class and assign the Teller object to the Teller attribute.

b.   In the Teller class, remove the references to ATMController that result from being imported from a previous lab. Add the window Listener to the frame as shown here:

```
frame.addWindowListener(new
ATMWindowHandler());
```

c.   In the main method of the Teller class, remove the code that was imported from the previous lab and instantiate a Teller class. Then compile and run the Teller class.

Step 3: Review Questions

a.   Name an advantage of using an adapter class.

_____

_____

_____

b.   How is a marker interface different from an interface class?

_____

_____

_____

c.   What is the function of an interface class?

_____

_____

_____

Step 4: Documentation

a.   Using the document "How to Use UMLTestTool," follow the instructions to verify that the JBANK classes match the JBANK UML diagram shown in Figure 10-3-4-1.

b.   Write all needed javadoc comments and document elements for the lab. Then, using BlueJ, select **Tools** and create the javadocs by selecting **Project Documentation**.

Figure 10-3-4-1: JBANK Application—Phase IV

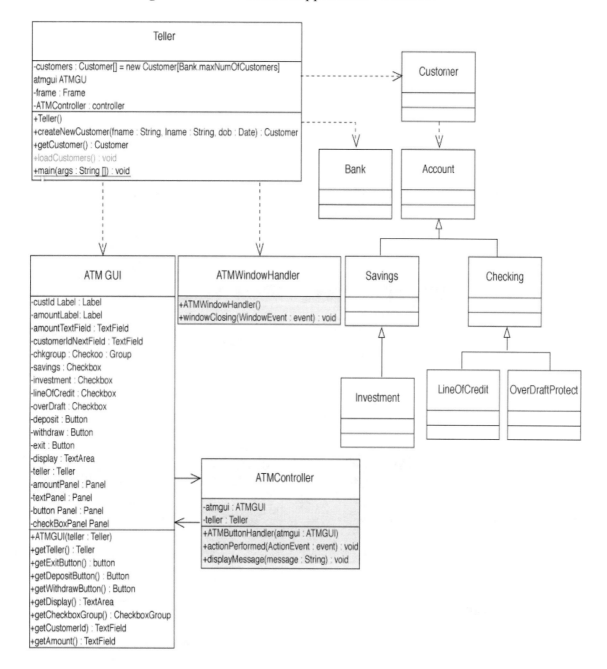

Lab 10.4.1: Finalizing the Model View Controller Pattern for the ATMGUI Class

Estimated Time: 60 minutes

Learning Objective

In this lab activity, the student will implement the business logic for handling banking transactions through a GUI.

Description/Scenario

The ATMController class will be modified to implement the business logic that is required to enable the withdrawal and depositing of money into a customer account. The student will create some sample customer objects and use the GUI to transact banking activities. Refer to the ATMGUI layout shown in Figure 10-4-1-1.

Figure 10-4-1-1: ATMGUI Layout

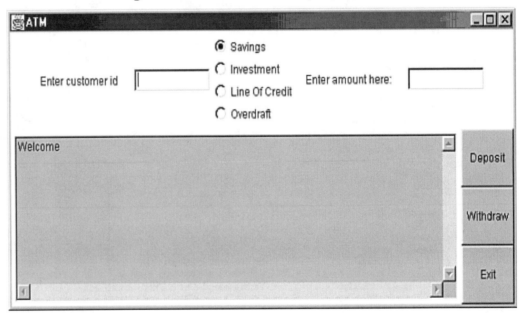

File Management

Retrieve the previous lab, Lab10.3.4. Continue to save completed work in the same Chap10 folder. Use Save As and title the file Lab10.4.1.

Tasks

Step 1: Implementing Actions

a.   In the ATMGUI class, define methods to get the attributes chkgrp (CheckboxGroup), customerIdTextField, and amountTextField.

b.   Modify the actionPerformed() method in the ATMButtonHandler class to implement the actions that represent the business rules for the JBANK application. When a user types a customer ID and selects the type of account and amount for deposit or withdrawal, he interacts with one of three buttons. To provide a response to the user interaction, the ATMButtonHandler class uses the actionPerfomed() method to identify the button pressed. Modify the ATMButtonHandler class by first removing any code from the actionPerfomed() method of the previous version.

c.   When the Deposit button is pressed, the actionPerformed() method should check the ID of the customer against elements of the customer array. If an account exists for the customer, call the deposit() method of the account. Display in the TextArea a message that states "Depositing amount" and the amount the customer entered. After the deposit method has completed, test the Boolean value that is returned by the deposit() method. If this method returns true, display a message that states that the deposit is complete along with the current account balance. If the deposit method returns false, display this message: "Unable to complete transaction. Your current balance is" and the account balance.

d.   When the Withdraw button is pressed, the actionPerformed() method should check the ID of the customer against elements of the customer array. If an account exists for the customer, call the withdraw method of the account. Display in the TextArea a message that states "Withdrawing amount" and the amount entered by the customer. After the withdraw method has completed, test the Boolean value that the withdraw() method returned. If this method returns true, display a message that states the withdrawal is complete along with the current account balance. If the withdraw method returns false, display the message "Unable to complete transaction. Your current balance is" and the account balance.

e.   When the user presses the Exit button, the TextArea content should be cleared and replaced by the message "Thank you for your business. Good-bye. This ATM will now close." Invoke a call to the System.exit(0) method to close the window.

Step 2: Code Questions

Which code would be included to address the following issues?

a.   The user enters an incorrect customer ID.

_____

_____

_____

_____

b.   The user enters an incorrect account type.

_____

_____

_____

_____

Implement this logic into the JBANK application.

Step 3: Testing the GUI

In the Teller class, define a method called loadCustomers. (Go to the Resource folder and under Chap10, you will find the template for the loadCustomers method.) This method is going to create customers with the information provided in the suggested data shown next.

Suggested Data:

FirstName: John

LastName: Doe
City Address: Phoenix
Street Address: 4128 West Van Buren
E-mail: Rman@theriver.com
Phone Number: 111-111-1111
zipOrPostalCode: 67777
DOB: 2/1/50
Account SAVINGS: 3000

Customer 2
FirstName: Betsy
LastName: Smith
City Address: Glendale
Street Address: 123 East Pine Street
E-mail: betsy@aol.com
Phone Number: 222-222-2222
zipOrPostalCode: 9999
DOB: 5/7/70
Account SAVINGS: 3210

Account LINEOFCREDIT: 5000

Customer 3
FirstName: Joe
LastName: Smith
City Address: Mesa
Street Address: 890 West Elm Street
E-mail: joe@java.com
Phone Number: 333-333-3333
zipOrPostalCode: 9999
DOB: 2/8/80
Account SAVINGS: 4500
Account OVERDRAFTPROTECT: 3500
Account LINEOFCREDIT: 2000

Step 4: Documentation

a.   Using the document "How to Use UMLTestTool," follow the instructions to verify that the JBANK classes match the JBANK UML diagram shown Figure 10-4-1-2.

b.   Write all necessary javadoc comments and document elements for the lab. Then, using BlueJ, select **Tools** to create the javadocs by selecting **Project Documentation**.

Figure 10-4-1-2: JBANK Application—Phase IV

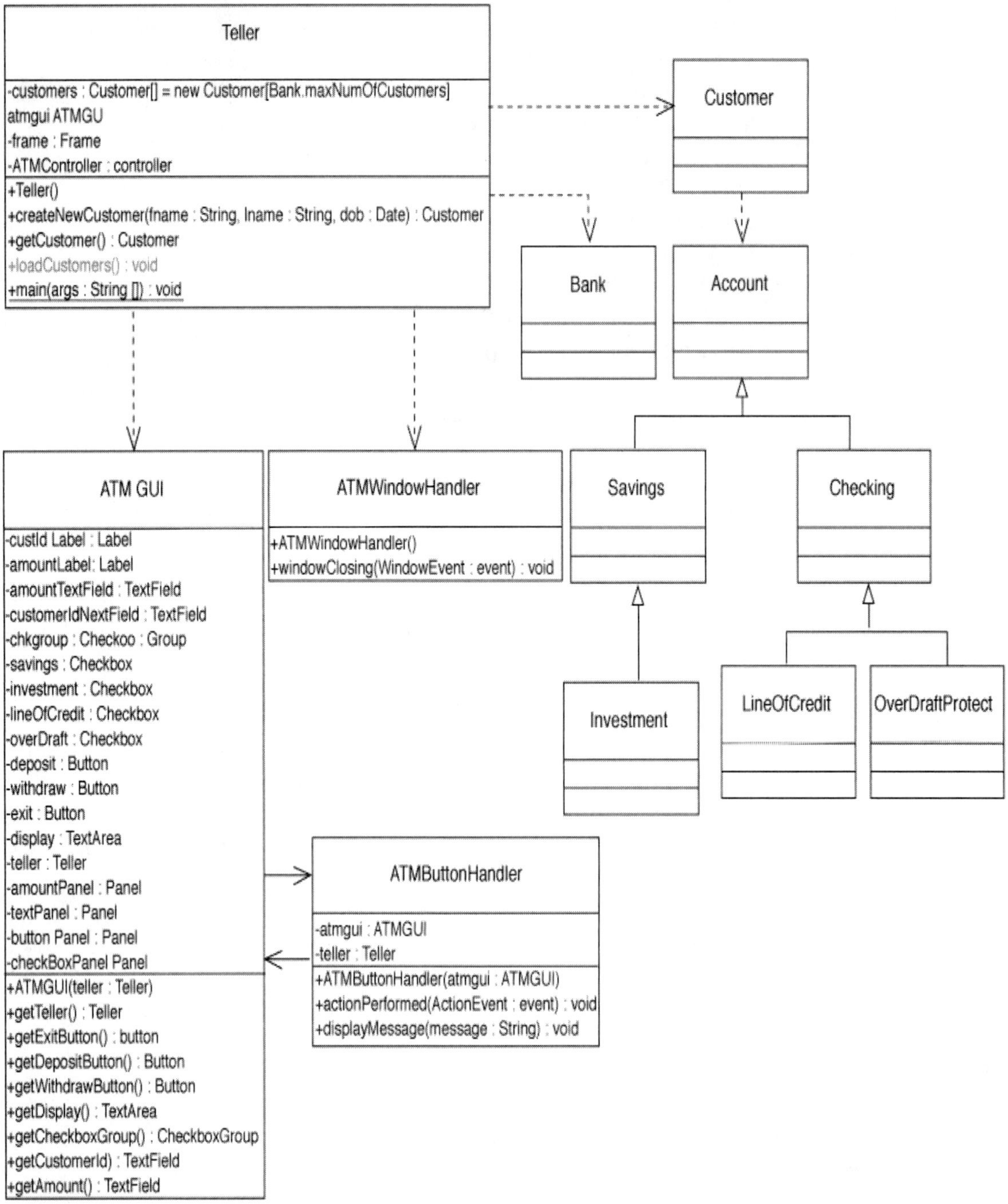

Chapter 11 Labs – Applets and Graphics

Lab 11.2.1: Creating an Applet to Display Employee Information

Estimated Time: 20 minutes

Learning Objective

- In this lab activity, the student will create an applet to display information.

Description/Scenario

- The basic steps followed in the creation and use of applets are outlined here:

  ⇒ Design the GUI that you want to display.

  ⇒ Create a class that extends from the Applet class.

  ⇒ Compile the applet.

  ⇒ Create an HTML file and insert the statements that call the applet class.

  ⇒ Open a browser or use the appletviewer program to call the HTML file.

- An applet cannot be run directly. Displaying the HTML file requires an HTML file and a browser. The Java platform also provides the appletviewer program to test run the applets.

- Writing an applet class requires several things:

  ⇒ Adding more import statements (in addition to others such as java.awt.* and java.awt.event.*)

  ⇒ Adding components

  ⇒ Implementing the methods to handle what happens to the applet when the window is resized or minimized

  ⇒ Including the use of the Font and Color classes to set the properties of text and graphics

  ⇒ Including the use of the Graphics class to draw images on the display

  ⇒ Implementing event handling through WindowListener and ActionListener objects

- Create an applet to display information about an employee.

218

- Create an Employee class that will extend from Applet.

- Use the AWT components TextField and Label to display employee information.

- Create the .java file and compile it to create the .class file.

- Remember that you cannot display the applet unless you have the .java file compiled to its corresponding .class file.

- The HTML document references the .class file and not the .java file.

- Create an HTML document to display the .class file or use BlueJ's ability to run an applet from an appletviewer or a browser when you right-click on the class and select Run.

File Management

Open BlueJ, click on Project from the BlueJ main menu, and select New. In the New Project window and in the Look In list box, select C:\. If you double-click the javacourse folder listed in the text window, a different New Project window opens with javacourse in the Look In list box. Then double-click the chap11 folder listed in the text window, and a different New Project window opens with chap11 in the Look In list box. Next, in the File Name text box, type lab11.2.1 to create a lab11.2.1 subfolder in the chap11 folder.

Tasks

Step 1: Creating an Applet

a. Create a class named Employee that extends Applet. To create an applet, you need import statements such as these:

```
import java.awt.*;
import java.awt.event.*;
import java.applet.*;
```

b. The applet's class must be public, and its name must match the name of the file. The class must be subclassed from the class java.applet.Applet, which extends from java.awt.Panel.

c. Create a Label for first name, last name, street address, city, and state.

Sample code:

```
Label firstName = new Label("First Name");
```

d. Initialize the Labels to the appropriate names.

e.   Create a TextField for first name, last name, street address, city, and state.

f.   Initialize the TextFields first name to "John", last name to "Smith", street address to "123 North Fifth Street", city to "Mesa", and state to "Arizona".

Step 2: Running the Applet

a.   In the init( ) method, set the layout of the applet to GridLayout(5,2).

b.   Add the Label and then the TextField until all five sets have been added to the applet.

Sample code:

```
add(firstName);
```

c.   Compile the program, right-click on the **Employee** class, and click on **Run Applet**. Set the height to **150** and the width to **300**. You will be able to view the applet.

OR

d.   If you want to create an HTML document, open **Notepad** and write the following sample code:

```
<HTML>

<APPLET CODE =Employee.class WIDTH = 300 HEIGHT = 150>
</APPLET>
</HTML>
```

e.   Save the file as emp.html in your working folder. Open the browser and run the HTML file.

Lab 11.5.4: Graphical User Interface (GUI) Components in Applets

Estimated Time: 20 minutes

Learning Objective

- In this lab activity, the student will create an applet to calculate and display a value based on user input.

Description/Scenario

- Create an applet to calculate the result of dividing two values, and then display this result on the screen.

- Convert the calculated value into a String to display on the screen.

- The data the user entered is stored as a String object.

- Write code to convert this text object to a Double object, and then extract the Double value to perform calculations.

- Convert the calculated value into a String to display on the screen.

- This lab provides further practice in the use of wrapper classes.

- Review the API docs on the wrapper classes. Remember that wrapper classes have the same name as the primitive value they store.

- Remember that you cannot display the applet unless you have the .java file compiled to its corresponding .class file.

- The HTML document references the .class file and not the .java file.

- Create an HTML document to display the .class file or use BlueJ's ability to run an applet from an appletviewer or a browser when you right-click on the class and select Run.

File Management

Open BlueJ, click on Project from the BlueJ main menu, and select New. In the New Project window and in the Look In list box, select C:\. If you double-click the javacourse folder listed in the text window, a different New Project window opens with javacourse in the Look In list box. Then double-click the chap11 folder listed in the text window, and a different New Project window opens with chap11 in the Look In list box. Next, in the File Name text box, type lab11.5.4 to create a lab11.5.4 subfolder in the chap11 folder.

Tasks

Step 1: Creating a Class Named Divide That Extends Applet and Implements ActionListener

    a.   Create a label that states "Enter two integers".

    b.   Create two TextFields to store the integers.

    c.   Create one TextField to store the answer.

    d.   Add the label, three TextFields, and the button button1 in the init() method.

    e.   When you add components to an applet, additional methods must be implemented:

          1.   The init() method lays out all the components of the applet. The init() method is called only once when the applet loads. In the actionPerformed() method, perform the calculations and set the result in the answer TextField. Because your applet implemented ActionListener, it is the ActionListener object and will handle any ActionEvent objects that button1 generates.

          2.   This statement can be described as the registering of an ActionListener object with a component (button1) that generates events. When a user presses the button on the applet screen, an action event object is generated.

Step 2: Running the Applet

    a.   Run the applet in the appletviewer/browser that BlueJ provides or create an HTML file to run the applet.

Lab 11.6.1: Changing the Location of Components in an Applet

Estimated Time: 30 minutes

Learning Objective

- In this lab activity, the student will display text information and place it in different locations on the screen, use setLocation() to place components in different locations, and use validate() methods to change and add components to an applet's display.

Description/Scenario

- The important concept explored here is the use of setLocation(), validate(), and invalidate() methods to change or add components to an applet's display.

- Remember the applet cannot be displayed unless the .java file is compiled to its corresponding .class file.

- The HTML document references the .class file and not the .java file.

- Create an HTML document to display the .class file or use BlueJ's ability to run an applet from an appletviewer or a browser when you right-click on the class and select Run.

File Management

Open BlueJ, click on Project from the BlueJ main menu, and select New. In the New Project window and in the Look In list box, select C:\. If you double-click the javacourse folder listed in the text window, a different New Project window opens with javacourse in the Look In list box. Then double-click the chap11 folder listed in the text window, and a different New Project window opens with chap11 in the Look In list box. Next, in the File Name text box, type lab11.6.1 to create a lab11.6.1 subfolder in the chap11 folder.

Tasks

Step 1: Creating a Class Named Personality That Extends Applet and Implements ActionListener

a. Create three labels as follows:

```
Label question = new Label("What's your favorite color?")

Label profile = new Label("Personality profile will show up
here")

Label instruction = new Label("Press the button until the
question returns).
```

b. Create a Button as follows:

```
Button button1 = new Button( "Press Me");
```

c. Create a TextField as follows:

```
TextField response = new TextField(8);
```

d. Create three int variables. One variable will be a counter, and two variables will store x and y coordinates.

Step 2: Creating Components

a. Create an init() method to add all components, request focus for the TextField, and add a listener to the Button.

b. Create an actionListener(ActionEvent e) method that, after the button is pressed, checks to see which of three colors is typed in the TextField (blue, red, or green).

c. If any of the three colors is typed, have your code remove the question label, the instruction label, and the response TextField.

d. Set the text of response to ("").

e. Set the profile label to "Hot tempered" if the color is red; "You are serene" if the color is blue; or "Very friendly" if the color is green.

f. Use the setLocation() method to move the profile label to a different location every time the button is pressed until the y coordinate is greater than 100, at which time everything is returned to the original condition. The init() method is called only once when your applet loads. If the applet code adds or removes components, you must call two methods to have the applet redraw the components. These are the invalidate() and validate() methods. When moving out of the window or resizing the window, the applet knows that the window needs to be redrawn. The applet redraws based on the original information about the components. When adding a component, the applet does not know that its information is out of date. The programmer needs to call the invalidate() method for the applet to mark it as out of date. The validate() method then redraws any invalid windows, allowing the changes to take effect.

g. The re-creation cycle occurs only three times, at which time the button must be disabled.

h. Run the applet using an HTML document or BlueJ.

Lab 11.7.2: Calculator

Estimated Time: 30 minutes

Learning Objective

- In this lab activity, the student will create a GUI by using a grid layout to position components.

Description/Scenario

- This lab will create the following:

  ⇒ A class called Calculator that has methods to add, subtract, divide, and multiply

  ⇒ A class called CalculatorGUI that displays the calculator user interface and instantiates the Calculator class that performs the number crunching

  ⇒ A class called CalculatorApp that creates a frame to display the calculator

  ⇒ A class called CalculatorApplet that displays the calculator in the appletviewer or a browser

File Management

Open BlueJ, click on Project from the BlueJ main menu, and select New. In the New Project window and in the Look In list box, select C:\. If you double-click the javacourse folder listed in the text window, a different New Project window opens with javacourse in the Look In list box. Then double-click the chap11 folder listed in the text window, and a different New Project window opens with chap11 in the Look In list box. Next, in the File Name text box, type lab11.7.2 to create a lab11.7.2 subfolder in the chap11 folder.

Tasks

Step 1: Creating the CalculatorGUI

a.   Create the class CalculatorGUI, which uses the design shown in Figure 11-7-2-1.

Figure 11-7-2-1: Calculator

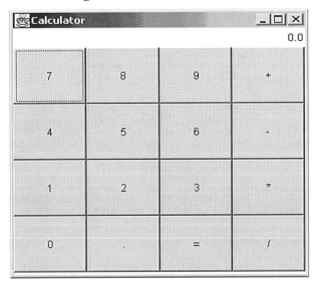

b.   In the CalculatorGUI class, create buttons for 0 to 9 digits and six buttons for the period, equal sign, plus, minus, multiply, and divide. Use a 4 x 4 grid layout for the buttons.

c.   Use panels and layout managers to assist you in the CalculatorGUI design.

d.   Add a constructor to instantiate the Calculator class and create all attributes.

e.   Add a getContentPanel() method to return a panel that has all necessary buttons and action listeners added to it.

f.   Add two nested classes: OpButtonHandler and NumberButtonHandler. The OpButtonHandler class contains an actionPerformed() method that uses the Calculator class methods to compute answer to math operations.

g.   The NumberButtonHandler class contains an actionPerformed() method that assigns text to the TextField named answer. Use the following sample code to create the NumberButtonHandler class.

Sample code:

```
private class NumberButtonHandler implements ActionListener
{
   public void actionPerformed(ActionEvent event)
   {
      if ( readyForNextNumber )
      {
         answer.setText(event.getActionCommand());
         readyForNextNumber = false;
      }
      else
      {
         answer.setText(answer.getText() +
         event.getActionCommand().charAt(0));
      }//end of if else
   }//end of method
}//end of class
```

h.   Modify the code that creates 12 separate buttons and have it create an array of buttons. Use a for loop and the button array to:

- create the buttons,

- add the buttons to the buttonArea panel, and

- add the correct action listener to each button.

Step 2: Creating a Class Calculator

a.   Create a class named Calculator that follows the UML listed next.

b.   Note that you will need a class (static) method parseNumber() to take a String argument and convert it into float.

c.   Use the main method to test the math operations of the class. Use the following data for the test:

```
Calculator calc = new Calculator();
System.out.println("2.0 + >> " + calc.opAdd("2.0"));
System.out.println("3.0 = >> " + calc.opEquals("3.0"));
System.out.println("15.3 * >> " + calc.opMultiply("15.3"));
System.out.println("2.0 / >> " + calc.opDivide("2.0"));
```

Step 3: Creating a Class CalculatorApp

a. Create a class named CalculatorApp that follows the UML shown in Figure 11-7-2-2. Have this class create a frame to display the CalculatorGUI class, and then have the main method launch the frame.

b. Test the operation of the calculator by using the frame.

Step 4: Creating a Class CalculatorApplet

a. Create a class named CalculatorApplet that extends Applet and follows the UML diagram shown in Figure 11-7-2-2. Have this class instantiate the CalculatorGUI.

b. Launch this applet by using the appletviewer. Or with the BlueJ IDE you can use the browser to launch your applet:

- right-click of the CalculatorApplet class
- select 'Run Applet' from the menu
- select 'Run Applet in web browser'
- select 'OK'

c. Test the operation of the calculator by using the applet.

228

d.   Which launches faster: the frame or the applet?

Figure 11-7-2-2: Calculator UML

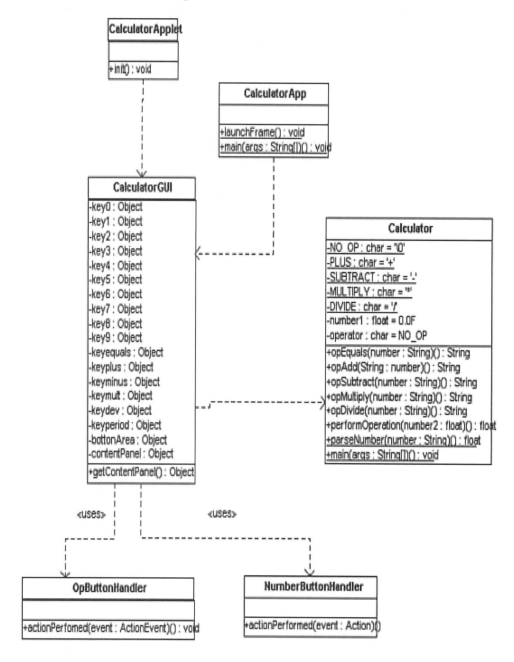

Lab 11.8.1: Creating an ATM Applet

Estimated Time: 30 minutes

Learning Objective

- In this lab activity, the student will create an applet to display the ATM GUI, utilizing the listener classes that were defined in previous labs.

Description/Scenario

- Creating applets includes the use of the java.applet class and other java.awt classes. A Java applet can be embedded in an HTML document. In all of the classes thus far, a main method is the starting point of your program. An applet cannot be run directly; displaying the HTML file requires both an HTML file and a browser. Browsers run by using HTML commands also known as HTML tags.

- To run a Java applet, you need to learn only two HTML tags. HTML tags are special keywords that are enclosed in < > symbols. To embed applets in an HTML document, you will use <HTML> </HTML> and <APPLET> </APPLET> tags.

- Inside the applet tag, you will place three attributes: CODE, WIDTH, and HEIGHT.

- The applet's class must be public, and its name must match the name of the file it is in. The class must extend from Applet.

- Applets represent container objects. The Browser window or frame serves as this container.

- The applet is a Panel that inherits the default layout manager FlowLayout from the Panel class.

- Writing an applet class require that you do the following:

    ⇒ Add import statements for:

    ```
    java.awt.*;
    java.awt.event.*;
    ```

    and others.

    ⇒ Add components.

    ⇒ Implement the methods to handle what happens to the applet as you resize.

⇒ Include the use of the Font and Color classes to set the properties of text and graphics.

⇒ Include the use of the Graphics class to draw images on the display.

⇒ Implement event handling through WindowListener and ActionListener objects.

- The Applet class inherits methods from Component, Container, and Panel classes. An applet is a container, so you can layer your presentation to include panels that have different layout managers. You can add panels to the applet and then add labels, buttons, text boxes, and scrollbars to your panels or directly to the applet. Every applet includes the four methods init(), start(), stop(), and destroy(). If you do not write code for one of these methods, the compiler creates it for you. The first method the browser calls is the init() method. This is the method in which you must write code to present the components. When you close the window, the destroy() method is called. In this method, your program should initiate actions to release resources and close input/output streams and any network connections.

- Learn about object reuse and the benefits of developing a GUI to a panel.

- Use the **instanceof** operator to enable sharing of the same button handler class.

- You will use the set of classes from Chapter 10 labs. You will then create a new class named ATMApplet that will extend Applet and add the ATMGUI to itself. Because the applet can launch itself from an HTML document, it will not need the Teller class.

File Management

Retrieve the previous lab, Lab10.4.1. Continue to save completed work in the Chap11 folder. Use Save As and title the file Lab11.8.1.

Tasks

Step 1: Creating an Instance

a.   Create an ATMApplet class that extends Applet.

b.   Create an instance of ATMGUI.

c.   Create an instance of the Teller class.

d.   Because an applet doesn't have a main method, add the following to the init() method:

```
teller.loadCustomers(); //teller is an instance of the Teller
class
```

To this, add the ATMGUI, which is a Panel, and setVisible to true. (The pack is not needed.)

e.   Your applet is now complete.

Step 2: Running the Test

In the constructor of the applet, create an instance of the Teller class. In the init() method of the applet, call the loadCustomers() method of the Teller class. Set the applet visibility to true. Run the applet in the appletviewer/browser that BlueJ provides or create an HTML file to run the applet. To launch the applet by using BlueJ, right-click on the **applet** class and select **Run Applet**.

Step 3: Review Questions

a.   Why is it important to determine which controller is running?

_____

b.   Does an applet have a constructor?

_____

c.   What are the imports needed for your ATMApplet?

_____

d.   What is the major item reused in this lab?

_____

e.   Could the event handling have been done in the applet?

_____

232

Step 4: Documentation

a.	Using the document "How to Use UMLTestTool," follow the instructions to verify that your JBANK classes match the JBANK UML diagram shown in Figure 11-8-1-1.

b.	Write all needed javadoc comments and document elements for the lab. Then, using BlueJ, select **Tools** and create the javadocs by selecting **Project Documentation**.

Figure 11-8-1-1: Calculator

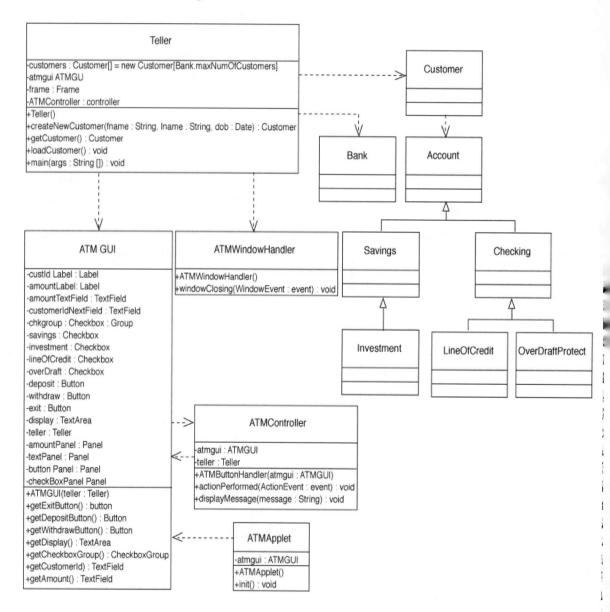

Chapter 12 Labs – Exceptions

Lab 12.5.3: Testing for Run-Time Exceptions

Estimated Time: 30 minutes

Learning Objectives

- In this lab activity, the student will implement try-catch blocks to handle exceptions.

Description/Scenario

- Use try-catch blocks to handle run-time exceptions.

  The sample syntax for a try-catch block is as follows:

  ```
  try
  {
      System.in.read(); //code that might generate an exception
  }
  catch(IOException ioe) // first exception type being handled
  {
      // code to handle exceptions of first type
  }
  catch(Exception e)
  {
      // code to handle other type of exceptions
  }
  ```

- The try block will always contain the code you need to execute. The catch block consists of an argument that defines the specific type of exception that the catch block will handle. Programmers can have more than one catch block to catch different types of exceptions.

- Code that can throw a known exception must be enclosed in a try block; otherwise, the possibility of an exception must be advertised by using the throws Exception clause as part of the method signature. A try block can enclose code that might give rise to one or more exceptions. A try-catch block has one try block and one or more catch blocks.

- The code in the catch block encloses code that is intended to handle a specific type of exception. There can be several catch blocks, each catching a different type of exception. If the code is expected to give rise to different errors and each error needs to be handled differently, then make sure to code specific handlers for each error. If multiple catches are used, the subclassed exceptions must occur before their parent; that is, in the preceding example, the catch for the Exception object should not occur before the catch for the IOException object. If it does, an IOException object will be caught by the first catch block (designed to handle Exception objects), preventing it from being caught by the IOException catch block (designed to handle IOExceptions).

234

- The syntax of the catch code block consists of the keyword catch, a single argument specifying the Exception class type, and a variable to hold the reference to the object of that type.

- Create a class called NumberDivision. This class accepts two Strings from Console. The Integer.parseInt() method is used to convert the Strings to the int type. If the Strings are not valid numbers, the parseInt() method raises a NumberFormatException. This exception is caught and an error message is displayed. The second number is used to divide the first number. If the second number is zero, an ArithmeticException is raised. This exception should be caught and an error message displayed.

File Management

Open BlueJ, click on Project from the BlueJ main menu, and select New. In the New Project window and in the Look In list box, select C:\. If you double-click the javacourse folder listed in the text window, a different New Project window opens with javacourse in the Look In list box. By double-clicking the chap12 folder listed in the text window, a different New Project window opens with chap12 in the Look In list box. Next, in the File Name text box, type lab12.5.3 to create a lab12.5.3 subfolder in the chap12 folder. Import the Console class from the resource folder.

Tasks

Step 1: Handling Exceptions by Using Try-Catch Blocks

a. An *exception* is a representation of an error condition or any situation that is not the expected result of a method. Exceptions can be errors at runtime, such as an unexpected response of a user or unexpected results of an expression.

b. Define a class called NumberDivision. In the main method, use the Console class readLine() method to read two numbers in the form of Strings. Use the parseInt() method to parse the Strings to the int type and save them in two int variables: number1 and number2. Divide number1 by number2 and display the result.

c. Compile and run the program, using two valid numbers as input. What is the result?

d. Run the program; enter two invalid numbers, such as "12A12" or "324B1", as input. What is the output?

_____

_____

_____

_____

e. The method Integer.parseInt() converts numbers from type String to type int. If the String cannot be parsed as an integer, it throws NumberFormatException. Handle the exception by using try and catch blocks. The Java language provides two code constructs to test code and handle exceptions when they occur. These are known as try-catch blocks.

f. The try block will always contain the code you need to execute. The catch block consists of an argument that defines the specific type of exception that the catch block will handle. You can have more than one catch block to catch different types of exceptions. Define try-catch blocks in the program to handle the exception encountered.

Sample code:

```
Try
{
    num1 = Integer.parseInt(number1);
    num2 = Integer.parseInt(number2);
}
catch(NumberFormatException error)
{
    System.out.println("Invalid number");
}
```

Compile and test the program with two valid numbers and two invalid numbers.

g. Run the program and enter the value of the second number as zero. What is the output?

_____

h. When you divide a number by zero, an ArithmeticException is raised. Use try-catch blocks to handle the exception.

Lab 12.5.6: Using the Finally Block

Estimated Time: 15 minutes

Learning Objectives

- In this lab activity, the student will use a finally block and demonstrate re-throwing exceptions.

- The student will practice throwing, handling, and closing exceptions based on logic in the methods.

Description/Scenario

- Exceptions are handled as soon as they occur. The execution of the try block of code terminates and the code in a catch block is executed. This occurs regardless of the importance of the exception or the code in the try block that follows the statement that caused the exception. For example, in a code block that writes data to a file, an exception in this block will result in the file writing operations ceasing. This will leave the file that was being written to open. In this execution, no instruction in the try block that closes the file will be executed.

- The try-catch block of constructs includes a construct finally, which is optional. This block of code is always executed, regardless of the exception that occurred or was caught, and even when there are no exceptions. The finally block provides a means to clean up at the end of executing a try block, which enables the programmer to exit gracefully.

- The finally block is executed when any of these conditions occurs:
  - ⇒ When the code in the try block executes properly
  - ⇒ When the code in the applicable catch block is executed after an exception occurs
  - ⇒ When the code in the try block includes a break or continue statement
  - ⇒ When the code in the try block includes a return
  - ⇒ When the code in finally does not execute when the System.exit() method is called in a try or catch block

- Modify ExceptionDemo class created in lab12.5.3 to include a finally block. In the finally block, display a message to show the end of the program.

File Management

Open BlueJ, click on Project from the BlueJ main menu, and select New. In the New Project window and in the Look In list box, select C:\. If you double-click the javacourse folder listed in the text window, a different New Project window opens with javacourse in the Look In list box. By double-clicking the chap12 folder listed in the text window, a different New Project window opens with chap12 in the Look In list box. Next, in the File Name text box, type lab12.5.6 to create a lab12.5.6 subfolder in the chap12 folder. Import classes from lab12.5.3.

Tasks

Step 1: Using the finally Block

a.   Exceptions are handled immediately. The execution of the try block code terminates and the code in the catch block is executed, regardless of the importance of the exception or the code in the try block that follows the statement that caused the exception. The try-catch block of constructs includes a construct finally.

b.   This block of code is always executed regardless of the error that occurred or was caught. The finally block provides a means to clean up at the end of executing a try block, which allows the programmer to exit gracefully.

c.   In the class ExceptionDemo, include a finally block. In the finally block, display a message "End of Finally block".

Step 2: Running the Class

Compile and test the class.

Lab 12.6.3: Creating Your Own Exceptions

Estimated Time: 30 minutes

Learning Objectives

- In this lab activity, the student will create a user-defined exception, declare and throw the exception, and test it in a try-catch block.

Description/Scenario

- In addition to the extensive library of Throwable classes, you can define individual exception classes. These are used in many applications to alert the program of errors that represent unexpected activity (or results that are unexpected from a business point-of-view) so that the program can take corrective action. These steps describe how to create and use customized exceptions:

  1. Create a class that extends from Exception.
  2. In a method of another class, "throw" a new instance of the exception.
  3. Use the method that throws the exception in a try-catch block.

- User-defined exceptions need to be thrown in some method.

- Handling user-defined exceptions is no different from handling any other checked exception:

  ⇒ Declare the exception and do nothing further.

  ⇒ Enclose the method that throws the exception in a try-catch block and handle the exception.

  ⇒ Enclose the method that throws the exception in a try-catch block and rethrow the exception.

- Create your own exceptions by extending the core Java Exception class.

- Use try-catch blocks to handle the exceptions.

- The water tank holds a maximum of 20 units of water, and the user is notified when the tank is too full or empty.

File Management

Open BlueJ, click on Project from the BlueJ main menu, and select New. In the New Project window and in the Look In list box, select C:\. If you double-click the javacourse folder listed in the text window, a different New Project window opens with javacourse in the Look In list box. By double-clicking the chap12 folder listed in the text window, a different New Project window opens with chap12 in the Look In list box. Next, in the File Name text box, type lab12.6.3 to create a lab12.6.3 subfolder in the chap12 folder.

Tasks

Step 1: Creating and Throwing Your Own Exceptions

a. To create your own exception, you have to create the subclass of the java.lang.Exception class. Using BlueJ, create a class called TankIsFullException that extends Exception. Similarly, create another class called TankIsEmptyException that extends Exception.

b. Create a class called tank that has a private int attribute called capacity. Implement a method called fillTank(int units) that throws TankIsFullException if the tank capacity is incremented beyond 20 units.

Code sample:

```
public void fillTank(int units) throws TankIsFullException{}
```

c. Similarly, implement another method called drainTank(int units) that throws a TankIsEmptyException if the tank capacity falls at or below 0 units.

Step 2: Handling Exceptions

a. Implement the main method in the tank class. In that main method, instantiate a Tank object called waterTank.

b. Use the waterTank.fillTank(19) method to fill the tank object and compile the program. Can you successfully compile the program?

c. Because the fillTank() method throws TankIsFullException, try and catch blocks must be used to handle the exception. In the main method, define try and catch blocks. Include the waterTank.fillTank(19) statement inside the try block and in the catch block print "Tank is full" message. Can the program be compiled and executed?

d. In the try block, include one more fillTank() statement to fill the tank with two more units of water. Compile and run the program. What is the output?

_____

_____

Similarly, use the waterTank.drainTank() method inside a try block and catch the TankIsEmptyException to print the "Tank is Empty" message.

Lab 12.9.1: Exceptions for the JBANK Application

Estimated Time: 60 minutes

Learning Objectives

- In this lab activity, the student will create a user-defined exception based on the business rules for the JBANK application and then throw and test it using a try-catch block.

Description/Scenario

- Deal with exceptions.

- Define and use custom exceptions.

- Create custom exceptions by extending the core Java Exception class.

- Use try-catch blocks to handle exceptions.

Business Rules

- A customer cannot have more than one of each type of account.

- To deposit or withdraw money from a particular account type, the corresponding account type should exist for the customer.

- A customer is not permitted to withdraw money from an account in an amount that is more than the balance or credit limit.

File Management

Open BlueJ, click on Project from the BlueJ main menu, and select New. In the New Project window and in the Look In list box, select C:\. If you double-click the javacourse folder listed in the text window, a different New Project window opens with javacourse in the Look In list box. By double-clicking the chap12 folder listed in the text window, a different New Project window opens with chap12 in the Look In list box. Next, in the File Name text box, type lab12.9.1 to create a lab12.9.1 subfolder in the chap12 folder. Import the JBANK classes.

Tasks

Step 1: Defining Your Own Exception Classes

a. Create a class named AmountOverdrawnException that extends from the Java core Exception class.

b. Define an attribute that holds the account type using char acctype.

c. Define a constructor that accepts a char for the account type (AmountOverDrawnException(char acctype)). In the constructor code, pass a String message to the parent constructor. The call to super("Insufficient funds"); will assign this String to the private message attribute of the exception. The message attribute is a String to hold any message that the programmer designs. Because this is a private attribute, a getMessage() method is provided in the parent class. Also assign the argument from the constructor to the acctype attribute of the Exception class.

d. Override the inherited getMessage() method. This method is defined in the parent class Throwable. The getMessage() method returns a String. Because all of the Account subclasses will use this exception, implement the logic by using a switch statement. All instances of this class will hold an account type. Use this attribute to test its value, and then concatenate the message of the Exception object with messages that are specific to each account. An example for one of the tests is provided:

S- "in Savings Account"

I - "in Investment Account"

L- "in Line-Of-Credit Account"

O- "in Overdraft Protect Account"

Sample code:

```
switch (acctype){
      case 'S' :
            return super.getMessage() + "in Savings Account";
      case 'L':
      // rest of switch statements.
      // Do not forget the default statement.
```

Step 2: More User-Defined Exception Classes

a. Create the AccountTypeAlreadyExistsException class extending from Exception. Define an attribute of type char to hold the account type called acctype. Implement a constructor that accepts a char for the account type, AccountTypeAlreadyExistsException (char acctype). In the constructor code, pass a message String to the parent constructor. The call to super(" account exists. If you're unable to create a duplicate account, ") will assign this String to the private message attribute of the exception.

b. Override the inherited getMessage() method. Because all of the Account subclasses will use this exception, include logic using a switch. All instances of this class will hold an account type. Use this attribute to test its value, and then concatenate the message of the exception object with messages specific to each account. An example for one of the tests is provided:

```
switch (acctype){
    case 'S':
        return "Savings" + super.getMessage();
    case 'I':
        return "Investment" + super.getMessage();
    // rest of switch code. Do not forget the default statement.
```

c. Create an AccountTypeNotFoundException class extending from Exception. Implement a constructor that accepts a char for the account type: AccountTypeNotFoundException (char acctype). In the constructor code, pass a message String to the parent constructor. The call to super(" account does not exist ") will assign this String to the private message attribute of your exception.

d. Override the inherited getMessage() method. Because all of the Account subclasses will use this exception, include logic using a switch. All instances of this class will hold an account type. Use this attribute to test its value, and then concatenate the message of the Exception object with messages that are specific to each account. An example for one of the tests is provided:

```
switch (acctype){
    case 'S':
        return "Savings" + super.getMessage();
    case 'I':
        return "Investment" + super.getMessage();
    // rest of switch code. Do not forget the default statement.
```

Step 3: Throwing AmountOverDrawnException in Classes That Implement the withdraw() Method

a. In the Account class, use the throws keyword to show that withdraw() method throws the AmountOverDrawnException.

Code sample:

```
public abstract double withdraw(double amt) throws
AmountOverDrawnException
```

The abstract withdraw() method is implemented in the concrete classes (Savings, OverdraftProtect, LineOfCredit, Investment). Make sure that the withdraw method of these classes is modified to include throws AmountOverDrawnException, and throw an instance of the AmountOverDrawnException. For example, in the withdraw() method of the Savings class, replace the statement and return false; with the following statement:

```
throw new AmountOverDrawnException (getAcctType());
```

Note: The constructor for the AmountOverDrawnException requires a char representing the account type (S, I, L, O).

Repeat this for each of the concrete classes that implement the withdraw method.

Step 4: Throwing AccountTypeAlreadyExistsException and AccountTypeNotFoundException in Classes That Create and Use Account Objects

a. In the Customer class modify the addAccount() method . This method throws an AccountTypeAlreadyExistsException if the account type of the account to be created already exits and an AccountTypeNotfoundException if an OverdraftProtect account is created without a matching savings account existing for the customer. The value passed to the constructor is the char 'S'. (Note: Business rule states that the Overdraft protect account will cover withdrawals in excess of the balance in the account if there is money in the savings account. This requires that the overdraft protection account be associated with the savings account). This method also throws an AccountTypeNotfoundException if none of the values provided for account type are correct. In this case the AccountTypeNotFoundException constructor is passed the value of the addAccount() method of argument 'type'.

b. Modify the getAccount() method to throw AccountTypeNotFoundException if a particular account type does not exist. Remember to declare the throws AccountTypeNotFoundException as part of the method signature.

Step 5: Handling Exceptions

a. In the ATMButtonHandlerclass, use try and catch blocks to handle the exceptions thrown by withdraw(), addAccount(), and getAccount(). In the catch block of each try-catch block, use the getMessage() method of the Exception object to display the exception message in the TextArea of the ATMGUI. Test and run the program. Use a test data that will cause the exceptions to be thrown.

b. Revise the catch block from the previous step to print the stacktrace.

Step 6: Review Questions

a. What blocks are used for exception handling?

_____

_____

b. What statement is used to throw an exception?

_____

_____

_____

Step 7: Documentation

a. Using the Document "How to Use UMLTestTool," follow the instructions to verify that your JBANK classes match the JBANK UML diagram shown in Figure 12-9-1-1.

246

b.   Write javadoc comments to the classes introduced in this lab.

Figure 12-9-1-1: JBANK Application—Phase IV

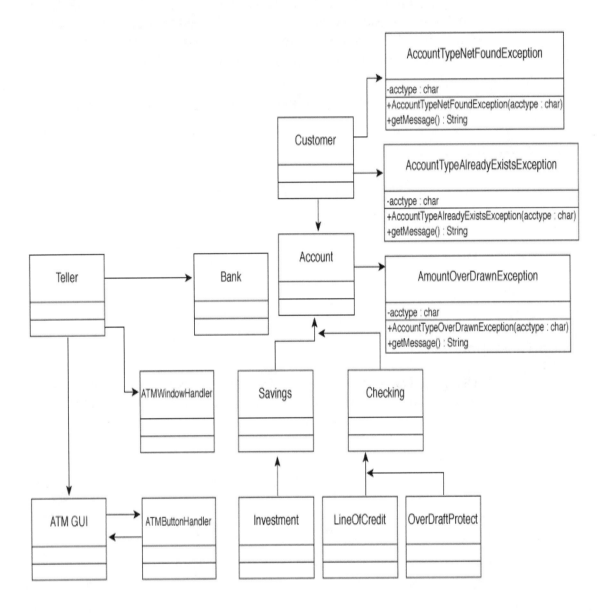

Chapter 13 Labs – Files, Streams, Input and Output

Lab 13.1.1: Displaying File Statistics

Estimated Time: 120 minutes

Learning Objectives

- In this lab activity, the student will use objects of the File class to obtain information on files created and stored on the system.

Description/Scenario

- The Java platform provides the File class to store information about a file or directory. The File objects can read the contents of the underlying file system or directory of files, but not the contents of a file. *Note:* The File class provides functionality for navigating the local file system. The File object describes the directories, files, and access status of these files. The File class does not create a file or add data to a file.

- The simple constructor for the File class holds the name of a file and directory as a String. The second constructor holds the information for a file as a String and the information for a directory as a File object.

- The information for a file includes directory information and a filename. The directory information for a file can consist of the absolute or relative pathname.

- The programmer should create a File object to hold information about a file and then verify the file's existence before reading or writing to the file. A File object is immutable, as are instances of the File class. This means that after the abstract pathname represented by a File object is created, it never changes.

- The File object can only point to the file described in the constructor. After a File object is created, it cannot be changed to point to a different File object. It should be noted that this is in reference to the File object, not the variable that references the File object.

- Create a file called fileExample.txt in Notepad in the working directory. Using BlueJ, create a class called FileDemo. This class will use the File class methods to display the filename, the file size, the file's date of creation and modification, and the file location.

File Management

Open BlueJ, click on Project from the BlueJ main menu, and select New. In the New Project window and in the Look In list box, select C:\. Double-click the javacourse folder listed in the text window, and a different New Project window opens with javacourse in the Look In list box. Then double-click the chap13 folder listed in the text window, and a different New Project window opens with chap13 in the Look In list box. Next, in the File Name text box, type lab13.1.1 to create a lab13.1.1 subfolder in the chap13 folder.

Task

Step 1: Creating a File

a. Open the API document and look for the java.io package. Find the class File and go through all the methods.

b. Open Notepad, type your name, and save the file as fileExample.txt in your working directory.

c. Open BlueJ and create the FileDemo class. Define a File object that represents the file fileExample.txt.

Sample code:

```
File newfile = new
        File("c:\\javacourse\chap13\lab13.1.1\fileExample.txt");
```

d. Include the statement:

```
import java.io.*;
```

The File class provides functionality for navigating the local file system. The File object describes the directories, files, and access status of these files. The File class does not create a file or add data to a file.

e. Check whether the file exists. If the file exists, use the getName() method of the File object to get the name of the file. Similarly, use the getParent() method to find the file pathname, the getSize() method to find the size of the file, and the lastModified() method to find the date of file modification.

Lab 13.1.2: Using RandomAccessFile to Seek Positions Within a File

Estimated Time: 120 minutes

Learning Objective

- In this lab activity, the student will use objects of the RandomAccessFile class and its methods to store and retrieve data randomly from a file.

Description/Scenario

- Storing data in files can occur sequentially or through random-access file techniques. To store and read data from a file in a random order, the RandomAccessFile class and its methods are used.

- Although a File object cannot read or write to a file, a RandomAccessFile object can. With a RandomAccessFile object, the programmer can use reading, writing, and seeking methods of the class to find a specific position within a file, read it, or write to it.

- The constructors of the RandomAccessFile class accept the name of the file as a String or as a File object. The programmer should use a File object to hold information about the file or verify the existence of the file before reading or writing to the file. In addition to information about the file, the constructor accepts the mode for file operations as String values. The values are "r" for reading and "rw" for reading and writing. The file is opened for operation in the specific mode provided in the constructor argument.

- With random-access files, if a file does not exist and the mode is read only ("r"), a FileNotFoundException is thrown. If the file is not found and the mode is read-write ("rw"), a zero length file is created.

- Create the SeekPosition class. This class accepts an integer from the user and accesses the requested position reading the character in that position and displaying. This class also displays one or more characters, with the user providing input for the seek position and the number of characters to be displayed.

File Management

Open BlueJ, click on Project from the BlueJ main menu, and select New. In the New Project window and in the Look In list box, select C:\. If you double-click the javacourse folder listed in the text window, a different New Project window opens with javacourse in the Look In list box. Then double-click the chap13 folder listed in the text window, and a different New Project window opens with chap13 in the Look In list box. Next, in the File Name text box, type lab13.1.2 to create a lab13.1.2 subfolder in the chap13 folder. Import the Console class from the Resource folder.

Task

Step 1: Creating RandomAccessFiles

a. A typical feature for input and output is the ability to randomly access data within a file. In Java, random access in a file is through a RandomAccessFile object. The File object cannot read or write to a file, but the RandomAccessFile object can.

b. Define the class SeekPosition, and in the main method, define a RandomAccessFile object called inFile. The constructors of the RandomAccessFile accept the name of the file as a String or as a File object. In addition to information about the file, the constructor accepts as String values the mode of operation. Like values are "r" for reading and "rw" for reading and writing.

Sample code:

```
RandomAccessFile inFile = new
RandomAccessFile("c:\\fileExample.dat", "r");
```

c. The RandomAccessFile class contains read(), write(), and close() methods as InputStream and OutputStream. In addition, a seek() method selects the starting position within a file before the user can read or write data.

d. Use the Console class readInt() method to read the seek position from which to begin reading from the file into a variable position. Define an OutputStream object for output called ostream.

e. To start reading the file from the selected position, type the statement inFile.seek(position);. Read a character from the selected position into an int variable c and write the character. The File operations throw an IOException. Include the throws IOException clause in the main method and use try and catch blocks to catch the IOException object. In the finally block, close the files that were opened for reading and writing.

Lab 13.5.1.1: Writing Customer Objects to a File

Estimated Time: 30 minutes

Learning Objective

- In this lab activity, the student will use the ObjectOutputStream to store Customer objects in a file implementing the Serializable interface for persistence of data in the JBANK application.

Description/Scenario

- Use the Serializable interface to identify the Customer class and the Account class. If the Account class is Serializable, all its subclasses inherit this behavior. Any data that should not be written should be marked as transient. This lab uses the ObjectOutputStream class to write the Customer objects to a file.

- Create a class called CustomerFileWriter. The CustomerFileWriter implements a method called saveCustomers() to save Customer objects to a file called customers.dat. All the customer data except the numberOfCurrentAccts is written to the file.

File Management

Open BlueJ, click on Project from the BlueJ main menu, and select New. In the New Project window and in the Look In list box, select C:\. If you double-click the javacourse folder listed in the text window, and a different New Project window opens with javacourse in the Look In list box. Then double-click the chap13 folder listed in the text window, and a different New Project window opens with chap13 in the Look In list box. Next, in the File Name text box, type lab13.5.1.1 to create a lab13.5.1.1 subfolder in the chap13 folder. Import the JBANK classes from Lab 12.9.1.

Task

Step 1: Writing Customer Objects to a File Called customer.dat

a. To write objects to a file, make use of ObjectOutputStream. The Customer class and Account class should implement the interface Serializable. The Serializable interface is part of the java.io package. Make sure to include the following statement:

```
import java.io.*;
```

If the Account class is made serializable, then all the classes that inherit from the Account class are serialized. There is no need to store the value of the attribute numberOfCurrentAccts to the Object file, so make use of the transient keyword in the variable definition.

Sample code:

```
import java.io.*;
public class Customer implements Serializable {
    private String lastName;
    --
    private transient int numOfCurrentAccts;
}
```

b. Using BlueJ, create a class called CustomerFileWriter. Include attributes to store references to File, ObjectOutputStream, and FileOutputStream objects.

c. Implement a method called saveCustomers() that takes an array of Customer objects as arguments. In the saveCustomers() method, create a File object called objectFile for the customer.dat file. Use File class methods to check whether the customer.dat file already exists. What method is used to check the existence of a file? If the exists, delete it. (*Note:* The customer.dat file can be created on any drive or folder. Make sure to define the path properly in the argument to the File constructor.)

d. The save() method creates the output stream required to write the data from the object to the file. To do this, create an instance of ObjectOutputStream. The constructor of the ObjectOutputStream takes an argument of type FileOutputStream. In a try-catch block, create an instance of FileOutputStream called fileOutputStream, and use the objectFile as the argument to the constructor. Use the FileOutputStream object as an argument to create an instance of ObjectOutputStream called objectOutputStream. The try block has the code to create the streams. The catch block catches any IOExceptions and prints the messages from the exceptions. In the try block, test to make sure the fileOutputStream or objectOutputStream objects are not null, and call the close() method of these objects. Remember that an objectOutputStream (ObjectOutputStream object) could not have been created if the FileOutputStream object was not created. Therefore, if you call the close() method of the objectOutputStream object, all the streams that are attached (connected) to it close also.

e. In the try block, iterate through the customer array and use the writeObject() method of the ObjectOutputStream to write the Customer objects. After the last object has been written, make sure you call the objectOutputStream.flush() method.

Step 2: Writing CustomerObjects

Test the CustomerFileWriter class by modifying the Teller class. For this lab, the ATMGUI class is not used. Instead, modify the Teller class by removing the code in the Teller Constructor. In the Teller class main method, create three customers with the suggested data.

Suggested Data:

Customer 1
FirstName: John
LastName: Doe
City Address: Phoenix
Street Address: 4128 West Van Buren
E-mail: Rman@theriver.com
Phone Number: 111-111-1111
zipOrPostalCode: 67777
DOB: 2/1/50
Account SAVINGS: 3000

Customer 2
FirstName: Betsy
LastName: Smith
City Address: Glendale
Street Address: 123 East Pine Street
E-mail: betsy@aol.com
Phone Number: 222-222-2222
zipOrPostalCode: 9999
DOB: 5/7/70
Account SAVINGS: 3210
Account LINEOFCREDIT: 5000

Customer 3
FirstName: Joe
LastName: Smith
City Address: Mesa
Street Address: 890 West Elm Street
E-mail: joe@java.com
Phone Number: 333-333-3333
zipOrPostalCode: 9999
DOB: 2/8/80
Account SAVINGS: 4500
Account OVERDRAFTPROTECT: 3500
Account LINEOFCREDIT: 2000

At the end of the main method, create a CustomerFileWriter object and call the saveCustomers() method, passing it a reference to the Customer array variable of the Teller class.

a. Locate the customer.dat file in your current directory.

b. If this file is opened, notice that the data is not stored as characters, but as bytes. Do not modify or change the data in this file; this ensures that the data is available for retrieval in the next lab.

Step 3: Documentation

Using the document "How to Use UMLTestTool," follow the instructions to verify that the JBANK classes match the JBANK UML diagram shown in Figure 13-5-1-1.

Write javadoc comments to the classes introduced in this lab.

Figure 13-5-1-1: JBANK Application—Phase V

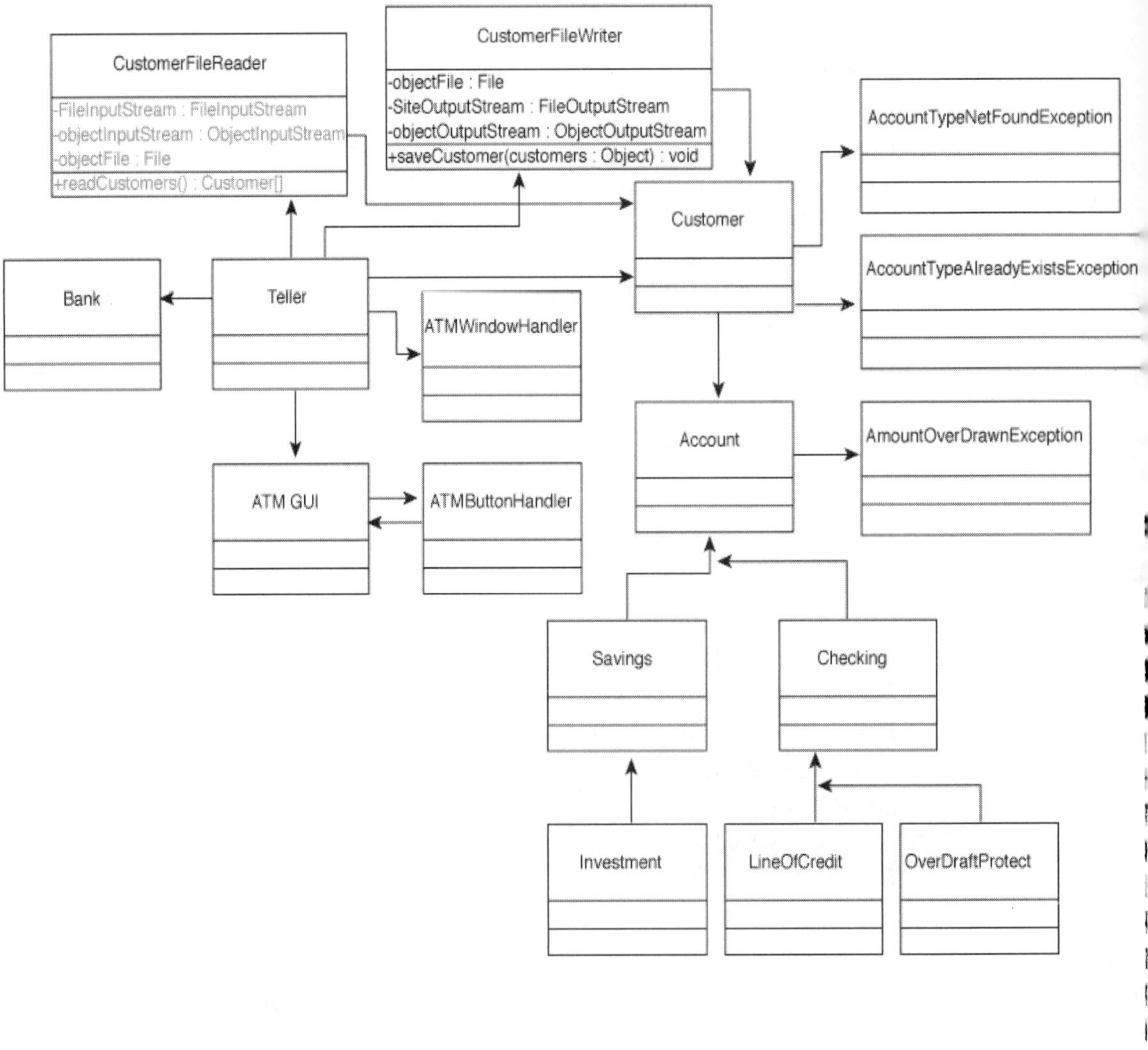

Lab 13.5.1.2: Reading Customer Objects from a File

Estimated Time: 20 minutes

Learning Objectives

- In this lab activity, the student will read the Customer objects saved in the previous lab by using the ObjectInputStream.

Description/Scenario

- Create a class called CustomerFileReader to read customer objects from the file customer.dat. The CustomerFileReader will have a method called readCustomers(), which reads the customers stored in the file.

File Management

Open BlueJ, click on Project from the BlueJ main menu, and select New. In the New Project window and in the Look In list box, select C:\. By double-clicking the javacourse folder listed in the text window, a different New Project window opens with javacourse in the Look In list box. Then double-click the chap13 folder listed in the text window, and a different New Project window opens with chap13 in the Look In list box. Next, in the File Name text box, type lab13.5.1.2 to create a lab13.5.1.2 subfolder in the chap13 folder. Import the JBANK classes from Lab 13.5.1.1.

Task

Step 1: Reading Customer Objects from the c:\\customer.dat File

a. To read objects from a file, make use of ObjectInputStream. For this purpose, the Customer class and Account class should implement the interface Serializable. This is already defined from the previous lab.

b. Using BlueJ, create a class called CustomerFileReader. Define attributes to store references to File, ObjectInputStream, and FileInputStream objects. Implement a method called readCustomers() that returns an array of Customer objects. This method should throw an exception if the file does not exist. In this method, create a File object called objectFile for the customer.dat file. Use File class methods to check whether the customer.dat file already exists. Read the Customer objects from the files. If the file does not exist, throw an instance of the Exception object, setting the message of the exception to display "File does not exist". You can do this with the following syntax:

```
throw new Exception(objectFile.getName() + "  File does not
exist");
```

(*Note:* If you created the file customer.dat in a different directory or under a different name, you should modify your code to reflect this.)

c. The class holds a reference to an array of customers. The maximum number of customers can be set using the following:

```
Customer[] customers = new Customer[Bank.maxNumOfCustomers];
```

d. In a try-catch block, read the Customer objects from the files. To read the objects, create an instance of ObjectInputStream. The constructor of the ObjectInputStream takes an argument of type FileInputStream. Create an instance of FileInputStream called fileInputStream, and use the objectFile as the argument to the constructor. Use the FileInputStream object as an argument to create an instance of ObjectInputStream called objectInputStream. Use try and catch blocks to handle the IOException and ClassNotFoundException.

e. In a loop, use the readObject() method of the ObjectInputStream and read the Customer objects into a Customer array; the read method returns a reference to an instance of the Object class. Include a cast expression to cast the object to that of a Customer class. In the catch block (if no objects are read), rethrow the IOException. The last statement of this method must return a reference to the Customer array. Do not place this in the try block. Place it after the definition of the catch block or in the finally block.

f. In the Teller class main method of the class, create a reference to a Customer[] array, setting its size to the maxNumberOfCustomers static variable of the Bank class. Then create an instance of the CustomerFileReader class identified by custFileReader. Next call the readCustomers() method of the CustomerFileReader object referenced by custFileReader, which returns a reference to the Customer array object. Assign this value to the Customer array object.

g. Include a for loop to traverse through the array. Keep in mind that you might not have created the maximum number of customers. Be sure to include some tests that end the loop if the Customer array element is null. The System.out.println() statement can print each Customer object. The Customer class overrides the toString() method.

Step 2: Documentation

Using the document "How to Use UMLTestTool," follow the instructions to
verify that your JBANK classes match the JBANK UML diagram shown in
Figure 13-5-1-2.

a.   Write javadoc comments to the classes introduced in this lab.

Figure 13-5-1-2: JBANK Application—Phase V

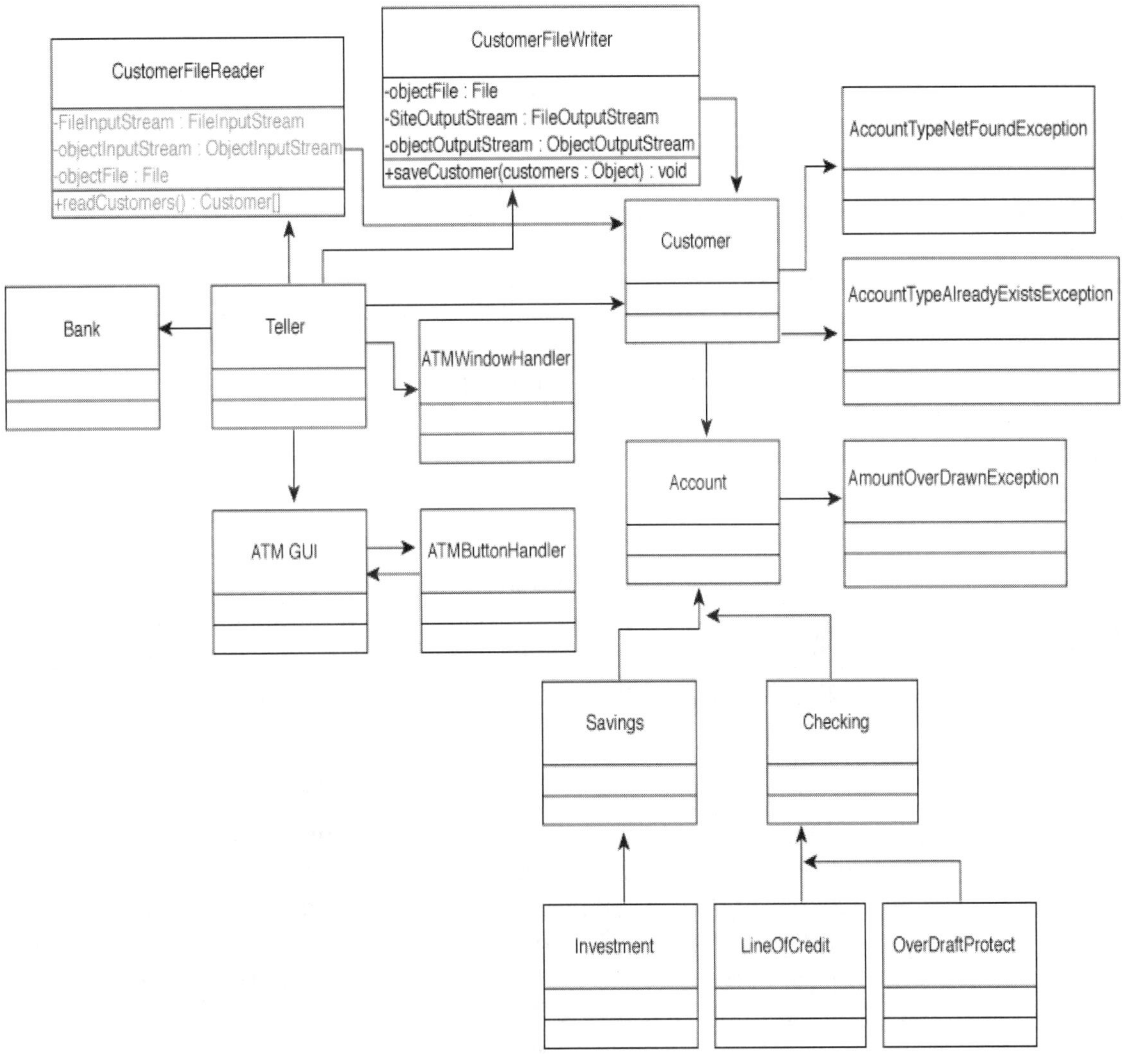

Chapter 14 Labs – Collections

Lab 14.3.5: ArrayList

Estimated Time: 30 minutes

Learning Objectives

- In this lab activity, the student will use the Collections class ArrayList to store objects.

Description/Scenario

- Collection objects represent references to other objects.

- Four basic storage technologies are available for storing objects: array, linked list, tree, and hash table.

- Objects that can serve as containers for other objects can be categorized as collections, lists, sets, or maps.

- Lists are ordered collections, and they can have duplicates. The order can be the natural order, which is the order in which the objects were added to the list. Because the list is ordered, objects in a list can be indexed. An array is an example of a list. The collection framework includes classes that provide for dynamic lists. This type of storage is also known as a *bag* or *multiset*. Other names for this type of storage include list and sequence.

- The programmer can create classes that implement the collections interface to manage and store objects. However, an extensive group of classes is available that has implemented one or more of the collection interfaces and storage methods. The ArrayList class extends from AbstractList, which extends from AbstractCollection. ArrayList implements the List interface.

File Management

Open BlueJ, click on Project from the BlueJ main menu, and select New. In the New Project window and in the Look In list box, select C:\. By double-clicking the javacourse folder listed in the text window, a different New Project window opens with javacourse in the Look In list box. Then double-click the chap14 folder listed in the text window, and a different New Project window opens with chap14 in the Look In list box. Next, in the File Name text box, type lab14.3.5 to create a lab14.3.5 subfolder in the chap14 folder.

Tasks

Step 1: Using ArrayList

a. Define an ArrayList called points to store Point objects in a class called Line. Lists are ordered collections that can have duplicates. The order can be the natural order (the order in which the objects were added to the list). Because the list is ordered, objects in a list can be indexed. An array is an example of a list.

b. Define an addPoint(Point p) method that takes a Point object as an argument. The class Point stores the x and y coordinates of a two-dimensional point and implements the toString() method to return a textual representation of a point.

c. Include the import java.awt.Point statement to implement the Point class. The addPoint() method uses the add() method of the ArrayList points to add the points.

d. Define a method numberOfPoints(), which returns the number of points (*Hint:* Use the size() method of the ArrayList to determine the size of the list).

Step 2: Testing the Program

a. In the main method, create an instance of Line called line. Use the addPoint() method to add points to the ArrayList.

Sample code:

```
line.addPoint(new Point(17, 102));
```

Similarly, add points such as (678, 56). Using the System.out.println() method, print the number of points.

Lab 14.3.7.1: ListIterators

Estimated Time: 20 minutes

Learning Objectives

- In this lab activity, the student will use ListIterators to scan through a collection.

Description/Scenario

- A collection can be scanned by using an iterator. Two iterator interfaces are available in the collection framework: the Iterator and its subclass, the ListIterator. Use the ListIterator with list objects. Iterators provide methods for scanning through any collection. In a set, the order is nondeterministic. This means that the order is not determined by the sequence in which the set was added or by some special key value. When using an iterator to move over a set, the iteration moves forward (but not backward) through the list elements.

- Iterator objects allow scanning through the list and adding and removing elements from the collection.

- A List object also supports a ListIterator, which allows the list to be scanned backward.

- Use ListIterators to traverse through a collection of Point objects created in the previous lab, 14.3.5.

File Management

Open BlueJ, click on Project from the BlueJ main menu, and select New. In the New Project window and in the Look In list box, select C:\. By double-clicking the javacourse folder listed in the text window, a different New Project window opens with javacourse in the Look In list box. Then double-click the chap14 folder listed in the text window, and a different New Project window opens with chap14 in the Look In list box. Next, in the File Name text box, type lab14.3.7.1 to create a lab14.3.7.1 subfolder in the chap14 folder. Import the Line class from Lab 14.3.5.

Tasks

Step 1: Using the ListIterator

a. Import the Line class from the previous lab. Add another method called listIterator(), which returns a ListIterator object that can be used to iterate through the collection of Point objects. You can use an iterator to scan a collection. Two iterator interfaces are available in the collection framework: the iterator and its subinterface, the ListIterator.

b. Use the ListIterator with list objects. When you are using an iterator to move over a set, the iteration moves forward through the list elements. The ListIterator provides additional methods for scanning forward and backward through the collection.

Step 2: Testing the Program

Add statements to the main method to test the listIterator() method and the ListIterator object it returns.

Lab 14.3.7.2: Creating a Collection to Store Integer Objects

Estimated Time: 20 minutes

Learning Objectives

- In this lab activity, the student will use the HashSet object to store integers by using objects of the Integer class. The lab will also include a user-defined exception that will be thrown whenever an attempt is made to enter a duplicate integer values into the set.

Description/Scenario

- The two Set objects discussed in this chapter are HashSet and TreeSet.

- The HashSet class extends from AbstractSet, which extends from AbstractCollection. HashSet implements the Set interface. A Set object does not allow duplicate objects to enter the collection. The collection is unordered and unsorted. Note that the collection fails when it tries to add duplicates. The HashSet class overrides the toString method and creates a sequence of the items separated by commas, delimited by the open and close braces.

- Create a collection class called IntegerSet. This class stores only integers, and duplicate values of integers are not allowed. This class has methods for adding and removing values, always ensuring that the rule stated here is followed. The class also has a method to display the objects in the collection by using an Iterator object.

  ⇒ Create an 'InvalidIntegerObjectException' class and use it in the IntgerSet class. This exception is thrown in the methods that enforce the rules disallowing duplicates or other objects being added to the collection.

File Management

Open BlueJ, click on Project from the BlueJ main menu, and select New. In the New Project window and in the Look In list box, select C:\. If you double-click the javacourse folder listed in the text window, a different New Project window opens with javacourse in the Look In list box. Then double-click the chap14 folder listed in the text window, and a different New Project window opens with chap14 in the Look In list box. Next, in the File Name text box, type lab14.3.7.2 to create a lab14.3.7.2 subfolder in the chap14 folder.

Tasks

Step 1: Defining the IntegerSet Class

a. A *set* is an unordered and unsorted collection of objects with no duplicates. Define a class called IntegerSet. In this class, define a private variable of type Set called integerElements to reference the Set object.

Sample code:

```
private Set elements = new HashSet();
```

b. Define a method called addElement() that takes an Integer object as an argument. In the addElement() method, use the add() method of the Set class to add the Integer objects to the set.

c. Define a method called exists() that takes an Integer object as an argument. In the exists() method, use the contains() method of the Set class to check whether the element exists in the set.

d. Define a getIterator() method that returns an Iterator of the Set object.

e. Define a removeAllElements() method that removes all the objects in the set. This method uses the clear() method of the Set class.

f. Define a removeElement() method that takes an Integer object as an argument and removes the object from the list. Use the remove() method of the Set class to remove an object from the set.

g. Define a toString() method that returns a String object containing the values of all the objects in the set.

Step 2: Adding the InvalidIntegerObjectException

a. This program should not allow duplicate integer values to be entered into the set. Define an Exception class called InvalidIntegerObjectException that extends from the Exception class. This exception is thrown by the addElement() method, which checks whether a duplicate element exists and raises the InvalidIntegerObjectException.

Step 3: Testing Your Program

a. In the main method, create an instance of the IntegerSet class. Add integer elements to the set by using the addElement() method.

b. Test your program by removing an element from the set, displaying all the integer elements in the set, and removing all elements in the set. Use try and catch blocks to handle the exception.

Lab 14.4.1.1: File I/O Using Collection Classes

Estimated Time: 60 minutes

Learning Objectives

- In this lab, the student will use Vector objects to store Customer objects that are retrieved from a file.

Description/Scenario

- This lab combines the use of I/O and collection technologies. The skills developed in this lab will be useful for creating classes to extract data from databases.

- Modify the CustomerFileWriter class to accept a Vector, and save the contents of the Vector to the customers.dat file.

- Modify the CustomerFileReader class to read back the Vector from the customers.dat file.

File Management

Open BlueJ, click on Project from the BlueJ main menu, and select New. In the New Project window and in the Look In list box, select C:\. If you double-click the javacourse folder listed in the text window, a different New Project window opens with javacourse in the Look In list box. Then double-click the chap14 folder listed in the text window, and a different New Project window opens with chap14 in the Look In list box. Next, in the File Name text box, type lab14.4.1.1 to create a lab14.4.1.1 subfolder in the chap14 folder. Import JBANK classes from Lab 13.5.1.2.

Tasks

Step 1: Using Object Vectors to Write and Read Customers Objects

a. Modify the saveCustomers() method signature of the CustomerFileWriter class to accept an argument of type Vector. In this method, pass the Vector object as a parameter to the writeObject() method of the ObjectOutputStream objectOutputStream.

b. Modify the readCustomers() method signature of the CustomerFileReader class to return a Vector object. Modify the Customer class attributes to hold a Vector. In this method, typecast the output of the readObject() method of the ObjectInputStream objectInputStream to the Vector type and return the Vector.

c. In the Teller class, modify the attribute customers of the type Customer array object to Vector type. Include the import statement import java.util.*;. In the Teller class constructor, read the customer data stored in the file by calling the readCustomers() method of the CustomerFileReader. Handle the IOExceptions in a try-catch block. Modify the createNewCustomer() method in the Teller class to add customers to the Vector. Modify the getCustomer() method by using an iterator to traverse through the Vector and return a Customer object.

d. In the Teller class main method, create customers with the suggested data and save them in the file.

e. Use the Console class to accept a customerId. Call the getCustomer() method, which takes a customerId as an argument. Display the Customer with a customerId of 1002.

Step 2: Documentation

Using the document "How to Use UMLTestTool," follow the instructions to verify that the JBANK classes match the JBANK UML diagram shown in Figure 14-4-1-1.

Write javadoc comments to the changes introduced in this lab.

266

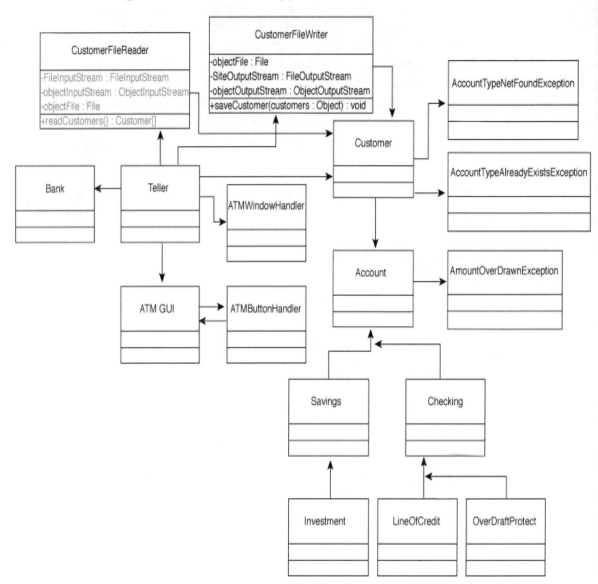

Figure 14-4-1-1: JBANK Application—Phase V

Lab 14.4.1.2: Sets and Iterators

Estimated Time: 60 minutes

Learning Objectives

- In this lab activity, the student will create a SortedSet object to hold a collection of Customer objects sorted by customer information (such as ID or name) and scan through them using iterators.

Description/Scenario

- Modify the Teller class to make use of SortedSet to maintain Customer objects sorted by customerIDs. Use the Iterator to scan through the set to access a customer object by its customerID.

File Management

Open BlueJ, click on Project from the BlueJ main menu, and select New. In the New Project window and in the Look In list box, select C:\. If you double-click the javacourse folder listed in the text window, a different New Project window opens with javacourse in the Look In list box. Then double-click the chap14 folder listed in the text window, and a different New Project window opens with chap14 in the Look In list box. Next, in the File Name text box, type lab14.4.1.2 to create a lab14.4.1.2 subfolder in the chap14 folder. Import JBANK classes from Lab 14.4.1.1.

Tasks

Step 1: Storing Customer Objects in a SortedSet

a.   SortedSet is an interface; the class that implements the SortedSet is the TreeSet. In the Teller class, change the variable Customers to type SortedSet. The Customers variable can now reference an object of type TreeSet.

b.   An object that is inserted into a SortedSet should implement the interface Comparable. In our case, the Customer class should implement the interface Comparable. Change the class definition of the Customer class to implement Comparable and define a method called compareTo(). The compareTo() method is used in the SortedSet methods to insert or search for an object by comparing its value with the other objects in the set. In

268

our case, the Customer objects are sorted by the customerID. Use the following code sample to implement the compareTo() method based on customerID:

```
public int compareTo(Object objectToCompare)
{
    Customer c = (Customer) objectToCompare;
    return (this.custID - c.getCustID());
}
```

c.   In the Teller class, read the Customers objects stored in the "customers.dat" file using Vector output of the CustomerFileReader class from the previous lab, and use the following syntax to create a TreeSet of customers:

```
customers = new TreeSet(customerFileReader.read());
```

d.   To add a new customer to the Customers set, use the add() method of the SortedSet.

Step 2: Scanning the SortedSet Using Iterators

a.   To search for a customer in the Customers set by customerID, use the iterator() method of the SortedSet to get the reference to the SortedSet. Within a while loop that uses the hasNext() method to break the while loop, iterate through the set. Use the next() method to get the reference of the object in the set and verify the customerID of the object to find the match.

Sample code:

```
public Customer getCustomer(int customerID) {
    Iterator iter = customers.iterator();
    while (iter.hasNext())    {
        Customer c = (Customer) iter.next();
        if (c.getCustID() == customerID) {
            return c;
        }
    }
    return null;
}
```

Step 3: Documentation

Write javadoc comments to the methods introduced in this lab.

Using the document "How to Use UMLTestTool," follow the instructions to create a JBANK UML diagram.

Step 4: Preparing Your Application for Deployment

This is the final phase of the JBANK application. Save the classes in Lab 14.4.1.2 to the phase4 folder to complete your packaging.

Figure 14-4-1-2: JBANK Application—Phase V

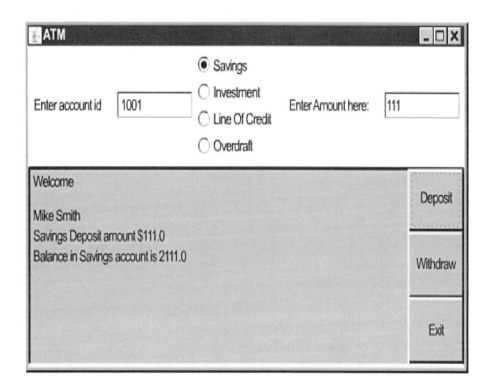

Chapter 15 Labs – Threads

Lab 15.3.2: Threads and Priorities

Estimated Time: 30 minutes

Learning Objective

- In this lab activity, the student will create multithreading solutions by using the Thread class to run several threads that display the same information.

Description/Scenario

- In the Java language, the Virtual CPU that is created to manage a thread is an instance of the java.lang.Thread class. In other words, a *Thread object* is a virtual CPU that runs code and uses data. More than one Thread object can share the code and data.

- Any class whose instances are intended to be executed by a thread should implement the Runnable interface. The class must define a method that contains no run() arguments. A class that implements Runnable can run without subclassing Thread by instantiating a Thread instance and passing itself in as the target.

- One way to create a thread is to create it in a class and pass it a reference to an object that implements Runnable. A second way to create a thread is to extend it from Thread.

- A thread starts with the start() method. This calls the run() method of the thread or the object that is implement Runnable.

- The run() method can be that of an object that implements the Runnable interface or a Thread object that overrides the run() method. A programmer cannot control the schedule for a thread, but it can assign a priority to a thread. The Java virtual machine (JVM) schedules threads of the same priority. Other method calls can be used to yield to a thread of the same or a higher priority. Use the getPriority() method to determine the current priority of the thread, and use the setPriority() method to set the priority of the thread. The priority is an integer value. The Thread class includes the following constants:

  ⇒ Thread.MIN_PRIORITY

  ⇒ Thread.NORM_PRIORITY

  ⇒ Thread.MAX_PRIORITY

- This lab covers creation of a Thread class and instantiation of three different threads.

- The student will set thread priorities and observe the results.
- This lab covers thread priorities and the affects that priority has on thread processes.

File Management

Open BlueJ, click on Project from the BlueJ main menu, and select New. In the New Project window and in the Look In list box, select C:\. If you double-click the javacourse folder listed in the text window, a different New Project window opens with javacourse in the Look In list box. Then double-click the chap15 folder listed in the text window, and a different New Project window opens with chap15 in the Look In list box. Next, in the File Name text box, type lab15.3.2 to create a lab15.3.2 subfolder in the chap15 folder.

Import the JBANK classes from Lab 15.3.2.

Tasks

Step 1: Creating the IntThread Class

a. Create a class named IntThread that extends Thread and has a constructor that accepts an int as an argument.

b. Add a run() method with a for loop that displays the int argument 15 times.

Step 2: Creating the TestThread Class

a. Create a class named TestThread that contains a main method.

b. Have the main method instantiate three threads of the IntThread class and pass the ints 1, 2, and 3. Use the start() method to start each thread.

c. Run the TestThread class and observe which int displays first.

Step 3: Creating the TestThread2 Class

a. Create a class named TestThread2 that contains a main method.

b. Have the main method instantiate three threads of IntThread class and pass the ints 1, 2, and 3.

c. Add setPriority() methods to set the priorities for each thread as follows:

```
one.setPriority(Thread.MIN_PRIORITY);
two.setPriority(Thread.MIN_PRIORITY + 1);
three.setPriority(Thread.MIN_PRIORITY + 2);
```

d. Run the TestThread2 class and observe which int displays first.

Lab 15.5.2: Controlling Threads by Using Methods of the Thread Class

Estimated Time: 30 minutes

Learning Objective

- In this lab activity, the student will use methods of the Thread class to control threads.

Description/Scenario

- A program launches a thread's execution by calling the thread's start() method, which calls the run() method. After start() launches the thread, start() returns to its caller immediately. The caller then executes concurrently with the launched thread. The start() method throws an IllegalThreadStateException if the thread it is trying to start has already been started.

- Threads can be placed in a blocked state to allow other threads to run or to wait for resources to become available. The programmer has several methods of the Thread class that can be used to place threads in a blocked state, assign threads a priority, or notify other threads when it is finished. When a blocked thread becomes runnable, it is placed back into the appropriate runnable pool. Threads from the highest priority nonempty pool are given CPU time.

- When a sleep() method is called in a running thread, that thread enters the sleeping state. A sleeping thread becomes ready after the designated sleep time expires. A sleeping thread cannot use a processor even if one is available. The static method sleep() is called with an argument specifying how long, in milliseconds, the currently executing thread should sleep. While a thread sleeps, it does not contend for the processor; therefore, other threads can execute. This can give lower-priority threads a chance to run.

- Create an applet that creates a thread.

- Test the Thread sleep() method.

- Create an applet, and inside the applet, create a thread.

- Create and start the thread inside the init() method of the applet.

- Inside the run() method, have the thread sleep() method pause the thread.

- Have the paint() method draw a String that is moved across the screen by the run() method.

File Management

Open BlueJ, click on Project from the BlueJ main menu, and select New. In the New Project window and in the Look In list box, select C:\. By double-clicking the javacourse folder listed in the text window, a different New Project window opens with javacourse in the Look In list box. Then double-click the chap15 folder listed in the text window, and a different New Project window opens with chap15 in the Look In list box. Next, in the File Name text box, type lab15.5.2 to create a lab15.5.2 subfolder in the chap15 folder.

Tasks

Step 1: Creating an AppletThread Class

a.   Create a class named AppletThread that extends Applet and implements Runnable.

b.   Create and start a thread inside the init() method:

```
t = new Thread(this);
t.start();
```

Step 2: Adding a String

a.   Have the paint() method draw a String:

```
g.drawString("Help!",x, y);
```

b.   Have the run() method move the String down the window in a diagonal line from the left side to the right. When it reaches the change point, the String moves down and to the left.

c.   Have the String change color when the direction changes.

d.   Have a try block inside the run() method that uses the Thread sleep() method to pause the movement of the String.

Step 3: Running the Applet

a.   Run the applet in the appletviewer that BlueJ provides.

b.   Notice the speed of movement of the String.

c.   Change the sleep time and run the applet in the appletviewer.

d.   Notice the String's speed of movement.

Lab 15.5.5: Digital Clock

Estimated Time: 40 minutes

Learning Objective

- In this lab activity, the student will create an applet that will display a digital clock with the hour, minute, and second.

Description/Scenario

- Create an applet that displays a digital clock.

- Display the hour, minute, and second.

- Use the Thread sleep method to repaint the clock every second.

- Have the clock update the time every second by using a thread.

File Management

Open BlueJ, click on Project from the BlueJ main menu, and select New. In the New Project window and in the Look In list box, select C:\. Then double-click the javacourse folder listed in the text window, and a different New Project window opens with javacourse in the Look In list box. If you double-click the chap15 folder listed in the text window, a different New Project window opens with chap15 in the Look In list box. Next, in the File Name text box, type lab15.5.5 to create a lab15.5.5 subfolder in the chap15 folder.

Tasks

Step 1: Creating the DigitalClock Class

a.   Create a class named DigitalClock that extends Applet and implements Runnable.

b.   In the init() method, create the thread and start the thread.

c.   Use the run() method to call the Thread sleep() method and the repaint() method to repaint the clock every second.

d.   Use this code to get the current hour, minute, and second:

```
Date myHours = new Date();
        Date mySeconds = new Date();
   Date myMinutes = new Date();
   hrs = myHours.getHours();
   sec = mySeconds.getSeconds();
   mins = myMinutes.getMinutes(); //Note: these methods are
       deprecated but work.
```

Step 2: Running the Applet

Run the applet in the appletviewer that BlueJ provides.

Notes

Notes

Notes

Notes